WANDERINGS OF A NATURALIST IN INDIA

WANDERINGS OF A NATURALIST IN INDIA

THE WESTERN HIMALAYAS, AND CASHMERE

ANDREW LEITH ADAMS

GYAN

Published by

GYAN

Gyan Publishing House
5, Ansari Road
Daryaganj, New Delhi-110002
Phone: 011-47034999, 9811692060
E-mail: books@gyanbooks.com

Distribution Network
gyanbooks.com
India, USA, Canada, UK, Australia, France

ISBN : 978-81-212-4211-0 (PB)
First Published, Edinburgh, 1867

2nd Impression 2020

Printed at: Gyan Press, Delhi.

Wanderings of a Naturalist in India
Author: Andrew Leith Adams

WANDERINGS

OF A

NATURALIST IN INDIA

THE WESTERN HIMALAYAS, AND CASHMERE

BY ANDREW LEITH ADAMS, M.D.

SURGEON 22D REGIMENT.

EDINBURGH

EDMONSTON AND DOUGLAS

1867

I DEDICATE THIS VOLUME

TO THE MEMORY OF

FRANCIS ADAMS, A.M. M.D. LL.D.

AS A

SMALL TOKEN OF FILIAL DEVOTION,

AND IN GRATEFUL REMEMBRANCE OF THAT TRAINING

IN EARLY LIFE

BY WHICH HE DIRECTED MY MIND

TO AN APPRECIATION OF THE WORKS OF NATURE,

AND A LOVE FOR ALL INTELLECTUAL

AND IMPROVING STUDIES.

CONTENTS.

CHAPTER I.

CHAPTER II.

CHAPTER III.

CHAPTER IV.

CHAPTER V.

CHAPTER VI.

CHAPTER VII.

CHAPTER VIII.

CHAPTER IX.

CHAPTER X.

CHAPTER XI.

CHAPTER XII.

CHAPTER XIII.

CHAPTER XIV.

CHAPTER I.

Introductory—Departure—Ocean-life—Accidents at Sea from falling overboard—Birds—Albatross—A Gale—Tropical Sunsets—Seychelle Islands—Becalmed—Arrival at Bombay—Caves of Carlee—Advice to Indian Residents from a Sanitary point of view.

DURING a sojourn in the East of nearly seven years, with frequent change of place, I had many opportunities afforded me of making a lasting acquaintance with various objects of natural history, the local scenery of Northern India, and the Western Himalayan mountains. My leisure hours were also not unfrequent, and leave of absence was always most willingly granted me whenever my professional services could be dispensed with; for which I shall ever retain a grateful remembrance to the highly-esteemed commanding and medical officers under whom I then served.

In the following reminiscences I have aimed at preserving the objects in the order they appeared to me, and attempted to describe the scenes and circumstances with which I was brought in contact as minutely as the incidents of travel would allow, and in a belief that my jottings by the way would add zest to the drier descriptions of animals. To a few such a proceeding may seem a work of supererogation, but it must be borne in mind that it is not to the professors of natural science that these pages are devoted, but to the young and ardent, who may enjoy such opportunities for enlarging their ideas and improving their minds ; therefore, should I weary the reader, I must confess that my best endeavours have been directed to the opposite, for I have too lively a recollection of my own difficulties when I began inquiries into the natural history of India, and the perplexity and confusion occasioned by dry details, catalogues, and detached papers, devoid of lively incidents to excite my ardour or increase my interest in the study. It would be useless to dilate on the advantages India offers to the naturalist; and with respect to the Himalayas, perhaps few regions afford like inducements for study. Their vast ranges are often clothed with verdure to the summits, and on the highest to the confines of perpetual snow. In the rich and fertile valleys animated nature appears in all its loveliness and beauty. The mineralogist and geologist will find ample materials of the greatest interest on their mountains and the lesser ranges. In the latter especially—what is called the Sewalik range—are to be found remains made known to us by the labours of Falconer and Cautley. But although we are in possession of much interesting and valuable data regarding the palæontology of the Himalayas, great mines are yet undiscovered. The zoologist may ramble over hill and dale, mountain and plain, and after a lifetime of constant observation find his delightful pursuit more attractive than ever. It is on these noble mountains that the sportsman can enjoy his favourite pastime unscathed by the burning Indian sun ; in their lovely glens bears stalk undisturbed, whilst various species of deer, wild sheep, goats and the ibex, feed unmolested on the craggy steeps. In the forests and valleys along the sub-Himalayan range tigers and leopards prowl, and the wild dog and various foxes seek subsistence wherever their peculiar prey is plentiful. Add to these the numerous pheasants and partridges, whose elegance and beauty are unsurpassed by the allied birds of any other country. The endless variety of plants, from the lichen on the mountain-top to the deodar and Himalayan oaks in their native forests, present one of the choicest fields to the botanist.

There can be no doubt that he who constantly keeps his mind and body in healthy exercise is accumulating stores which, if they do not produce intense happiness at the time, will be the source of many pleasant after-reflections. If a journal registers only the leading events of every-day life, and describes the most prominent occupations of its author, it does a great deal; for if these occupations had not been recorded, where is the intellect however clear—the memory however good—that could have retained them with any degree of accuracy? I therefore present them as they were registered years ago among the busy and changing scenes of an active life. If I fail in benefiting others with the information obtained, I have at least the consolation of knowing that my exertions, as regards myself, have borne good fruits; insamuch as they have kept mind and body in pleasant and improving occupation; or rather, as the author of the *Rambler* has exquisitely expressed it, "He that enlarges his curiosity after the works of nature, demonstrably multiplies the inlets to happiness; and therefore the younger part of my readers, to whom I dedicate this vernal speculation, must excuse me for calling upon them to make use at once of the spring of the year, and the spring of life; to acquire, while their minds may be yet impressed with new images, a love of innocent pleasures and an ardour for useful knowledge; and to remember that a blighted spring makes a barren year, and that the vernal flowers, however beautiful and gay, are only intended by nature as preparatives to autumnal fruits." *

However invaluable are the labours of him whose field of observation is entirely confined to the naming and arranging of objects in the cabinet or in the museum, it will, I think, be conceded, that a proper acquaintance with the subject means something more than a mere knowledge of the appearances and classification of species; in fact, that nature is best studied in her own wide chamber. This it is that gives the intense zest to the writings of such original observers as Humboldt, Darwin, Audubon, and a host of distinguished names, whose labours are not only valued for their depth of learning and acumen, but also for the homely lessons they convey to the youthful mind. Were the lives of the most eminent students of science carefully inquired into, it would no doubt be found that their tastes for the study of natural phenomena were first aroused and developed by having their attention early directed to the subject.

It is not often that a member of the medical profession in active employment can devote the necessary time and attention to enable him to form a close acquaintance with the collateral sciences; at the same time, by husbanding one's leisure hours, it is wonderful how much may be done in intervals of rest even in the most engrossing avocations of life. In the army especially, where the calls of duty are not always onerous or frequent, together with the advantages offered by constant change of scene, opportunities present themselves to military officers very rarely enjoyed in civil life. It has been my good fortune to participate largely in these respects, and whilst I am sensible of having made a fair use of my hours of freedom, at the same time I cannot conscientiously re-

* *Rambler* for April 1750.

proach myself with having done so at the expense of the requirements of my profession, or the service to which I belong.

As a mental and bodily gymnastic during the long tedious hours of idleness that frequently fall to the lot of officers in the army and navy, more particularly on foreign stations, there is perhaps nothing equal to the outdoor pursuit of natural science,—whether in setting to work with head and hands to study the natural objects which everywhere surround them, or even simply collecting specimens without evincing any particular desire to become better acquainted with their characters—which, however, I must allow, is a faint-hearted essay at gaining information.

In thus attempting to suggest a remedy for idleness, I trust my readers will not accuse me of the narrow-mindedness that excludes all rational and manly pastimes, inasmuch as, if he will take the trouble to peruse the contents of this volume, he will find that both admit of wholesome combination.

Voyages by the Cape of Good Hope to India have been so frequently narrated, and present in general the same monotonous uniformity, that I shall content myself with transcribing only a few of the chief and most interesting incidents in that portion of my journal.

I left Queenstown (then better known as the Cove of Cork) on the 29th of January 1849, with a detachment of the 64th Regiment bound for India.

The first few days were marked by very rough weather, and the never-failing accompaniment, sea-sickness, until about the latitude of Madeira, when a change for the better took place, and we began to get our sea-legs, and observe the novelties of the deep, such as flying-fish and shoals of porpoises, whilst an occasional shark would show its great fin and tail above water.

As we neared the Line, sudden squalls and heavy rains were of frequent occurrence, and now and then vast numbers of that beautiful tunny-fish, the bonito, were seen charging past us at great speed.

Thus sped the even tenor of our ways. No troop-ship at sea should be without a netting around the forecastle. It is notorious that more soldiers are drowned by falling from the fore-chains than any other part of the vessel. A sudden lurch will suffice to throw a landsman off his balance; and if the forecastle is on a level with the bulwarks, there is every chance of his falling overboard. In this way we lost a soldier, who was washing his clothes, when a wave struck the vessel, and he missed his footing and fell into the sea. I have moreover records of several cases of a similar nature, all showing that many lives might be saved if more attention were paid to prevent that and such-like accidents. Lifeboats ought to be *always* in immediate readiness, and supplied with buoys, and all the requisite contrivances to secure the quickest and most efficient assistance.

On the 5th of March we sighted the island of Trinidad, and having gained a strong westerly breeze, our good bark scudded along, our almost constant companion being the little petrel; a few of a square-tailed species were also observed, and now and then a solitary individual of the great black petrel.

In lat. 30° 52 S., and long. 27° 12′ W., an albatross made its appearance for the first time, and as we approached the Cape, they became more numerous.

The brown booby and Cape pigeons were plentiful off the African coast, where we encountered a heavy gale of three days' duration. At length the hurricane abated, and was succeeded by a dead calm, during which several land birds were seen hovering around the rigging.

In lat. 36° 37′ S., long. 33° 9′ E., a little gray fly-catcher flew on board exhausted. Flocks of greedy albatrosses, petrels and Cape pigeons crowded around the ship's stern. A hook was baited with fat, when upwards of a dozen albatrosses instantly rushed at it, and as one after another was being hauled on deck, the remainder, regardless of the struggles of the captured, and the vociferations of the crew, kept swimming about the stern. Not even did those birds which were indifferently hooked, and made their escape, desist from seizing the bait a second time! The poor animals seemed half-starved. The wing-bones of the albatross are much in request for pipe-stalks, and purses are made of the skin of the feet.

Our sailors prognosticated that the unusual familiarity and tameness of the albatross were certain harbingers of another storm; and assuredly, towards evening, a mass of dark clouds was seen lowering in the east, and by sunset we had again "hove-to," under close-reefed sail, and were weathering one of the most fearful tropical hurricanes our gray-headed captain had ever witnessed.

We saw no more albatrosses or petrels after passing lat. 25° S. Flying-fish began to reappear in great numbers, and seldom a day passed without a tropic bird (*Phaëton*) to keep us company. The weather, as we again drew near the Line, became more settled; and we had frequent opportunities of beholding the splendid sunsets of these latitudes—such pictures as a Turner never could have painted, or, had he done so, none but those who had witnessed them in nature would credit.

At daybreak on the 19th of April we sighted the Seychelle Islands, and were soon at anchor in the little harbour of Mahe.

After a long imprisonment on board ship, one feels a schoolboy's longing to take a run on shore, and when the foot touches *terra firma* for the first time, especially in a new country, how eager are we to be off and see the lions of the place!

The desolate and barren appearance of the Seychelles, when viewed from a distance, dies away as you approach.

Their mountains rise as high as 2000 feet above the level of the sea, and are clothed with verdure to their summits. For the first time we observed the bamboo, cocoa-nut, tamarind, plantain, orange, coffee-plant, mango, date, and sugar-cane, growing in all their tropical luxuriance. A coral reef surrounds the island of Mahe, which is said to be composed of granite, and consequently forms an interesting geological feature compared with other oceanic islands.

The Seychelles are likewise famous from being the only locality where the celebrated coco-de-mer (*Lodoicea Sechellarum*) is found. This graceful palm attracts the stranger's attention on landing at Mahe, where several may be seen in the centre of the town. It has been introduced into the island of Mauritius, but is said not to produce fruit anywhere except in its native islands.

During our short stay we were much indebted to our excellent friend M. G., whose delightful retreat on the sea-coast we had the pleasure of visiting.

On the following morning, after a refreshing bathe in a mountain-stream, and a ramble through our friend's plantain-groves, among the clustering fruit of which I found a turtle-dove (*Turtur rostratus*) sitting on its nest and eggs, we bade farewell to our kind host, and left in his canoe, loaded with fruit and sugar-cane.

Turtles are plentiful, but the particular species I could not determine. The frigate, or man-of-war bird (*Tachypetes*), was often seen soaring at great heights. Its deeply-forked tail and aquiline flight are distinctive.

After passing the Line we were becalmed for several days, during which there was not a ruffle on the wide expanse, and our vessel lay like unto "a painted ship upon a painted ocean."

Every one was tired out by the monotony of a long voyage; and irrespective of that, and the failure of the winds, the heat was great, and seldom under 86° and 90° in our cabins. At length uncertain breezes came and went, and after days of suffocating heat and much discomfort we cast anchor in Bombay harbour on the 18th May, when the troops were disembarked into small boats, and sailed for Panwell, on the coast.

The weather was intensely hot at the time: in consequence we were obliged always to march at night, so as to arrive in camp before the burning sun of the Deccan made its appearance.

A hurried visit was paid to the celebrated Caves of Carlee, and we admired their wonderful galleries and colossal elephants, dug out of solid trap; but there was no time to examine anything minutely, for the short-lived evenings of these latitudes afford but scanty opportunities for a passing traveller to feast his fancy.

Soon after our arrival at Poonah we were joined by the other detachments of the regiment, which had arrived at Bombay after us; and then, once fairly settled down to habits of Eastern life, I found that even active or onerous professional toil and study may find an occasional leisure hour, which will be best employed in whatever tends to improve the mind and keep the body healthy. Accordingly, by rising early and going soon to bed, I had always a few hours at my disposal for outdoor amusements and recreations; and when the heat of the day kept me within the shade of my bungalow, I could still find occupation and study among the collection of natural objects I had gathered during my morning and evening rambles.

A physician of great Indian experience says: "Nothing is so destructive of energy of mind and body as habitual indolence and inactivity in a tropical climate. Those persons are undoubtedly the most happy who have sufficient opportunities and inducements to keep themselves always employed in useful occupations, and they alone preserve their vigour of body and mind unimpaired during a long residence in India."*

Such, I will confess, has been my experience, and I appeal to those who have made themselves conversant with the habits and mode of life of Englishmen in India whether or not the most part of the so-called insalubrity of the climate is not attributable to the neglect of the simplest of hygienic rules?

It might be no unprofitable study for the political historian to trace how far the habits and modes of life of Englishmen in India may have influenced their characters as rulers, and whether the great mutiny was in any way the result of our selfish regard for personal comfort, to the neglect of the interests and welfare of the people we attempt to govern.

* Twining on *Diseases of Bengal.*

CHAPTER II.

Familiar Birds about Poonah—Hindoo Temple of Parbuttah—Scenery—Vultures—Large Bats—Habits of Parrakeet—Frogs—Sunbird and Frog-Flycatcher—Insects—Snakes—Cobra—Hog Rat—Tiger and Bullock—Kingfishers—Indian Roller—Pigeons—Warblers—Tailor-Bird—Govind-Kite a Public Scavenger—Hoopoe—Dial-Bird—Weaver-Bird's Nest—Egyptian Vulture—Common Trees—The Mango—Paradise Flycatcher—Ants—Coming of the Monsoon.

AMONG the chief ornithological denizens of the highlands of the Deccan, the following may be easily distinguished :—

The wire-tailed swallow (*Hirundo filifera*) is plentiful at Poonah during the summer months. It is on wing soon after daybreak, and may be observed skimming over the Great Parade, or around our bungalows, all day long, hunting its winged prey. In the calm and delightful evenings peculiar to Poonah they may be seen in hundreds, perched on stones and tufts of grass upon the plains and the river-banks, and just as night is closing in they rise and seek a roost on the tallest spires and mosques. It is seldom that the males have their delicate tail appendages perfect, and often, they are entirely wanting.

The allied swift (*Cypselus affinis*) is common, and builds in societies among the ruined palaces and domes : its nest is made of clay, intermingled with feathers and grass. In haunts and habits it much resembles the European black swift, which, it would appear, has not hitherto been found in Hindostan.

Of the Corvidæ we have only the Indian crow (*Corvus culminatus*) and Indian jackdaw (*C. splendens*) about Poonah. Both are plentifully distributed. The latter is a bold marauder, and fearlessly disputes his rights with the govind-kite (*Milvus migrans*, Bodd.) and the Egyptian vulture (*Neophron percnopterus*); like the rook, the Indian crow breeds in societies. In plumage and habits the Indian sparrow is very similar to the British species; the manner in which his nest is formed, and the materials of which it is composed, bear likewise a close resemblance to that of its brother in England. In the walls of the natives' huts, among the thatch of our bungalows, in every tree, it builds its nest. It is the same dirty little fellow amidst the mud and mire of an Indian city as on the house-tops of St. Giles.—Among the most common birds, I noted the Indian robin (*Thamnobia fulicata*). In manner and habits it is the Oriental representative of redbreast, just as the migratory thrush takes the place of the former with the Canadian emigrants.—The gray titmouse (*Parus cinereus*) represents the great ox-eye of Europe; it is, however, a poor rival in point of brilliancy of feather, nor is his call-note so clear and joyous; it is, however, more familiar, and may be constantly seen in our gardens.—The intensity of the red on the sides of the bay-backed shrike (*Lanius hardwickii*) is peculiar to the breeding-season. It is the most common butcher-bird, and may be seen perched on the lower branch of a mimosa, watching an opportunity to dart on some luckless beetle: down it pounces on its prey, which it bears away to a neighbouring thorn, impales and devours; then flits within a few feet of the ground to a new perch, from whence, with head awry, it examines intently the ground beneath, now and then answering the harsh scream of its companion on some neighbouring tree.

The bulbul (*Pycnonotus hæmorrhous*) is very common.—There is considerable variety in the plumage of the green bee-eater (*Merops viridis*), sufficient to puzzle one at first.—The black Indian redstart frequents gardens.—The pied wagtail (*Motacilla dukhunensis*) is very plentiful.—After some trouble, I had the good fortune to obtain a specimen of the great pied wagtail (*Motacilla maderaspatana*) ; it is rare in this district, seen only by the sides of streams, and generally alone.—Here also is often found the yellow wagtail-lark (*Budytes viridis*) : the feathers on the head are blue-gray in spring and summer.

One of the finest views of the city of Poonah and the surrounding country is to be obtained from the fort of Parbuttah, once a Mahratta stronghold, now a Hindoo temple. It is said that, in 1802, the Rajah of Poonah witnessed from this place the defeat of his army at the battle of Kirkee. The approach leads through a shady avenue of tamarind, mango, and cocoa-nut trees, to a small lake with an island, clothed with fruit-trees to the very margin of the calm and glassy water, in which are reflected the broad leaves of the plantain and palm, festooned with a woodbine-like creeper. The scene is perfectly Oriental, and seldom will the beholder gaze on a prettier little spot. A broad flight of steps leads to the fort, on entering which the ears of the traveller are assailed by the deafening clamour of "*tom-toms*" and the discordant screeches of uncouth instruments. Among the dilapidated and ruined walls are dark and dismal dens, filled with grim idols, to which numbers of adoring natives bend the knee. From the parapet there is a fine view of the surrounding country. A range of high conical mountains stretches from north to west, while eastward lesser hills bound the view, and southward the eye roams over a vast level covered with fields of grain, orchards, and groves, wherein grow the lime, the orange, the vine, pomegranate, mango, plantain, and guava. Truly may the traveller say, "This land is fair to look upon!"

The remains of one of Holkar's palaces may be seen at the back of the artillery lines. At the time of our visit (5 A.M.) the carcase of a horse was lying close by; round it were congregated tawny eagles, Indian and Egyptian vultures, crows, pariah dogs and jackals. As we approached they quickly dispersed. One after another the great eagles disappeared, but the vultures gorged with their repast, sat perched on the ruined walls of the palace, while the jackals skulked away to their hiding-places, and the dogs, scarcely able to rise from the place where they had fed, lay listlessly around the skeleton, or, seated on their haunches, licked their lips, as though gloating over the remembrance of their recent meal. I believe, when an artillery horse dies, the carcase is never buried, but laid upon the plain, where it is quickly devoured by these useful scavengers.

The climate of the high northern ranges is delicious; several old forts remain upon their ridges, the chief of which is Poonadur, a favourite resort during the hot months.

There are few good shooting-grounds in the neighbourhood. Quail and partridge are found in small numbers, and after the rains snipe—common and jack-snipe—also the painted species (*Rhynchœa bengalensis*).

The antelope black-buck (*Cervicapra bezoartica*) is rare, and from having been so much hunted is very shy and difficult of approach.

The wokhab or tawny eagle (*Aquila fulvescens*) is common around Poonah, and is often seen on housetops or feeding with govind-kites on the refuse of the kitchen. It is by no means dainty in its choice of food, and has little of the majestic and noble mien of the golden eagle ; it roosts on the tops of tall trees in the immediate vicinity of cantonments. —The Indian vulture (*Vultur indicus*) I have seldom seen except in the circumstances described above, when almost incredible numbers congregate.

My attention was one morning directed to a colony of flying foxes (*Pteropus edwardsii*) which had taken up their abode on a banyan-tree situate in one of the most central and populous quarters of the city of Poonah. Each bat was suspended by the hind-feet, in which position it remained even when shot. Some were perfectly motionless, others swaying to and fro with noisy clamour, indifferent to the busy crowd moving onwards in the street below. The natives call this bat the "wurbagool." The species is very plentiful, and numbers are usually to be seen in the still evenings at high elevations, flying with an easy floating motion, now and then varied by the regular flap of their large wings as they steer their course towards the fruit-groves. They do not always rest during the day, for flocks of several hundreds may be observed at mid-day in the mango-topes—some attached to the branches, others flitting round the trees, and uttering an occasional harsh discordant cry. The half-caste Portuguese eat them, and look upon their flesh as delicious. Individuals of this species appear to differ considerably in size, which may, however, be owing to age. One I killed measured from tip to tip about five feet. Figs, mangoes, etc., constitute their favourite food.

The rose-ringed parrakeet (*Palæornis torquatus*) is abundant in every grove, where great flocks often assemble. Their harsh screams are deafening at times. In the evenings it was amusing to watch these birds. Minas and sparrows used to collect in a mango-tope close to my bungalow; several hundreds frequently congregated in the same tree, screaming and vociferating as loud as they could. If a shot was fired among them, the parrakeets, with a shrill scream, dived downwards in a dense mass, and swept circling round the grove. The minas rapidly returned to their roost, when the noise and clamour became louder and louder as fresh arrivals poured in, until night began to lower. Then the cries died gradually away, and except an occasional scream, no signs were heard of the vast assemblage crowding every branch and twig.

The streams about Poonah are subject to sudden inundations, owing to the proximity of the mountains. During the hot summer months, when there is no rain, they become dried pu, and, excepting small pools here and there, nothing is to be seen but the debris of the last storm. Frogs spawn in these situations. One species, a few inches in length, with the belly and throat pure white, is very plentiful; it basks on the sides of the pools, and takes to the water when one approaches, skipping over the pool something in the way a boy *skims* a flat stone. My attention was directed to the surface of the water, which appeared as though large drops of rain were falling on it. Having satisfied myself that this could not be the case, my next supposition was that bubbles of gas were ascending from decomposing matter at the bottom of the pool, which opinion was apparently confirmed by the bubble rising at the time the drop appeared on the surface. I discovered, however, that the water was alive with minute tadpoles. Vast numbers of these little creatures were darting to and from its surface with great rapidity. The frogs I had alarmed were poised upon the water, staring at me intently, and at the margin of the pool were hundreds of tadpoles with the caudal extremity still perfect; others, again, at a distance of some eight or ten feet, had the tail almost separated ; whilst a few here and there had lost the appendage altogether, being complete frogs.

About half-a-mile from my bungalow there were two large hedges of prickly pear, and between them a stagnant pool. I often took up a position under the cool shade of a peepul-tree close by, and watched the habits of the feathered tribe at mid-day. On one occasion, having shot a sun-bird, it fell on the margin of the pool, when some animal jumped from the muddy water, seized it, and instantly disappeared with its prey. A short time afterwards a large green frog appeared on the surface. I shot it, and discovered the bird in its mouth.

The purple honey-sucker of Jerdon, the beautiful blue-winged sun-bird (*Arachnechthra asiatica*, Lath.), is common, and nothing can exceed the grace and elegance of its congener, the Ceylon sun-bird (*Leptocoma zeylonica*). This exquisite little creature sports round the top of the prickly pear, sucking the nectar from its flowers like a humming-bird. Neither species, however, subsists altogether on honey, for flies and minute insects are frequently found in their gizzards. The brilliant green spot on the wing of the male is wanting in the female.

The gaudy lesser crimson-breasted flycatcher (*Pericrocotus peregrinus*) is a tenant of the woods and hedges. Sometimes flocks of males, at other times females only, are observed ; the rich and beautiful plumage of the former is very striking ; insects and larvæ constitute its favourite food. The shrill, clamorous cry of the koel, or black cuckoo (*Eudynamys orientalis*) was constantly heard in woods and groves ; it feeds on fruit. I shot a specimen of a young male European cuckoo (*Cuculus canorus*) on the 16th of October.

At their residence near Poonah the ex-Amirs of Scinde had several fine goshawks, trained for falconry; the species has been shot on the Nepal mountains and Neilgherries. Trained Bhyri falcons (*Falco jugger*) are sold at Poonah by the natives, and fetch high prices. They say these birds inhabit the mountains and woody parts of the district; but there is no more handsome falcon than the teesa (*Poliornis teesa*); its fine, clear, light-coloured eye, and in fact the whole appearance of the bird, indicates grace and strength of wing. In the stomach of a female I found a lizard 4 inches in length.

Among the many discomforts Europeans have to endure in the East are myriads of fleas, mosquitoes, snakes, centipedes, scorpions, etc. etc., which not only infest gardens, but penetrate into the interior of houses, especially at night. No sooner is the cloth spread than hundreds of beetles, attracted by the light of the candles, dash recklessly into the flame, and fall disabled on the table, intruding themselves into every dish; crickets chirp among the beams overhead, and the whole apartment resounds with the noise and buzz of insect-life. Nor is the scene without very different, though occasionally more attractive; for swarms of fire-flies assemble round the bushes, and with the lucid beam of their tiny lamps illumine the gloom of the tropical night.

On one occasion I was awoke by my servant pursuing a snake across my bedroom-floor: he killed it at my bed-side. It was a species very common about Poonah, of a greenish-black colour, and about 2 feet in length, with numerous white spots on its upper surface.

Snake-skins (so entire that even the covering of the eye is retained) were often found under the floor-matting; and a species, white-spotted on the back and sides of the body and about 5 feet in length, abounds in gardens; on that account one is often obliged to ride on horseback after nightfall, when numbers may be seen crawling about in the roads and gardens, searching for frogs, on which they principally feed. There is a green species, 2½ feet in length, said by the natives to be very venomous. My attention was directed to a circumscribed swelling in the centre of the body of one of these serpents, which on dissection proved to be a frog, fully three times as broad as any other part of the snake's body. Two minute wounds on the frog's back were the only marks of violence discernible.

The cobra di capella is tamed, and taught to dance to the pan-pipe-like sounds of a sort of flageolet. It is said to be plentiful in the cactus hedges, which seem to be a "rendezvous" for all kinds of snakes and vermin. One sultry day, while seated under an acacia tree, I heard a hissing sound behind me, and turning, saw a cobra close by, with raised head and inflated hood, knocking its nose against the stem of a cactus. One of the first injunctions a native servant gives his newly-arrived master is, "*always to shake his boots well before putting them on,*" scorpions being apt to take up their abode in the toe!

A green lizard is common in gardens, and on the thatch of bungalows: it preys on scorpions, especially a small black species, abundant beneath stones and the matting of rooms. Centipedes of large size are very plentiful.

The moongus, or gray ichneumon (*Herpestes griseus*), is found in this district, and frequently domesticated. It is exceedingly useful in destroying centipedes and scorpions, but I have never seen it attack serpents; and the story regarding the antidote it obtains for snake-bites in the root of a certain plant called moonguswail, like most Indian tales of that description,* is perfectly mythical.

The bandy-coot or hog-rat (*Mus giganteus*) was frequently seen in our houses. This animal is very destructive, and creates much disturbance at night. Sometimes it coursed across the canvas covering of our ceiling—a signal always for "drawn swords," and a *prod* through the "dungaree,"† together with the pleasing uncertainty as to whether you are transfixing a ghous (as the Mahrattas call it) or a mangur (*Felis bengalensis*), a species of wild-cat which prowls about at night, and hides during the day in hedges, or under the thatch of bungalows.

Several species of chameleon are abundant: they frequent bushy places, and are seen basking on the stems of trees; while geckoes are common on the walls of houses: Tigers are found on the mountains and in the jungles. Not far from Kirkee is the village of Maun, where, during midsummer, both the common and jack-snipe are abundant in the rice-fields. They arrive about the beginning of November, when also a few painted snipe may be obtained.

Maun is situate close to a range of mountains covered with low dense jungle, extending some distance into the plain, which is studded with villages, rice-fields and gardens, separated by ravines and large tracts of waste and barren country. A dense jungle to the north of the village was said to have been the haunt of a man-eating tiger for some time previous to our visit, and we found the carcase of a bullock lying in a chilli field, not a stone's throw from the village. On both

* See an interesting account of a fight between a cobra and moongus in the *Times of India* for the 9th of August 1863, signed by three officers who witnessed the encounter.

† A coarse white linen used for lining the interior of rooms.

sides of the animal's neck were deep wounds caused by the tiger's teeth, and on the shoulder a long gash, where the claw had ploughed through the skin; the whole of the flesh on the belly and flanks was torn away, the stomach and entrails lying on the ground, where we could see distinct traces of a scuffle, and the footprints of a very large tiger. Pitching our tent within range, we sat up that night, expecting to get a shot at the marauder, as the moon was shining brightly; but after a fruitless vigil, and growing drowsy, I went to bed, and had scarcely been asleep an hour when my servant called me to say the tiger had arrived, and was carrying off the carcase. It was too late, however, as we were just in time to see him disappear in the cover with his prey. The following morning all that remained of the bullock was the skull, and a few pieces of the larger bones. A week afterwards I heard that the same tiger had killed another bullock near a village some ten miles distant.

The kestrel (*Tinnunculus alaudarius*), and also the sparrow-hawk (*Accipiter virgatus*), are common. The former may be observed hovering over the plains, and at dusk, not unfrequently in numbers, perched on stones and tufts of grass. Both prey extensively on mice, lizards, and beetles. The latter hawk is trained for quail-hunting. The broad-tailed flycatcher (*Rhipidura fuscoventris*) is plentiful in gardens and wooded localities. It is not shy, and for its size bold and fearless, and will attack birds much larger than itself. The song of the male consists of a few loud and pleasing notes, uttered while the little creature is dancing along the branch with tail and wings expanded like a fan.

The common kingfisher (*Alcedo bengalensis*, Gmel.), the black and white species (*Ceryle rudis*), and the Indian kingfisher (*Halcyon fuscus*, Bodd.), are often observed. The first is common in rice-fields, streams, and river-banks; the two latter are not so plentiful; the Indian kingfisher is a tenant of gardens and pools. On the broad tops of peepul, acacia, and mango trees, the lark-heeled cuckoo or Malabar crow (*Centropus rufipennis*, Illig.) perches; grasshoppers and coleopterous insects constitute its favourite food. These birds startle one, while passing under a tree, by the flapping of their large fan-shaped wings; their flight is a sort of sailing motion, which, with the expansive tail, makes them appear much larger than they are in reality. Frequenting like situations may often be seen the beautiful Indian roller (*Coracias indica*), it sports from one tree-top to another with a peculiar zig-zag flight; butterflies and large insects are its favourite food, and are caught on wing. Flocks of the black-headed finch (*Emberiza melanocephala*, Sykes) are common; it is dispersed over the fields during harvest, but disappears soon afterwards. Rock-pigeons (*Columba livia*) congregate in the deep wells, in the sides of which they breed. The natives capture them by suddenly throwing a net over the mouth of the well. There is no variety in the wild bird, and although the tame pigeons feed in the fields, the two do not appear to associate. By the sides of hedges, in gardens and way-sides, the Senegal dove (*Columba senegalensis*) is frequently observed. It passes the greater part of the day on the ground, but is often seen likewise on trees. In dissecting and preparing the skins of this species (in fact Columbidæ in general), great care should be taken to remove the fat from the skin of the back and sides, else the feathers will be sure to drop out.

The tailor-bird (*Orthotomus longicauda*), with its curiously-fashioned nest, displaying most marvellous skill and care, is plentiful in groves and gardens, where it may be seen flitting among the dense foliage, emitting its loud cry, resembling that of the mina. The tailor-bird is by no means shy or easily frightened; on the contrary, it is an inquisitive little fellow. I recollect once, when seated under a tree, employed in skinning a bird, one came within a yard of me, and attentively watched the proceeding. It has a droll way of inspecting objects *sideways*, jerking its tail unceasingly when moving. To those familiar with its habits it will not appear surprising that this strange little creature should be the architect of that wonderful nest, formed of cotton, wool, hair, etc., enclosed between leaves, beautifully *sewn* together with vegetable fibre. The young resemble their parents, except in length of tail; also the rufous on the head is not so clear.

Of all rapacious birds the govind-kite is the most useful and abundant; wherever offal exists there this bird is to be found, hovering over the butcher's shop, the kitchen, or the barrack—now leisurely sailing in circles—now darting like an arrow upon its prey, which it devours while on the wing, uttering a clear shrill cry whenever a companion disputes its possession. Its boldness is almost ludicrous. Once, when a servant was bringing mutton-chops from the cook-house to our mess, one of these birds darted upon the dish, and tore away the contents in its talons. The plumage of this species is subject to considerable variety: some are very dark (these I take to be the old birds), others have the under parts light rufous, darkly lined.

The govind-kite, Egyptian vulture, crow, Indian jackdaw, and mina, may justly be termed "*the great scavengers of India.*" What would its large cities be without these useful birds? and lean and degraded as the pariah dog is, abused and cowed by the natives, still he clings to man, and picks up a scanty meal on the dunghill, or feasts with the jackal

From constant ill-treatment he has become the very picture of abject misery, crouching at the sound of the human voice; yet, from some strange instinct, unsolicited he protects the dwelling of the native, and the midnight robber would find it hard indeed to pass his post unchallenged.

The hoopoe (*Upupa epops*) is very common on lawns and in fields. I have been informed that the black-headed bustard (*Otis nigriceps*) was at one time common in this district. It is now seldom met with, having been so much sought after by sportsmen; one specimen was brought to me from the mountains near Poonah with its eyelids sewn together to prevent it running away!—The naturalist is likely to be led into error in studying the appearance and habits of the dial-bird (*Copsychus saularis.*) The more sombre plumage of the female (which is seldom seen with the male, except during the breeding season) has deceived many. The song of this species is rich and sweet, and frequently imitates the notes of other birds. In habits familiar, it is a common tenant of the gardens, where it pours forth its welcome notes in the afternoon or early morning, and like its rival *redbreast*, sings a bar, and then waits a short time for another individual to reply. This species is the "*nightingale*" of English residents.—Among flocks of mina birds (*Acridotheres tristis*) may often be seen numbers of the roseate pastor (*Pastor roseus*). The smaller size, peculiar sailing flight, and more pointed wings, will distinguish the latter at a distance.

The rain-quail (*Coturnix coromandelica*) is plentiful during the monsoon. I have shot it in lucerne fields close to my house, and the bush-quail in low jungle near the mountains. We have the Indian golden oriole in woods and groves. It is shy and difficult of approach. The nest, which is placed in the fork of a tree, is formed of dry grass, with a finer description in the interior. The large purse-shaped nest of the weaver-bird (*Ploceus baya*) would fall an easy prey to its enemies, did not the little architect, with surprising intelligence, place it in situations not easily accessible; hence several may be seen suspended from the tips of branches overhanging deep wells, or on the topmost boughs of acacia and thorny trees. The weaver-bird builds in societies, and is docile and familiar in its habits.—The common king-crow (*Dicrurus macrocercus*) is often seen on the backs of cattle.

The Egyptian vulture is a native of Eastern Europe, Asia, and Africa. On the temperate regions of the Himalayas it follows man wherever he congregates; and on the plains of India its gaunt forbidding figure is seen stalking among all animal refuse. It is the smallest of the tribe found in the East; its total length seldom exceeding 26 inches. In the adult the skin of the head and front of the neck is bare, yellow and shrivelled, giving the animal a melancholy, poverty-stricken appearance. The general colour of the plumage is white, except the quills and their coverts, which are black; the iris is red in the old bird, but brown in the young, which also have the naked part about the head of a leaden colour until the second year. There is great diversity of plumage, from the brownish-black of the young bird to the white of the adult; this latter is attained at the third moult. The habits of this species are strictly domestic. It is usually met with in the filthiest parts of towns and military cantonments. As soon as dinner is announced by the bugle-sound in barracks, Egyptian vultures and kites may be seen hastening towards the scene, which soon assumes a lively aspect from the numbers and activity of the kites, as they dart like arrows on the bones and refuse; while others, with head erect, lifting their legs (much after the manner of rooks), are silently devouring whatever comes in their way. Now and then a vulture in the act of bolting a piece of flesh has to relinquish the morsel to his more nimble companion, whose sharp talons soon tear it off, and he is seen devouring the prize as he sails away. The two species often roost together, and seem to agree very well except at feeding-time. Flocks of both accompany troops for hundreds of miles, and regularly at daybreak, as the new camp is forming, they may be seen approaching from the direction of the previous day's halt.*

The mango is the most common fruit-tree in this district, but the fruit is not equal to that of Mazagon mango of Bombay. The turpentine flavour of the mango is less perceptible the oftener the fruit is eaten. There are many persons, however, never become reconciled to it—a peculiarity which unfortunately has deprived me of enjoying what many consider the most highly-flavoured and luscious of Eastern fruits. The tree grows to a considerable size, and is tall and spreading, with dense foliage of a dark green; it studs the country over, forming little groves (called *topes*), which break the sameness of the scenery, and offer a grateful shade from the sun. I have spent many happy hours in these mango-topes, during the fiercest heat of summer, searching for birds, especially warblers. Here may frequently be seen the paradise flycatcher (*Tchitrea paradisi*, Linn.), and though not common, its singularly attractive plumage can scarcely escape observation. The adult male has a blue head, white body, with two of the tail-feathers prolonged for upwards of

* Armies in the field have been followed by flocks of vultures, kites, and crows. It has been stated to me, on good authority, that the crows of New Brunswick and state of Maine decreased very much in number during the American war, and returned afterwards.

8 inches beyond the tip; these, in the female, scarcely extend beyond a quarter of an inch. The young birds are chestnut. The Paradise flycatcher does not possess great powers of flight, except when hunting for insects; then its movements are quick, it suddenly appears on a branch beside you, and the next moment is seen shooting like an arrow through the grove, at times uttering a harsh chirp—now perched on the upper bough of a tamarind, now on the lower one of a neighbouring tree—spectre-like it suddenly appears and is as quickly gone. Before I knew the difference between the sexes and young birds, a friend remarked to me, in one of our rambles, "Did you see that *red* flycatcher with the whip-tail?" I insisted that he had mistaken the colour; then immediately afterwards two birds were shot, one white, and one chestnut, both males. Towards the end of summer the species leaves this district for the warmer climate below the Ghauts.

The sweet-lime produces abundance of delicious fruit, and with the graceful tamarind, the tall peepul, the palm, cocoa-nut, and acacia, forms a leading feature in the landscape. The fig is reared extensively in gardens, where the thick-peeled orange, guava, pomegranate, melon, and pumpkin flourish, as well as an endless assortment of vegetables. Spreading over the land are fields of bageree and jowaree, the staple grain of the country. The former attains the height of a man on horseback. In India, as in most hot climates, ants are plentiful, the Termitinæ or white-ants being the most destructive. Besides several smaller species, there is a great black ant, of the family Attidæ; it has a large knobby head, is usually seen in columns stretching across the plain, occupied in carrying provender from one nest to another, and in storing up supplies for future consumption. These black moving trains of insect life are sometimes a foot in breadth, and from their strange appearance on the highway are very apt to frighten horses.

Among the dried-up watercourses running from the mountains, good specimens of agate are met with, and I have occasionally seen a small onyx from the same situations.

In summer the temperature is very equable, the heat never so great as to necessitate the use of punkhas or thermantidotes;* and in winter the cold is never so severe as to require a fire. The monsoon terminates in October, when the cold weather sets in, lasting until March or April. Then the heat begins to be felt, and nature pants for rain: the plains and mountains present a sunburnt and desolate appearance; at length clouds collect in the east, and the monsoon bursts with great violence. For some time previous there is lightning every night, and the atmosphere feels close and heavy,—a fierce wind then rises, tearing the thatch off the houses, and sending clouds of dust, dense and suffocating, into the rooms. Bang go doors and windows — distant thunder is heard, and the dark mass of cloud is lighted up by vivid flashes of lightning,—the air, at first hot and dry, becomes cool and grateful,—the dust suddenly subsides, and the peculiar smell from the plains tells that the longed-for rain is coming. At last big drops fall, louder and nearer sounds the "artillery of Heaven," as if all the ordnance of British India were roaring around! Gradually the storm-cloud sweeps away—the thunder dies in the distance, and a steady down-pour of rain sets in for days.

During the monsoon the temperature in the shade ranges from 75° to 85° Fahrenheit; vegetation progresses rapidly—the mountains becoming clothed with verdure in a few days.

* A machine, resembling that used in winnowing corn, by which a current of air is forced on a damp matting suspended in front of the door.

Now and then the sun breaks out strong and fierce, the atmosphere becoming laden with vapour from the dank soil. Then it is that sickness appears, and cholera sweeps over the land. It has, however, seldom time to seize many victims before the cold weather begins, and the climate becomes cool and healthy.

Dr. Maury, in his *Physical Geography of the Sea*, says, with reference to the formation of monsoons—"They evaporate, from the Bay of Bengal, water enough to feed with rains, during this season, the western shores of this bay, and the Ghauts range of mountains. This range holds the relation to these winds that the Andes of Peru hold to the south-east trade-winds—it first cools, and then relieves them of moisture, which they tumble down on the western slopes of the Ghauts."

CHAPTER III.

Departure for Scinde, Western Ghauts again—Kandala—A Man drowned—Discomforts of the Sea Voyage—Cholera—Kurrachee—Scenery—Familiar Birds—Climate—Flora—Pearl-oyster—Caucasian Ibex—Pelicans—Game Birds—Woodpecker—Bush-thrushes—Bulbul—Serpent-eagle—Insects—Crocodile Pond—Indus—Scenery—Alligators—Audacity of the Govind-Kite—Sutluj—Ferozepoor to the Himalayas.

On the road between Poonah and Bombay there is much to interest and delight; at Kandala the traveller is surrounded by a varied fauna and flora. What finer sight than that which greets him at day-dawn on some cool November morning, as he wends his way through the defiles, or by the sides of the little rice-fields?—

> "See how at once the bright refulgent sun,
> Rising direct, swift chases from the sky
> The short-lived twilight; and with ardent blaze
> Looks gaily fierce through all the dazzling air."

The roads are covered with heavy-laden waggons, toiling up the steep ascent, while groups of natives are enjoying their hookahs by the road-side, under the grateful shade of the mango and banyan.* The mountain-breeze is cool, even in the heat of summer. The European houses are situated on the sides of the great ravines, with shady avenues and pathways winding through the groves and around the rocky ridges. Kandala is a little highland paradise, and a fitting

* The author refers to some sixteen years since, before any railways existed in India.

place for the climate-worn European, who may seek to restore his health by its pure and invigorating air. I spent a delightful day toiling over these rugged ravines, and after a hard scramble at length gained the camp, and was reclining on my couch, when a soldier rushed into the tent, to inform me that one of his comrades was drowning in a pond close by, and no one could attempt to save him, in consequence of the dense weeds which covered the surface. On repairing to the spot we found the poor fellow in his last struggle, manfully attempting to extricate himself from the meshes of rope-like grass that encircled his body; but, to all appearance, the more he laboured to escape, the more firmly they became coiled round his limbs. At last he sank, and the floating plants closed in, and left not a trace of the disaster. After some delay, a raft was made, and we put off to the spot, and sinking a pole some 12 feet, a native dived, holding on by the stake, and brought the body to the surface. I shall never forget the expression of the dead man's face—the clenched teeth, and fearful distortion of the countenance, while coils of long trailing weeds clung round his body and limbs, the muscles of which stood out, stiff and rigid, whilst his hands grasped thick masses, showing how bravely he had struggled for life. Such was the end of Private John Malony. He had been the life and soul of the detachment with which I sailed from England; and used to keep his companions in roars of laughter, on many a dull evening on shipboard, with his merry Irish songs.

The descent from the Deccan plateaus into the plains brought us into a very different climate. The thermometer rose from 65° to 92° in tents; this, however, was little, compared with the miseries of an over-crowded vessel. The fatigue and discomforts of the officers and men were great, but not to compare with those of 100 women and 150 children, during the four days we spent on board the E.I.C.'s steamer Mozzufur during the voyage to Kurrachee. To call it discomfort is a mild term, when it is considered that 1100 human beings were huddled together like sheep in a fold, lying down at night anywhere, as best they could, unprovided with covering beyond the clothes they wore, exposed to the biting cold of a December night and the scorching heat of mid-day. The regiment had suffered from cholera before leaving Poonah, and a few cases continued on the line of march; twenty-five persons died immediately after we arrived at Kurrachee. We imported the disease to Scinde, and had it not been that the sick were isolated from the inhabitants and other corps in garrison, by being placed in barracks at a distance, there is no saying what might have been the result; yet, in those days, no one seemed inclined to admit that the disease was communicable in any way. The doctrine of the non-infectious and non-contagious character of cholera no doubt received considerable support from the desire on the part of communities to prevent panic; but we find now that the contrary principle is the best, by arousing public attention to the threatened danger, and the adoption of sanitary measures to prevent the spread of this formidable and fatal malady.

After Poonah the scenery of Kurrachee, in 1849, wore no very inviting aspect—long tracts of sandy waste and level shore; everything, animate and inanimate, appeared as though just emerged from a dust-storm. Hedges, trees, and dwellings looked hoary, as if covered with the frost of an English winter, not a blade of grass visible; and except the palm, cactus, and a few stunted shrubs, the surrounding country was one desolate and dreary wilderness.

During the cold months the sun is powerful at mid-day,

but the nights are cold and frosty. We waded along, ankle-deep in the heavy sand, towards the station, about 1½ mile, with a companion who (by way of cheering our drooping spirits) informed us, that four years previously he had lived at Kurrachee, *in a tent*, where the thermometer was often 130°! This, however, we found was not a common occurrence, for during the forepart of the day the sea-breeze sets in and lasts for several hours, so that, take it all in all, the heat of Kurrachee is not so severe as that of many inland stations. The native city is built on an eminence near the sea. Like many Oriental towns, its streets and bazaars are abominably filthy; and, besides the usual hubbub of crowds of natives, goats, and sheep, there is a sickening atmosphere, redolent of rancid butter, assafœtida, and divers other powerful, and not particularly pleasant, odours. Although the Turkish cemeteries at Scutari and Constantinople greatly exceed, in extent of area, anything of the sort I have seen in Hindoostan, the size of that outside the city of Kurrachee is very striking. Nothing shows the antiquity of Eastern towns more than their graveyards; and, even without the testimony of history, those around Kurrachee give evidence of its existence for many centuries. The gravestones are painted white, and covered with various devices in red, becoming thus prominent objects in an otherwise desert plain. Here and there are tall poles, from which float triangular flags of divers colours. We may wander through miles of sepulchres without meeting a symptom of animated nature. Now and then a solitary pied stone-chat (*Saxicola picata*) may be seen hopping about. This familiar little creature I observed at Poonah. It is plentiful in and around Kurrachee, and is, in fact, the "robin" of Scinde.

To one just arrived from the Deccan, the chimney-tops at Kurrachee are suggestive of the comfort of "my ain fireside"—

a pleasure that none appreciate but those who have long been strangers to its genial influence. In consequence of the constant shifting of the sand, there are no regular highways in Lower Scinde. About noon, when the west wind sets in, clouds of sand sweep across the country, penetrating through the minutest chinks and crevices. Whirlwinds (or *devils*, as they are commonly called by Europeans) are of frequent occurrence. At a distance they look like revolving clouds of smoke, shooting upwards fully 200 feet. These cycloidal movements often last for upwards of half-an-hour, and carry with them whatever light substances they may encounter. After gliding along for some distance they finally disappear. The meeting of two opposite currents of air is no doubt the cause, inasmuch as a whirlwind was always seen to commence at the corners of two ranges of buildings placed at right angles to each other.

There is a remarkable difference in the temperature of the wind, after it has traversed two miles of the desert. I made the experiment on horseback, in order to avoid as much as possible reflection from the sand, and found, during a hot forenoon in December, that the thermometer stood in the sun at 75° on the sea-shore, while two miles inland it was 90°.

There are few countries more devoid of natural beauty than Scinde. Pyramids seem only wanting to render its scenery Egyptian, and viewed from any eminence, the neighbourhood of Kurrachee is by no means prepossessing. Northwards, as far as the eye can reach, is one vast plain of sand, studded with *scrub*, or heaps of shingle. Westward, in the distance, are seen the desolate and sun-burnt mountains of Beloochistan. Looking seaward, we have various lines of building, the European barracks and dwellings,* half-hid

* I speak of the year 1849; since then Kurrachee has risen to a good-sized town.

among cactus and euphorbia hedges, which surround gardens, where the usual tropical fruit-trees and vegetables struggle for existence. Among others may be observed the graceful, prickly Jerusalem thorn, a laburnum-like tree, with feathery foliage, and pretty yellow flowers in loose and pendulous racemes. Here and there, at long intervals, are little clusters of date or cocoa-nut, while on the hills and rocky eminences

> "Th' acacia waves her yellow hair,
> Lonely and sweet—nor loved the less
> For flowering in a wilderness."

As Scinde does not come under the influence of the south-west monsoon, its barren and sterile nature is to be attributed to this cause. Beyond an occasional shower, during the cold months, rain seldom falls. Were it not for the dews, nothing would grow on its arid plains; these are often so profuse that in the morning the sand appears as though a heavy shower of rain had fallen. The sun, however, soon dissipates the coolness of the morning breeze, and the sand getting dried begins to blow about with the sea-breeze, and drives us to seek the shelter of our bungalows, where every door, window, and verandah, is closed to prevent its entrance; but in spite of all our endeavours it penetrates into drawers and boxes, and, what is still more uncomfortable, into the bedding.

During December, and the two succeeding months, the cold at night is often severe, being frequently 32° Fahrenheit at daybreak, while at noon it often mounts to 75° or 86° in the shade. Such sudden transitions cannot be otherwise than injurious to European constitutions, and though many have stood these shocks for years, there is no mistaking the effects of the Scinde climate on those who long brave its influence—for tardy, and almost imperceptible as are its manifestations to the individual, or those around him, the new comer is struck with the absence of anything like colour or freshness in the faces of his country people,—especially the gentler sex, whose rosy cheeks soon lose their northern bloom.

The natives of Scinde are a manly-looking race, but in point of physical powers the Beloochees greatly excel. Their well-knit frames, dark complexions, and flashing eyes distinguish them from their more peaceable brethren of the plains. Accoutred with sword, shield, and matchlock, the Beloochee has proved himself a valiant warrior in many a hard fight, from the day he first met the British on the field of Meanee, to the last grand struggle in the Northern Provinces.

The turban is the usual head-dress of the natives. They likewise wear a cap very like a black hat turned brim uppermost.

The pearl-oyster abounds in eleven or twelve fathoms of water all along the coast of Scinde. There was a fishing in the harbour of Kurrachee, which had been of some importance in the days of the native rulers, but was gradually declining.

The shore was covered with heaps of shells—each having a little perforation in its centre, marking the place where the pearl is found. Workmen were employed clearing away the sand, and carefully winnowing the dust and detritus of the shells, in which, now and then, minute pearls are found. The largest shown us was scarcely bigger than a pin's-head, and evidently of very little value, for we could purchase for five shillings as many as would cover the surface of a sixpence.

A "porpoise" is very common in the harbour, and ascends the Indus and rivers of the Punjaub.

The Caucasian ibex (*Capra caucasica*) frequents the mountains of Beloochistan.

I was informed by my lamented friend, the late Dr. Gould,

that it is likewise a native of the Muree and other ranges on the north-western frontier of Scinde. The Caucasus, Asia Minor, Syria, and Arabia, are also countries which it inhabits. It does not appear to travel any great distance eastward, and is probably replaced on the higher ranges of Afghanistan and Persia by its noble congener the Himalayan ibex.

The Caucasian ibex has the hair short and dark brown, with a black line down the back. The beard is also black. Like the European and Himalayan animals, the horns are also bent backwards, but they differ in being more slender and tapering. In the latter, moreover, the horns are three-sided, and the anterior and posterior surfaces sharp, and generally smooth, with the exception of a few irregular tuberosities on the frontal aspect.

Like the other species, it frequents dangerous and inaccessible places, such as bleak and barren mountain-tops.

The chukore, or Cabool partridge, imported from Afghanistan, is sold in the bazaars. Both the gray and black partridges are common in cultivated localities of this neighbourhood. In the Government Gardens I killed a woodpecker, said to be peculiar to this country.

The Scinde woodpecker (*Picus scindianus*) is distinguished from the other pied species by having the sides of the body dirty-white, and a broad streak of black down the side of the neck from the base of the lower mandible.

The Mahratta woodpecker (*P. mahrattensis*) is also not uncommon. Sand-shrikes (*Lanius arenarius*) are plentiful in cactus-bushes in the open country; and in the dense foliage of the gardens the white-fronted flycatcher (*Rhipidura albofrontata*) is often seen. In habits it resembles the broad-tailed species, but the clearness of the white on its body and forehead will suffice to distinguish it from the other.

The striated babbler (*Malacocircus candatus*) is known by the light brown striæ on its back—lower parts dirty-white. It is less in size than the pale-eared babbler (*M. malcolmi*), likewise found here. The habits of the two are similar, frequenting hedges and close cover, where they are usually seen in flocks.

The white-eared bulbul (*Rotocompsa leucotis*) is not, I believe, found in the Deccan, although plentiful in this country and the Punjaub.

The short-toed or serpent-eagle (*Circætus gallicus*) is often seen soaring over dwellings, but more frequently perched on a tree-top in the centre of a field, watching for its favourite prey; it lives principally on reptiles. I killed one whose stomach contained many small frogs. At a distance this bird might be mistaken for the common buzzard (*Buteo vulgaris*). It is, however, easily distinguished by the rufous white of the lower parts, with brown streaks. The total length is about 2 feet.

In Scinde (as in all desert countries) ants abound. The white ant (*Termitcs*), so plentifully distributed over Hindoostan, does not seem to be common at Kurrachee; at least I did not observe the sugar-loaf nests so characteristic of its presence.

There are many other species which make their nests in the open plains—entering by numerous holes in the surface of the sand. In some places the ground is literally riddled with these apertures. The large black species seen at Poonah is by far the most common. One day, during a ramble in the neighbourhood of Kurrachee, I observed a string of these ants extending from their nest across a plain for more than a quarter of a mile in the direction of an out-house or barn. Instead of carrying their eggs, these industrious little travellers were employed in stocking up supplies for future use. In the usual steady double file they were proceeding to and from their nest; one party moving slowly on, heavily loaded, each individual carrying a vetch-seed about twice the size of its bearer; while the returning party hurried back for a fresh burden. I passed them again at dusk, and on the following day found them as busy as ever. What a vast granary they must have collected even in twenty-four hours!

After rain, or heavy dew, they bring forth their store, and spread the grain round the entrances of their nests to dry; and, from some unknown cause, they often change their dwelling-places, carrying their grain with them.

Musquitoes are very abundant, and the common black fly, which seems to be indigenous to every clime, is here, as in all tropical countries, a perfect pest. In every stall of the bazaars it swarms in countless thousands, and, wonderful to relate, even in the centre of the desert, it continues to annoy and irritate the traveller.

During very cold weather in December a living female of the allied swift (*Cypselus affinis*) was brought to me, in a numbed state from cold, and the only one I saw during my short stay at Kurrachee. Its body was plump, and well covered with fat, but not a trace of food was discernible throughout the whole course of the intestinal canal. Perhaps this individual had been caught in the cold on its way to the more genial winter climates of Central or Southern India. Associating with minas and Indian jackdaws, are flocks of the common starling (*Sturnus vulgaris*). It frequents dunghills and fields.

The Indian wheatear (*Saxicola atrogularis*) is generally distributed over the sandy wastes in this neighbourhood. In general appearance and habits it bears a resemblance to its European allies. We see in this species the peculiar tinge of plumage common to many birds of desert countries. The feathers appear as if they had been tipped with a sandy-white, or isabel-colour, obscuring more or less the darker shades beneath.

They run with great agility along the level plains. In this respect there is no bird can beat the Coromandel courier (*Cursorius isabellinus*). Flocks of these plover-like birds are often seen on the sandy wastes of Kurràchee and Lower Scinde. They are not easily observed, in consequence of the similarity of their plumage to surrounding objects. Locusts seem to be their principal food, and on these they feed sumptuously, for sometimes clouds of these insects scour across the country. The flesh of the courier is well-flavoured, pale, and delicate. They are easily shot, and as many as four or six may be killed at one time, in consequence of their crowding together when feeding on the plain.

The whimbrel (*Numenius phæopus*) and curlew (*N. arquata*) are both found in the harbour; and associated with these birds, may often be observed a large pied species of plover. The flamingo (*Phœnicopterus roseus*) is often seen in flocks upon the coast.

The jackal (*Canis aureus*) is seldom visible during the day. At night packs of these animals prowl about the station, and at early morning may be observed skulking across the plains in the direction of their caves in ravines. Their wailing cry is very discordant. Often, in a dark night, the traveller is suddenly startled by the bark of a jackal—another at a short distance replies, and soon he is surrounded by ten or twenty—whose howlings are sometimes mingled with the hoarse bark of the hyena (*Hyæna striata*). Like the other, the hyena hunts at night, and is equally partial to carrion and putridity.

The cry of the jackal is peculiar; it is composed of a succession of half-barking, half-wailing cries, on different notes. When properly pronounced there is no better illustration of it than the following words, set to the music of the animal's voice—

"Dead Híndōō—Dead Hindōō!
Whĕre—whĕre—whĕre—whĕre?
Here—here—here—here!"

Being suggestive of a straggler, suddenly discovering a dead body, and calling on the scattered pack to "come and feast!" They have evidently a predilection for human flesh, and sometimes, especially during epidemics or on battle-fields, they have rare opportunities of indulging their appetites. It happened that during my stay at Kurrachee a pack of these animals found their way into a hospital dead-house and mutilated two bodies of persons who died of cholera.

In all the desert parts of Scinde the crested calandre lark (*Galerida cristata*) is plentiful. It is not unlike the skylark, but does not "up to heaven gates ascend." It is generally met with in flocks during the cold months.

Although I have not shot or seen the chimney-swallow in Scinde, I have observed specimens in collections made in Lower Scinde during the cold months; also the beautiful fairy roller (*Irena puella*), rare in the northern parts of India.

The Crocodile-pond, or "Mugger-peer," as it is called, lies to the north-west of Kurrachee. The journey for the first few miles is of the usual uninteresting description—sandy plains, intersected with deep fissures and ravines, or studded here and there with "scrub," the oleander-leafed spurge (*Euphorbia nerifolia*) plentiful in all waste and desert parts of Scinde.

Emerging from a defile which leads through a low range of hills, the traveller enters on a desert waste, stretching westward towards the mountains of Beloochistan. In the far distance two oases are visible, whose date and cocoa-nut trees are refreshing to the sight after eight miles of the most monotonous scenery. In the vicinity of the nearest grove is an ancient burial-ground, where may be observed several curiously-carved gravestones.

I visited the crocodiles (*Crocodilus palustris*) on two occasions at an interval of several years, and although during that time they had been seen by hundreds of Europeans, including a certain class of mischievous young Englishmen (whose chief amusement, we were told, had been to shy stones and sticks down the throats of the gaping monsters as they lay basking on the banks of the pond), yet there seemed no diminution in their numbers, and the wild and unearthly interest of the scene was to us as great as ever. From beneath a little banyan-tree on the verge of the pond, the spectacle, during the steaming heat of a mid-day sun, might call up to the mind of the geologist the eons of the world, when the "great monsters" wallowed in the seething waters of the Oolitic ages, when the mighty "Ichthyosaurus," and a host of "fearfully great lizards," dragons, etc., reigned supreme over sea and land. And as the date-palm now waves its shady boughs over the crocodiles of Mugger-peer, so then did the magnificent tree-ferns, gigantic reeds, and club-mosses, shelter their extinct predecessors.

The greater pond is about 300 yards in circumference, and contains many little grassy islands, on which the majority of the crocodiles were then basking; some were asleep on its slimy sides, others half-submerged in the muddy water, while now and then a huge monster would raise himself upon his diminutive legs, and waddling for a few paces, fall flat on his belly. Young ones, from a foot in length and upwards, ran nimbly along the margin of the pond, disappearing suddenly in the turbid waters as soon as we approached. The largest crocodile lives in a long narrow tank separate from the others. The Fakirs, and natives who worship in the neighbouring temples, have painted his forehead red,—they venerate the old monster, making a salaam to his majesty whenever he shows himself above water. A handsome young Beloochee, whose occupation it was to feed the animals, informed us that the said king was upwards of two hundred years old! (?) and that, by way of a "tit-bit," he was in the habit of devouring the young crocodiles. During our visit this enormous brute was asleep on the bank of his dwelling-place, and seemed quite indifferent to our presence, although we came within a foot of him, and even attempted to arouse him by rubbing his nose with a leg of goat's-flesh, which, however, a young one greedily seized and dived under water. Our attendant tried in vain to excite their ferocity, but beyond a feeble attempt to snap their trenchant teeth, the animals showed no disposition to attack us.

A pony was wading about in the pond and feeding on the grassy hillocks, but the crocodiles took no notice of him.

The water in the pool felt cold, although fed from two hot springs, one of which was of so high a temperature that I could not retain my hand in it; yet animal life existed, for I found where the water bubbled up from its sandy bottom, and in the little lade running to the tank, abundance of a species of small black spiral shell, which Mr. Woodward informed me is "very like some in the British Museum, named *Melania pyramis*, an allied species of which frequents the river Jordan."* The other spring gushes from under a bed of limestone, containing numbers of fossils, chiefly coral, and other marine zoophites. We had a refreshing bathe in a reservoir close by; the temperature, though not so high as the last, was still warm and pleasant. I should be sorry, however, to repeat the experiment, not from the chances of meeting with a crocodile (for, I believe, the Fakirs of the temple guard well against such accidents), but from the circumstance that (as is generally the case all over the East), lepers, and persons affected with loathsome diseases, repair to such localities.

The crocodiles dig deep in the sand, under the neighbouring date-trees, and there deposit their eggs. Quantities of deciduous teeth, of various sizes, were strewn along the slimy sides of the pond.

Strangers are expected to stand treat, not only by the Fakirs and natives, who gain a livelihood by hanging about the pond and showing the monsters, but even the crocodiles themselves seem to anticipate a feast, and on the arrival of a party come out in unusual numbers. Accordingly, we had a goat slaughtered, during which operation the brutes seemed to rouse themselves, as if preparing for a rush. Then our guide, taking piece after piece of the flesh, dashed it on the bank, uttering a low growling sound, at which the whole tank became in motion, and crocodiles, of whose existence we had been before ignorant, splashed through the shallow water, struggling which should seize the prize. The shore was literally covered with scaly monsters, snapping their jaws at one another.

They seize their food with the *side* of the mouth, and toss the head backward, in order that it may fall into the throat.

A few were observed to bolt their portion on shore after

* The temperature of the water in the lade was 127° Fahr.

very slight mastication, but the majority, anxious to escape from their greedy companions, made instantly for the water, and disappeared with the piece of flesh sticking between their jaws.

Our young Belooch friend informed us that they generally swallow their food at once, and do not, as has been asserted, bury it until it becomes putrid; also that other large individuals besides the old king frequently devour the young soon after they are hatched. Crocodiles wallowing in the mud of the Nile, or gavials in the Indus, are sights which one is prepared to encounter; but the traveller may wander far before he meets with a scene so strange and unexpected as that just described. How these animals found their way inland to this solitary oasis we could not discover. It can only be surmised that they had probably been introduced by the natives.

We left Kurrachee in a small steamer "one fine sunny morning" towards the end of January, and reached the Delta of the Indus in ten hours.

The scenery along the Scinde coast was devoid of interest until, nearing the river, the dreary and sandy wastes gave place to a rich green carpet, on which sheep, goats, and cattle were pasturing.

Tall reeds line the shore, out of which flocks of pelican and waterfowl, scared by the approach of our little vessel, rose and sought more secluded retreats among the numerous channels, creeks, and islands which abound at the mouths of the Indus. The porcupine is not uncommon in the neighbourhood; we came on a dead specimen.

The govind-kite followed in the wake of our vessel, sweeping obliquely downwards, and seizing with its talons any substance thrown overboard; and whenever we drew up to cook or take in fuel, numbers of Indian jackdaws hovered at the stern, within a few feet of the water, picking up whatever they could lay their bills on.

This noisy bird assembles in numbers, and assails one on entering a grove with a deafening clamour of cawing and croaking. The only alternative is to show *a gun*, when they decamp with all possible speed.

Its nest is built of twigs, and is lined with wool or any other soft substance. As many as twenty may frequently be seen in one tree. The Indian jackdaw has all the craft and more familiarity than any of its congeners, as it rivals them in the beauty of its glossy gray and black plumage.

We sometimes observed varieties with white markings on the wings and back, but these were dispersed throughout separate flocks, and did not seem to form any characteristic of what might be called a race.

A voyage up the Indus, after a lengthened sojourn at Kurrachee, is very exhilarating. To the lover of nature there are few better fields for research. Let him choose the cold months, when the river is well stocked with wild-fowl, and he will find ample occupation.

How different is the scene in June, when the inundation has taken place, and nothing is to be seen but a vast sheet of water, tenanted only by a few indigenous animals, such as the Indian alligator and pelicans—the greater part of the migratory birds have fled to the far north, and are rearing their young on the banks of the lakes of Central Asia. Again, as the hot season declines, long trains of cranes, storks, spoonbills, etc. etc., make their appearance; and in a few days every creek and shallow seems alive with myriads of these interesting wanderers. The scenery is constantly varying. At times the river looks like an almost boundless waste of water, stretching far away inland on both sides, intersected with numerous islands; or, gliding tardily between high banks of alluvium, dense jungles of tamarisk and underwood alternate with open and highly-cultivated tracts of country, which are irrigated from the river by means of Persian wheels worked by camels. At every turn of the river the traveller hears the dull creaking sound made by these machines.

Fields of wheat, barley, grain,* and mustard gladden the eye. The last is cultivated for its oil, which the natives burn instead of that of the cocoa-nut, generally used in the Deccan.

The mud villages are shaded by groves of mangoes, which may be seen stretching in lines across the country, while here and there dense shikargahs† (formerly the hunting-grounds of the Amirs of Scinde) vary the landscape. These are now fast disappearing, their wood being used as fuel for the river-steamers.

The channels of the Indus, and indeed all the great northern rivers of India, are continually shifting, in consequence of the constant and copious deposit of alluvium going on; the mud banks are also wearing away at a greater rate than formerly, and since the introduction of steamers, for as the swell gradually undermines them, large masses fall in with a thundering noise.

The water of the Indus is thick and muddy, but filtering, or the addition of a few grains of alum, renders it clear and drinkable.

It is asserted that there is an undercurrent in the Indus, so powerful as to suck down whatever disappears beneath the surface of the water; we had, however, a pretty strong

* *Cicer arietinum.*

† Game-preserves.

proof of the contrary, in the case of a boy who fell overboard and passed under the steamer, reappearing on the other side, where he was picked up not much the worse for his ducking.

The native boats are of the rudest description—flat-bottomed, raised at front and stern, something like the ancient British galley. The large square sail is all the canvas they carry. Numbers of these primitive crafts may be seen upon the river in every direction. The Indus is seen to the best advantage when the sun is setting in all his fiery beauty, and long trains of pelicans sweep along close to the surface of the river, which, as far as the eye reaches, is studded with native boats, and here and there a sandbank lined by myriads of water-fowl; shoreway there is little attractive save a clump of date, or a tope of acacia, etc., which add however to the true Oriental character of the scenery. The handsome little black-billed tern (*Sterna javanica*) is abundant. It is to be seen searching for fish in the little shallows, or by the banks of the river, congregating in situations where its prey abounds —now hovering and flapping its long pointed wings—then, with a scream, darting downwards, with unerring accuracy, and bearing off its scaly prize in triumph.

Athwart the surface of the river, its little wings almost touching the water, shoots like an arrow the beautiful Bengal kingfisher (*Alcedo bengalensis*), now and then dipping its green and azure plumage in the muddy stream. So closely allied is this species to the European bird, that unless minutely examined there is no knowing the one from the other.

The brahminy kite (*Haliastur indus*) is a handsome bird of prey; although wanting the grace and rapidity of flight of the govind-kite, it has the advantage as regards beauty and colouring of plumage. Individuals may be seen frequently stooping on fish in the river, or hovering over the shallows. The head, neck, and irides are white—the rest of the body chestnut. The Luzonian (*Motacilla luzoniensis*) and Dukhun wagtails (*M. dukhunensis*), and common sandpiper (*Actitis hypoleucus*), are constantly seen on the river-bank.

Less frequently may be observed the greater and lesser white-rumped sandpipers (*Totanus glottis* and *stagnatilis*). Sand-martins (*Hirundo riparia*) build their nests in holes on the river-bank, which are sometimes riddled in this manner. Occasionally the rose-ringed parrakeet (*Palæornis torquatus*) takes possession of one of these nests for its own use, and is accused by the natives of robbing them and eating the eggs, which, however, seems doubtful.

One of the most striking birds to be seen on the Indus is the white-headed eagle (*Haliaëtus macei*); although closely allied to the bald eagle of America, the two species differ in many particulars. The Eastern eagle is usually seen perched on the stump of a tree, numbers of which are borne down by the annual inundations, and as the river subsides appear above water like the snags of the Mississippi. Fish are its chief, but not exclusive subsistence, as we many times saw them, during our journey, feasting with jackdaws and kites on the refuse of slaughtered sheep and oxen. The plumage of this eagle is subject to considerable variation—in reference to the young and adult bird.

Pelicans (*Pelicanus javanicus*) in pairs and in flocks were observed daily on the river, sailing leisurely down some narrow channel, their great bills resting on their crooked necks, or, scared at our approach, sought a safer retreat among the shallows and sandbanks far ahead. Their flight is in general heavy and laborious. In many the bill is bright orange—in some of a leaden-gray colour, varying with age. The two species are not easily recognised until observed closely; the roseate hue, however, of the white pelican distinguishes it from the Dalmatian, which is perhaps the more common. The barred-headed goose (*Anser indicus*) is very plentiful on the Indus and northern rivers of Hindostan, but only during the cold months. It is not so large as the gray-goose, and has a triangular-shaped black bar on the nape, another on the back part of the head. Both this bird and the crane arrive in vast flocks, during October, and spread all over the cultivated districts, where they do much damage to the young wheat and barley; nowhere are they more abundant than on the Jhelum, between the city of that name and its junction with the Indus. I have seen specimens of the white-fronted goose (*A. albifrons*) that were shot near Suckur, and recognised it on wing several times.

The capital of Upper Scinde is situated a short distance inland. Like most of the native cities, it has its mud wall, crumbling fort, narrow and filthy streets; its temperature is at all times very high—for, as a friend of mine remarked, "cold weather at Hyderabad is a delusion."

In addition to the usual pleasure of sight-seeing, I had an intense interest in tracing the scenes where the 22d Regiment had taken so glorious a part: we visited the fields of Meanee and Dubba, and the famous Residency, situated on the left bank, and shaded by a dense grove of mangoes.

Opposite is the village and station of Koteree, perhaps the most beautiful spot on the banks of the Indus in its course through Scinde.

The European houses are placed among terraces and groves of date and other trees; their gardens, tastefully laid out, well stocked with vegetables and fruit-trees. We shall long remember the shady groves of Koteree, and a walk we had there one cool morning in February—the Surat dove and Asiatic pigeon (*Turtur suratensis et humilis*) cooing over head, and the "little birdies blithely singing;" there was a freshness about the scene we had not enjoyed for a long time. Even its green leaves, after the desert sands, brought up thoughts and associations of the haunts of earlier days.

Proceeding up the Indus, the scenery improves. As you near Sehwan, high mountain-ridges are seen stretching across the country in a northerly direction. The banks are covered with tamarisk, or dense forest and jungle. Birds are in greater plenty, and the surrounding country teems with animal life. Nature wears a more glowing robe.

As the sportsman threads his way through the jungle in quest of hog-deer (*Hyelaphus porcinus*), pigs (*Sus scrofa*), hares (*Lepus nigricollis*), or partridges (*Francolinus vulgaris et ponticerianus*), he feels a sort of nervous twinge as he sees in the mud by the side of a pond the broad rounded footprint of a tiger. There the fierce lord of the jungle has been skulking only a few hours previously! Then there is excitement when, suddenly emerging from the bushy labyrinth, the eye of the young Indian sportsman lights upon the graceful figure of the Houbara bustard (*Houbara macqueenii*), feeding on the tender shoots of the young barley! The Houbara is migratory in Scinde, and is found in the desert; but is plentiful in the cultivated districts along the banks of the river.

The eye of the Houbara is large, clear, and prominent. The yellow and black of the eye give a peculiarly brilliant appearance to the bird. Its flesh is much esteemed as an article of food. Hunting the Houbara in the open plain requires great tact and dexterity. Mounted on a camel, the pursuer ranges the desert with his telescope until an individual is discovered.

This is by no means easily accomplished, in consequence of the plumage assimilating with the colour of the sand. He then commences to describe circles round the bird, gradually diminishing their circumference until he gets within shot, when he dismounts, using the saddle as a rest for his gun or rifle. The Houbara leaves Scinde at the beginning of the hot months, possibly for Persia, where it is said to be found at all seasons.

The bastard floriken (*Œdicnemus crepitans*) is very common on the banks of the river. It is tame and easily shot, consequently little sought after by sportsmen.

The gavial or Indian alligator (*Gavialis gangeticus*) abounds in all the great rivers of Northern India. It is found in the Indus, from its delta northwards to near Attock, and up the Punjaub rivers for a considerable distance, where it is most abundant. This may be owing to the constant traffic from Mooltan downwards driving them to seek the parts seldom frequented by steamers.

This species is easily distinguished from any of its congeners by its spoonbill-like snout. Its eyes are prominent, throat white, body long and tapering. The gavial delights to bask on the sandbanks and slimy inlets, lying on its belly, the snout at an obtuse angle with the neck. Ten or twenty may be frequently seen together, and as the steamer approaches they glide quietly one by one into their muddy bed. The larger are generally from 12 to 15 feet in length, but occasional individuals may be seen of far greater size. On shore the old are very tardy in their movements, but the young run nimbly along the sands. I have seen a gavial raise its head above water close to the paddle-box of our steamer, take a quick survey, and suddenly disappear.

The fishermen informed us that they now and then carry off a man; yet numbers of natives may be seen wading about regardless of their proximity.

The native mode of crossing the river is somewhat novel. Rolling in the folds of his turban all his goods and chattels, the Scindian inflates a dog-skin. This is fastened across his breast, and supporting his legs by means of a large chatty (mug of earthenware with a narrow mouth), which he holds firmly between his ankles. If his child has likewise to be conveyed, the youth seizes his sire round the neck, crossing his legs over his back, the head only above water, while the swimmer, with his arms free, paddles himself, his child, and property, across the muddy water of the Hydaspes.

With that bold and majestic flight so characteristic of the tribe, the white-bellied cormorant (*Graculus carbo*) is seen flying across the river, and although not so plentiful, the brown-necked species (*Graculus sinensis*) is not uncommon.

The stork is often seen in large flocks, distinguishable by their red bills and legs, white plumage, and black wings.

Wading in the shallows may be seen a solitary heron (*Ardea cinerea*), and

> "See where yonder stalks, in crimson pride,
> The tall flamingo, by the river's side;
> Stalks in his richest plumage bright array'd,
> With snowy neck superb, and legs of length'ning shade."

The pass of Sehwan has a picturesque appearance from the river, with its rocky mountains rising in terraces along the bank, and its old ruined castle, supposed to have belonged to the Alexandrian age.

For the benefit of sportsmen and naturalists, I would

recommend a visit to the pool near the village of Sehwan, which during the cold months is covered with wild-fowl; here we procured specimens of the shoveller (*Anas clypeata*), castaneous (*Fuligula nyroca*), and tufted ducks (*F. cristata*), also the Gargany teal (*Anas querquedula*), and here I met for the first time the spotted-billed duck (*Anas pœcilorhyncha*). It is much larger than the mallard, and has a black bill with a red spot at the base, and less yellow—body speckled. This species is said not to be a resident, and breeds in the jungles on the river's bank. Towards dusk, the tern-like sheerwaters or skimmers (*Rhynchops*) appear in companies of from four to eight, skimming so close to the water, that their curiously-shaped bills and the tips of their wings often touch; they never settle, but seem to glean their food as they fly along; what that was I could not discover, possibly small fish, moths, or locusts; the two last are often found floating on the surface of the river in great numbers.

One morning, at daybreak, I was amused at the curious evolutions of a species of water-gnat ephemera; it was about an inch in length, and of a white colour, with two very long hair-like processes (*setæ*) projecting from the tail. The rapidity with which these little creatures propelled themselves, with or against the current, surprised me. By the constant flapping of their wings upon the water, aided perhaps by their legs, and guided by their setæ, the least waver of which seemed to turn the little animal in less than a moment, they steered their way rapidly, facing the current boldly, leaving two tiny furrows in their lee like those of a steamboat; in fact they were in principle diminutive steamers. They evidently furnished food for fish, as we noticed myriads of small-fry catching them.

The tall minarets of Suckur are seen a long way off, and

the banks of the river, for some distance below the town, are densely clad with date and cocoa-nut groves. Opposite is Roree, looking like some stronghold, with its houses built one above another on a prominence overlooking the river.

The ancient fortress of Bukur is situated on an island opposite Roree. Here the river is considerably narrowed, and the stream powerful. The heat of Suckur is intense, and its climate unhealthy. The pulla or tamarind-fish is caught in abundance and by various methods, sometimes by fishermen perched on a narrow-necked earthenware mug, which serves the double purpose of support and a reservoir for his fish and tackle; others buoy themselves up by means of dog-skins kept inflated from a mouthpiece. Some ten or fifteen fishermen were dropping slowly down with the current.

A squall is a most exciting spectacle. From twenty to thirty boats may be seen tracking slowly up the river, each dragged by its own crew. Suddenly a breeze springs up, and all jump on board, and unfurl the large square sails, when away they speed; sometimes bumping up on sandbanks, or running into one another amid the yelling and screaming of the boatmen.

None earn their bread by the sweat of their brows more honestly than these simple boatmen of the Indus. From daylight to sundown they may be seen dragging a heavily-laden boat along the muddy river, often half the day knee-deep in water. When about to enter upon the day's toil, by way of wishing "God speed" to his little craft, her owner throws a handful of water on her bow, says his prayer, and then, arranging his toilette (composed only of a turban and waistband), he shoulders his rope, and singing some simple chaunt sets cheerily forth on his way.

As simple as his song are his modes of life. At night he

grinds his little hand-mill to make flour for his badgeree cakes, which, with a slight addition of curry, are washed down by the muddy water of the Indus. Yet in point of strength, and power of endurance, few surpass him.

The Indian owl (*Athene brama*) is numerous in the jungles.

The first time I met with the raven (*Corvus corax*)* in the East was on the banks of the Indus, some distance above Suckur.

Daily during the remainder of the boat voyage, and until we reached Ferozepoor, numbers of ravens, crows, jackdaws, and bald-headed eagles, assembled on the debris of the cattle slaughtered for our use.

On these occasions I witnessed the daring sallies of the govind-kite. One afternoon, in particular, when the steamer was drawn up by the river's bank, a native was eating his "curry," when down dropped a kite, and, by means of its talons, actually tore the wings of a fowl from his mouth, devouring the capture as it sailed away. Great was the poor man's amazement, but his wife, who seemed to understand the habits of the govind-kite better than her husband, seized a stick, which she brandished over his head during the rest of the meal.

On a subsequent occasion, during our voyage up the Sutluj, we halted on a wet and sandy beach for the purpose of cooking. As the soldiers and their wives were returning to the vessel, carrying their plates of beef and rice, a flock of kites assailed them; darting, like so many arrows, on the laden platters, and bore off the contents. The sight was ludicrous in the extreme. One woman, from the clayey nature of the soil, was unable to extricate her feet, and

* It is in every respect identical with the European bird.

remained, with outstretched arms, helplessly imploring assistance, as kite after kite, in quick succession, carried away her dinner!

The govind-kite is a great enemy to poultry, and sometimes pursues tame pigeons, which it tortures to death, by pursuing them until they fall to the ground breathless, and are thus easily despatched. The same predatory disposition seems common to other allied species, inasmuch as I have seen the black and Egyptian kites, in Nubia, capture pigeons in the same way.

The Indian peregrine falcon was seen several times during our voyage, and I found a nest on an acacia-tree, near the banks of the Sutluj. It was built of sticks and lined with wool, and contained two young birds newly hatched.

In dissecting an adult specimen, I found numbers of a species of round worm, from 8 to 12 inches in length, and the thickness of a common pack-thread.* Coils of these parasites infested the abdominal cavity, under its investing membrane, and smaller sizes, of about half-an-inch in length, were common in the throat, gullet, and intestines. Still the bird (a female) was plump and in good condition.

The gotah-finch—white-bellied or singing babbler (*Chrysomma sinense*)—is plentiful in the jungles. Flocks of these curious birds may be seen flitting from bush to bush with a peculiar, feeble, fluttering flight. When frightened, the parties assemble in some dense bush, and commence chattering in low, sweet, musical notes.

The Sardinian starling (*Sturnus unicolor*) is likely to be confounded with the common starling, to which it assimilates in habits as well as general appearance. Sometimes both species are seen feeding together on dunghills and in fields;

* I noticed the same in one killed in Nubia.

and although the former is the more common, the latter was often observed during our rambles on the banks of the river.

The pretty blue-throated warbler (*Cyanecula suecica*) frequents the mustard-fields and low scrub, frisking about like the robin redbreast. All specimens I have shot and examined in India had the spot on the breast rufous.

By the sides of tanks, and in damp situations overgrown with stunted rushes or carex, may be found the yellow-headed wagtail (*Budytes citreola*), generally perched on a tuft of the latter, its long hind-claw facilitating this position. There can be no difficulty in recognising this bird from other yellow wagtails, by the last-named peculiarity and the head, neck, and lower parts being yellow.

The Brahminy goose (*Casarca rutila*) is often met with above Suckur. The male is a fine-looking bird, and measures about 29 inches ; the general colour of the plumage is rufous, with brilliant green on the wing-coverts. It is shy and wary, and not easily approached.

Flocks of mallards, teal, Gargany teal, and spoonbills, line the shores and cover the little islands. The spoonbills are easily distinguished by their white bodies and black legs. The pintail-duck is not uncommon, and now and then we killed numbers of that fine duck the red-headed pochard, distinguished by a prominent rufous crest.

On gaining the mouth of the Sutlej our party disembarked from the steamers, and made the rest of the voyage in native boats, thatched and covered over. In this way I had a better opportunity of observing the natural history of the districts we passed through, which, in point of fertility, increased as we proceeded onwards. Luxuriant crops of barley and wheat covered the country ; the yellow tinge of the ripening grain contrasted beautifully with the brilliant green of the gram-fields.

On the 10th of April we arrived at Ferozepoor, where we were delayed some time making arrangements for our march.

The great heat of summer was rapidly approaching, and we were glad when fairly on our way to the Himalayas. The route led through Loodiana and Umballah. As usual in the East, we commenced our marches very early, so as to get under cover by 8 A.M. When the cooling effects of a mussiek* of water refreshed us for our breakfast, the remainder of the day was generally spent in endeavours to exclude from our tents flies, mosquitoes, and that prince of gallynippers, the sand-fly, whose bite produces a painful and irritable swelling.

The scenery of Ferozepoor, and for a few marches eastward, is not by any means attractive; beyond occasional cultivated patches, the country is covered with low, stunted scrub, sandy wastes, or jungles of tamarisk, acacia, cactus, or the milkweeds. This monotony was, however, compensated by the herds of antelopes (*Antilope bezoartica*) often met with in the open, and affording excellent long shots for our best riflemen.

The black buck rivals any of the deer tribe in grace and elegance, as it certainly excels in swiftness of foot. Its spring is particularly grand, as when, wounded or scared by the shot, it stands motionless for a moment, and then like lightning bounds across the plain, reminding us of Moore's beautiful lines,—

> "Our sands are bare, but down their slope
> The silvery-footed antelope
> As gracefully and gaily springs,
> As o'er the marble courts of kings!"

---

* A skin used for carrying water.

On approaching Loodiana* the landscape becomes really beautiful. Mango-topes, and fields of grain and sugar-cane, cover the plains, while here and there are seen the strongholds of the old Sikh chieftains.

The road leads through the field of Aliwal, on which we encamped.

It has been said that the descriptions of the Peninsular battles received additional grandeur from the spirit-stirring pen of the talented narrator—that many who witnessed them could scarcely recognise them when dressed in the glowing language of the soldier-historian. Much has been said of Aliwal, but candid witnesses give a far different account from that written at the time.

I wandered over the field with one who had been present at the engagement; he assured me, and his testimony has been corroborated by many others, that a fruitful imagination was at work when the official account was drawn up. His words were :—

"Aliwal was the *battle of the despatch,* for none of us knew we had fought a battle until the particulars appeared in a document, which did *more* than justice to every one concerned."

But the public gulped it down, and, like many of our Indian battles and Indian blunders, the final issue of the struggle disarmed criticism.

As an Irishman would say, "We gained a disadvantage at Budiwal," by the baggage of the army falling into the hands of the enemy; *that* no exaggeration could well turn into a victory; but shortly afterwards, a few shots, and the charge of a squadron or two in pursuit of a host of retreating Sikhs, were

* Bishop Heber, in his *Journal,* says, "Lions are met with near Loodiana and Almorah." I cannot vouch for such being the case with reference to the latter locality, but certainly no lions are seen nowadays in any part of the North-west Provinces.

magnified into a grand combat, and thus the plain of Aliwal has been recorded as the scene of one of India's Marathons.

The Indian ring-dotterel (*Hiaticula philippina*), peafowl, common quail, black and gray partridges, are plentiful in grain-fields. The green bee-eater is very common, and usually roosts at night in societies, perching as close to each other as possible; in that way a string of from ten to twenty may be often seen on one branch. The common mina and its close ally the bank or gingi grackle are often noticed; the last is distinguished by its reddish bill and eyelids. Flocks of this species were often seen on the banks of the Indus and with cattle in the fields. In the middle of a tamarisk jungle, many miles from human habitations, I found the skull of a bullock suspended from the branch of a tree, and much to my surprise a sparrow's nest and eggs were discovered in the interior, showing that this species is not partial to civilised life.

Soon after leaving Loodiana, the stupendous Himalayan chains, with their snow-clad summits, were seen far away against the blue sky eastward.

Daily, as we neared the lower or Sewalik range, the scenery became more attractive. Dense jungles, or wooded tracts of hill and dale, gladden the weary traveller, and cheer up the invalid, on his way from the torrid plains. He must indeed hail with delight the little village of Kalka, at the foot of the mountains, the starting-point for those proceeding to the sanatoria at Kussoulee, Subathoo, Dugshai, Simla.

I can never forget how eagerly I longed to mount the steep ascent before me; for in a few hours you can be transported to a temperature of 70°, instead of 80° in the shade—truly delicious, after the feverish heat of the plains, and the dust and fatigue of a march in the month of April.

CHAPTER IV.

Division of the Himalayas into Regions—Scenery of the Lower Ranges—Climate—Magnificent View—Productions—Strange Way of putting Children asleep—Familiar Birds—Cuckoo—Black Partridge; its Habits and Haunts—Barking Deer—Gray Partridge—Hill Wagtails—Storms—Woodcock—Snipe—Spotted Eagle—Bulbul—Bearded Vulture—Bare-headed Vultures.

THE Western Himalayas may be divided into three regions.

1st. The lower or Sewalik region, comprehending the lesser ranges which border the plains of India, and differ but little from the latter in climate and natural productions. This region extends to an elevation of about 3000 feet above the level of the sea.

2d. The middle or forest region embraces the highly-cultivated and forest tracts, where nature wears the garb of the temperate zone.

3d. The upper or snowy region, comprising the table-lands and mountains of Thibet, Ladakh, etc., extending from the stunted birch at 8000 to 9000 feet above the sea-level to the limits of perpetual snow. The fauna and flora of this region are distinct from the foregoing, inasmuch as its animals seldom descend to the lower zones unless driven by the rigors of winter, and its plants present an arctic facies. The geological features vary much, from the upper and mid tertiary beds of the lower hills to the secondary and azoic rocks of the middle and upper regions. But what gives a most characteristic appearance to each of these belts is their flora. Although perhaps not so well defined as that of the Andes, still the tropical, temperate, and arctic forms preserve their position with marked regularity. Thus the naturalist from Kalka, at the foot of the Sewalik range, on his journey by the hill-road to Simla, can trace without difficulty the gradual botanical changes, from the stunted palm-tree to the gnarled oak, on to the stately pine, and thence to the lichen and rhododendron. The journey through the mountains to Simla and other hill-stations is usually performed by a litter, sedan-chair, or on horseback. The stages are easy, and there is tolerably good accommodation at the various halting-places. So marked are the gradations of climate, and so rapid, that from the torrid heat of the plains, and 90° Fahrenheit in the shade, one may be easily transported in forty-eight hours to a temperature below zero. The scenery of the lower ranges is exceedingly striking and beautiful. I felt as if suddenly conveyed to the temperate zone, and more especially when the stately cheer-pines, wild roses, jessamines, violets and dandelion met my view; but, however, there was an admixture of stranger plants and trees peculiar to the region, then quite unknown to me, such as the coral-tree with its gorgeous red flowers, and oaks with laurel-shaped leaves.

The mountains forming the lesser ranges which border on the plains of India present in general great broken chains running for the most part parallel and from east to west, separated by broad valleys called khuds; in the interior this regularity is less observable, and the mountains, instead of rounded summits, have a bold and well-defined outline.

The rainy season commences on the lower ranges towards the end of June. After a few showers vegetation springs up almost magically. Mountain-sides, that before appeared bare and desolate, became clothed with luxuriant vegetation in a few days. The fir (*Pinus longifolia*) crowns the mountain-brow, while in the valleys flourish oak, walnut, and mulberry. Cherries, apricots, and plums, are ripe before the commencement of the rains; however, in point of flavour, none of these fruits are to be compared with the productions of Cashmere and Ladakh. A tendency to double returns in one year may be observed in some fruit-trees, for during genial November weather I have seen cherry-trees in bloom, and even the fruit ripening until checked by the cold of the following month.

The monsoon ceases towards the end of August, and is succeeded by clear skies and a mild temperature. About the middle of November the cold weather sets in, and the distant peaks are seen tipped with snow. In January it often falls on the ranges next the plains, and for six weeks at this season the climate is almost British.

From April to June the thermometer averages from 76° to 80° in European houses; but, though at mid-day the heat is often very oppressive, the mornings and evenings are cool and agreeable.

It is a splendid sight to behold the moon on a clear night rising over the tops of these mighty mountains, or the bright sun casting his last rays over the snowclad sides of the sacred ranges of Jumnootri and Ghangutri. I can never forget the magnificent panorama which burst on my view when hunting one afternoon:—I had wandered rather farther than usual, so that I found myself near the summit of a high peak as the sun was setting. Before me stretched, far as the eye could reach, from east to west, one vast chain of mountains. There was the noble peak of Kilas, 21,000 feet above the level of the sea, and others, shooting their crests to the sky; some capped with snow, others half-covered with bare dark patches intervening, and all the various shades of colour produced thereby. The sun's last rays gave a fine pink appearance to the snow, the cool breeze came puffing like a trade-wind, while I gazed on in wonder and astonishment. Anon the scene changed; no more the golden rays were visible, for the sun soon sank behind the lofty western mountains, and left the deep blue sky and the desolate waste of scenery dim and indistinct on the distant horizon.

The soil of the mountains and valleys is very productive. On the mountain-sides small terraces are made, one above another, and irrigated by turning on the nearest stream, which, if distant, is conveyed by means of hollow trees. Rice, wheat, barley, indian-corn, and batu,* constitute the staple products of this region.

Every valley (or khud) has its little stream, whose banks are covered with shrubs and trees, sometimes so dense as to be impermeable, thus contrasting with the higher elevations, where we find the rhododendron and forest trees in all their magnificence and beauty.

As the productions of the Himalayas vary, so are there varieties in their scenery. Each region has an attraction peculiar and distinctive, whether among the tangled jungle of the lesser ranges, or high in the region of forest, or still further up among the stunted birch, upon the confines of eternal snow.

The natives of the lower Himalaya ranges (Paharees, as they are called) have little in common with their neighbours in the plains of India.

They are rather under the middle height, spare and wiry, with copper-coloured skins. Some of the women are

* *Amaranthus cruentus.*

very fair and handsome, although they have not the erect and graceful carriage of the Hindoos.

Goitre is very prevalent after the age of thirty.

The habitations of the natives are usually flat-roofed, and built in the bottoms of ravines, where the heat is extreme in summer.

The following curious custom prevails during the summer months :—Children are placed on straw beds, generally covered over, and put beneath a small stream, which is made to play upon the temple, by means of a piece of bark shaped like a water-spout. In any shady spot one or two children may be seen undergoing this ordeal, while their mothers are toiling in the adjacent field.

Natives have informed me that the children soon get accustomed to this treatment, falling asleep when placed under the stream, and awakening so soon as the water ceases to play on their temples.

Although many are said to die from this novel hardening system, it must be confessed that a healthier race than the survivors are not to be anywhere met with.

It is a study for a painter to mark the fair mother, bending over her little child as it lies in some shady bower, formed of pomegranate, wild-fig, and acacia, wreathed with woodbine and the many gorgeous exotics of that region in all their wild luxuriance and beauty.

It is, moreover, in such situations that the ornithologist will find an endless variety of interesting objects. Let him stray by the clear and gushing mountain-stream, o'erhung and canopied by the umbrageous plantain, the mulberry, or willow. He must creep along gently, for the little fairies are shy and easily alarmed. See! the blue water-thrush (*Myiophonus temminckii*) perched on that half-submerged rock;

its sweet and melodious note is ringing through the dell. The paradise flycatcher is darting, fairy-like, from tree to tree. What is that wagtail-looking bird that flutters along the water's edge, and seems to delight in frisking about where the stream runs fastest, or where the rushing cataract sweeps and dashes on? That is the beautiful spotted forktail (*Enicurus maculatus*). The plum-headed and rose-ringed parrakeets (*Palæornis cyanocephalus* and *torquatus*) are chattering among the leaves overhead. He may look long ere he observes them, for their green dress suits well with the surrounding foliage. A harsh scream, and they are away, darting like arrows down the ravine.

See! that is the gaudy red-billed pie with its long tail, which it jerks so gracefully, and chattering like a magpie, as it hops along the branch of yonder walnut-tree. The yellow and red vented bulbuls are chirruping in bush and brake. The kalij pheasant (*Euplocomus albocristatus*) and peafowl start up before him and seek the denser parts of the jungle, while the barking-deer (*Cervus muntjac*) is seen but for a moment as he disappears in the thick cover.

Objects of interest such as these the admirer of nature contemplates in his solitary rambles through the valleys of this region of the Western Himalayas.

One of the first ornithological objects to be met with on ascending the grassy sides of the mountains is the graceful pipit, which I have taken the liberty of naming the Himalayan pipit (*Heterura sylvana*). It frequents verdant spots, usually at high elevations, and in appearance, as in habits, is a true pipit. This active little creature may be seen shooting upwards from the hill-side, uttering its rasping call-note "He, hoe," then downwards it darts, and is lost to view among the tall grass.

In rocky situations, and on the scarped sides of mountain-roads, the wall-creeper (*Tichodroma muraria*) is often observed. At a distance it looks like a very large gray and scarlet butterfly, as with expanded wings it noiselessy creeps over the rock, poking its long awl-shaped bill into every little nook and crevice. The cuckoo (*C. canorus*) chaunts its welcome note in bush and tree from the earliest appearance of vernation in March up to the end of May. The natives, who are familiar with its appearance, allege that it remains in the sub-Himalayan valleys throughout the year. As late as the 18th of September, I observed a pair hunting in my garden after insects. There is another species (*C. himalayanus*) closely allied to the above, which is not uncommon in the valleys. It is at once distinguished by its smaller size.

For strength of wing there are few birds with which I am acquainted equalling the Alpine swift; its congeners, the black and allied, cannot compare with it in that respect. After rain flocks are seen scouring across the great valleys, and around the mountain-tops; now dipping into the vast abysses, then rushing upwards with an elegance of swoop, they suddenly turn and dive downwards again with amazing rapidity.

The black partridge is one of the most handsome species found in Asia, where it enjoys a wide range, being plentiful in Syria, Persia, Afghanistan, Northern India, and the Himalayas. On the latter it prefers the more temperate and cultivated ranges towards the plains, to the high exposed mountains of the interior. However, neither the great heat of Bengal, nor the cold of the Himalayas, seem to affect this bird, for we find it equally common at all seasons in both climates. Black partridge shooting is a great source of amusement to the Eastern sportsman, especially on the mountain ranges, where, from the mildness and salubrity of the climate, he can enjoy himself without danger from the sun, so frequently injurious and even fatal to sportsmen in India. A small tent (*routee*, as it is called), changes of shooting-attire, and necessaries, with as few servants as possible, are all he requires; luxuries are out of the question. To those who wish to move with rapidity and ease, it is advisable that there be nothing more than is absolutely required. A good pack of dogs is a desideratum, and far preferable to beaters both for this and pheasant-shooting, as they can be used with more advantage, especially in thick jungles and grassy mountain-sides. The dogs usually procured in the stations of the North-west Provinces of India are called spaniels, but in England I fear would be looked on as curs of "very low degree." However, when better cannot be got, they answer the purpose. Thus equipped, the sportsman who starts with a light heart, and bent on combining instruction with amusement, need seldom know a dull moment. At every step something new or curious attracts his eye. He kills his birds, and when tired sits down with a keen appetite to enjoy the produce of his day's healthy amusement—his little tent pitched on some hill-side clothed with verdure and the fair exotics of that region.

The principal food of the black partridge consists of wheat, badgeree, rice, barley, tender shoots of plants, and insects. During the heat of the day it repairs to bushy places, and in the morning and afternoon makes excursions into the fields, where it may be found associated with the gray partridge (*Perdix ponticeriana*).

In choosing a shooting-ground for black partridge, preference ought to be given to well-cultivated districts, in particular, fields surrounded with low bushy jungle. Except during mid-day they are easily raised by beaters or dogs. The black, unlike the gray partridge, never perches on trees. On the Himalayas, during the cold months, the black resorts to the dense brushwood at the bottom of valleys. The species is not gregarious, and seldom more than a couple are seen together. Its flesh is pale and well flavoured, but neither the black partridge nor any of its Eastern congeners can compare in that respect with the British bird. The accusation of being a foul feeder, so objectionable in the case of its gray ally, may be sometimes brought against this species, but I must vindicate the red-leg or chukore (*Caccabis chukar*) from such bad habits; it is a game bird in every sense. The black partridge commences to pair about April in the Himalayas, but earlier in the plains; the young remain with their parents a long time, and are not fit for shooting until the middle or end of October. During the period of incubation the males can be heard answering each other all over the district; the call-note is harsh and composed of four distinct sounds, following each other in succession, and not unlike the words: "*Whee whá whick á-whick,*" which it repeats at short intervals when perched on a stone in bushy places. I doubt if this species would stand the cold of Britain. I brought several from India, but all died during wet and cold weather off the Cape of Good Hope. The gray species is much hardier, and would doubtless thrive well in our preserves at home. Both species are known to the natives of India by the same appellatives, *Tetur* or *Tetra.*

The barking deer, called by the natives "kakur," is generally distributed over the lower and cultivated tracts of the Himalayas, being seldom met with at elevations exceeding from 8000 to 9000 feet above the level of the sea. The prevailing colour is a reddish-brown above, white underneath, inclining to ash on the inside of the legs of males, which have two short canine teeth in the upper jaw, resembling those of the musk-deer, but not so long. The bark of the kakur is loud and harsh, like a fox's, and generally heard at night or at early morn. Wooded dells by the sides of streams, oak-forests and grassy hill-sides are its favourite resorts. Although several may be found in one little belt, they do not herd together. Its movements are slow and stealthy, and it is by no means shy or timorous; on that account it is easily killed, and often met with when least expected. During progression it seems to strike the fore and hind hoofs, which occasions the clattering similar to a horse "over-reaching." Among the kalij-pheasant jungles of the lower ranges kakur may be looked for, and offer an occasional good snap shot to the dexterous sportsman.

One of the most common denizens of woods and jungles, flitting noiselessly among the dense foliage, and so tame as to approach within a few feet, is that beautiful warbler the yellow zosterops, known by the white downy ring round the eye, from which it has received its name (*Z. palpebrosus*); it is about the size of the blue titmouse; the general colour is olive, approaching a light yellow on the wings, forehead, and lower parts.

The gray partridge is one of the most common species found in Northern India. It is plentiful in the sub-Himalayan jungles, but does not travel any distance into the interior. As a game bird it has obtained some disrepute among European sportsmen from its foul feeding and propensity to perch in trees. It rises with a feeble wabbling flight, to which it doubtless often owes its escape by puzzling the sportman's aim. However much abused it may be, there are few, I am sure, who do "not" like to hear its loud ringing clang resounding across the plain. Poor little fellow! in this way he often betrays his hiding-place, and if not up and off on "whirring wing," he soon helps to fill the game-bag. The gray partridge runs with great rapidity, and unless the cover is low and scanty, is not easily flushed. Its habits are the same as the black species.

I have before alluded to the spotted hill-wagtail (*Enicurus maculatus*), one of the most handsome denizens of the mountain-stream. It is larger than the pied wagtail, and nearly 11 inches in length. The rich white and black colourings are particularly attractive, and its habits so eccentric as to arrest the attention of even the most indifferent observer—now running sprightly along the margin of the torrent, with its forked tail expanded like a beautiful black and white fan; anon with extended neck and wings it turns its well-marked body from side to side as if on a pivot, until, gathering up its snow-white legs, with an austere screech it shoots rapidly along the windings of the stream.

There is a species closely allied, but not by any means so common, and at best a rare bird on the streams of the lesser ranges. It is called the short-tailed fork-tail (*Enicurus scouleri*), about 5 inches in length, with a snow-white forehead and black upper parts, excepting a white band which crosses the back and wings. Its lower parts are also white. This active little creature delights in sporting by the sides of roaring cataracts in wooded situations, and is sometimes seen with the last.

Nowhere is a storm seen to such advantage as on the lower Himalayan ranges. There is a magnificence and grandeur about the scene perhaps in some ways peculiar to these regions. In April and May the dust-clouds generated on the plains are often carried inwards, and envelope the hill-stations of Dugshai and Kussoulee in dense and dark masses, so that objects are invisible at a few yards' distance, and the air feels close and oppressive. Such a state of matters may last for hours, or be broken by blinks of sunshine. Again, the thunderstorms which often burst with terrific violence on the Himalayan stations come most usually from the heated plains below. It was on the 17th of April that we experienced one of the most severe hurricanes that had taken place for many years. During the first part of the day, and until 3 P.M., it continued to blow a strong breeze from the direction of the low lands, over which heavy dark masses of cloud lay piled up. These began moving towards us, and gradually swept over the intervening range, curling and seething as they rushed noiselessly down the mountain-sides into the great valleys below, and ascended the ridge on which we were located, where they were preceded by a fierce wind and illuminated by occasional flashes of lightning. At length the mass rose up and enveloped the mountain-top in a dismal gloom almost like twilight, rain falling all the time in torrents, and the thunder rolling peal after peal; whilst now and then a powerful gust of wind cleared the mountain-top for a few moments, until the brightness was again dispelled by a fresh mass of dense cloud, so that the sun shone through it with a glare like the light produced by looking through coloured glass. Suddenly the vapour-clouds passed away, and we could see them moving northwards towards the great central snow-range.

The European woodcock is met with occasionally during the winter months on the Lower Himalayas. As many as four to six couples may be occasionally procured in one day. The species is not plentiful, however, anywhere.

In the lonely glen, by the side of the mountain-torrent, where the pine grows tall and dense, and the sun's rays seldom penetrate, may be found the great snipe (*Gallinago solitaria*), from the lower to the upper ranges of the forest region.

This bird differs in other respects besides size from the common snipe; at the same time I have procured solitary individuals of the latter on mountain-streams, in secluded alpine regions, far away from its ordinary haunts.

The spotted eagle is plentiful on the lesser ranges, and affects the vicinity of villages and European stations, where it may be seen feeding with kites and vultures, which it delights to torment when on wing.

The hooded bulbul is one of the most common denizens of jungles, and is easily recognised by its handsome top-knot and loud clanging chirp. It seems strictly Himalayan, and is seldom seen at any distance from the mountains.

Amid all the grandeur of the Himalayas, it is a most attractive sight to the naturalist to behold the vultures and rapacious birds soaring over the vast ravines and around the tops of the mighty mountains. Let him choose a summer evening, with that clear blue sky almost characteristic of the Himalayas, and just as the sun casts his last rays on the snow-clad mountains—when the quiet is only broken by the cry of the eagle, the bleat of the goat, or the shrill pipe of the black partridge—then the vultures, kites, and jackdaws may be seen wheeling in vast circles; some are gliding along, apparently without an effort, others appear suspended motionless in the vast canopy of heaven; while, careering in his majesty, the lammergeyer gathers up his great wings and stoops downwards, mayhap to rise again and join the medley he has just left, or stretching forth his pinions to their fullest extent, he sails along the mountain-brow to the projecting cliff on which his eyrie stands safe, for *there* who dare assail him?

On the Crol mountain, near Dugshai, on an inaccessible rock, I once saw a nest containing two young lammergeyers;

bones of sheep and cattle were strewn among the cliffs hundreds of feet below; they were found to be the remains of food carried by the parent-birds from the slaughter-houses of Dugshai or the neighbouring European stations.

It has long been a vexed question how vultures discover their food. Though divers authorities have pronounced opinions in favour of *sight*, some again contend that *scent* is the means employed, while a third considers both senses are concerned.

Mr. Darwin says—"Often, when lying down to rest on the open plains, on looking upwards I have seen carrion-hawks sailing through the air at great heights. Where the country is level, I do not believe a space of the heavens of more than 15° above the horizon, is commonly viewed with any attention by a person either walking or on horseback. If such be the case, and the vulture is on the wing, at a height of between 3000 and 4000 feet, before it could come within the range of vision, its distance in a straight line from the beholder's eye would be rather more than two British miles. Might it not thus readily be overlooked? When an animal is killed by the sportsman in a lonely valley, may he not all the while be watched from above by the sharp-sighted bird, and will not the *manner of its descent* proclaim throughout the district, to the whole family of carrion-feeders, that their prey is at hand?" *

In illustration of what has just been quoted, I may adduce the following as of familiar occurrence:—After a bear or other large animal is killed, the hunter soon finds himself surrounded by rapacious birds, where none were seen before; they are observed dashing down the glens, and sailing in

* "Narrative of the Surveying Voyages of His Majesty's ships 'Adventure' and 'Beagle,'" vol. iii. (Darwin) p. 223.

circles around his quarry. Some sweep within a few yards of him, others are soaring at higher elevations, and even at such vast altitudes that the huge bearded vulture appears only as a small speck in the blue sky, but gradually it becomes more distinct as its wide gyrations increase. It may gather itself up and close its wings, or dash in one fell swoop hundreds of feet, and the next minute is seen perched on the jutting rock beside him. Such, then, are the usual appearances observed soon after the death of a large animal, and the hunter wonders whence all these great vultures and carrion-crows have come ; but if, immediately after his noble ibex has rolled down the crag, he directs his eyes heavenward, he will observe carrion-crows or vultures, at various distances and elevations, sailing leisurely about, whilst the one nearest to him, observing the death of his quarry, instantly commences to descend ; then one follows the other until the valley resounds with the hoarse croakings of the crows, and the air seems alive with them. It is surprising the numbers that are sometimes observed to congregate on these occasions ; I have seen no less than sixty vultures and crows on and around the carcase of a newly-killed bear.

This subject is beautifully described by Longfellow in his "Song of Hiawatha,"—

> "Never stoops the soaring vulture
> On his quarry in the desert,
> On the sick or wounded bison,
> But another vulture watching,
> From his high aëriel look-out,
> Sees the downward plunge and follows ;
> And a third pursues the second,
> Coming from the invisible ether,
> First a speck, and then a vulture,
> 'Till the air is dark with pinions."

Every one at all conversant with the habits of Asiatic vultures must agree with me, that they discover a carcase as quickly when fresh as when putrid; it would be preposterous therefore to aver that *scent alone* guides these animals from such vast altitudes to their prey; moreover, I believe that in the former case scent has little to do in the matter, and even when putridity exists, I question whether the bird does not discover the presence of the substance *by sight*, long before it could possibly be within the influence of smell: one has only to consider the distance, currents of air, etc., intervening between the bird and its prey, to see at once the impracticability of scent being the only agent employed.*

The lammergeyer or bearded-vulture (*Gypaëtus barbatus*) is, without doubt, the "Roc" of *Arabian Nights*, and the "Nisser" mentioned by Bruce in his *Travels in Abyssinia.* Heber, in his *Indian Journal*, speaks of a large vulture as the "condor of the mountains," but evidently he had never examined one, as he describes it having a bald head and neck.† Specimens from the Alps, Africa, and the Himalayas, do not differ in any well-marked degree. It appears to me that the mistakes have arisen in the usual manner—by taking immature birds as types of the species, and in not making allowances for effects of climate, etc. In the *Journal of the Asiatic Society of Bengal*, vol. iii., Hutton describes a collar on the Himalaya bird as characteristic; but I agree with Mr. Hodgson this cannot be accepted as a specific distinction, being by no means regular. Again, in many Himalayan specimens the *hinder part of the tarsus is bare at the joint*, although not all the way down as in the Abyssinian indi-

* See the discussions of Audubon and Waterton.

† May he not be describing one of the large bald Indian birds?

viduals described by Rüppell,—"tarsis parte inferiore et interna plumis devestita." The plumes are particularly obvious in the Eastern bird, and project much backwards when it is feeding. These minor discrepancies are perhaps owing to climatic peculiarities, or the countries they frequent. The size and weight of this species vary considerably: Bruce mentions having killed one 22 lbs. in weight; but the heaviest out of many adults shot by me on the Himalayas did not exceed 14 lbs., the average being 12 lbs. Bishop Heber says, "One shot by Lieutenant Fisher near the Himalayas measured 13 feet between its extended wings." I have notes of many killed at different seasons of the year, none of which approached such dimensions—for instance the following:—"An adult female killed near Dugshai was 8 feet 2 inches between the tips of the wings, and from bill to extremity of tail 3 feet 8 inches; stomach contained a mass of bullock's hair, with large bones of sheep and oxen. An adult male, shot in the same ranges with the last, measured 9 feet between the tips of wings, and 3 feet 9 inches in length. A fine adult female had the greatest possible expansion of wings, 9 feet 2 inches; length, 3 feet 11 inches; weight, 14 lbs.; stomach contained the hoof of an old ibex half-digested."

The lammergeyer is easily distinguished from the other vultures by its pointed wings and wedge-shaped tail. The young bird differs considerably from the adult, whose plumage it does not fully attain until the third year. At first the head, neck, and lower parts are black; with a tinge of ash on the back and belly; the eye is black, while the old bird has the above parts an ochreous white, globe of the eye deep red with a white iris and black pupil, which add considerably to the boldness and majesty of his appearance. The eye is smaller than might be expected in such a large bird. In point of strength of wing he has few rivals. The bearded-vulture is usually observed sailing leisurely along the mountain-side, now and then flapping his great wings when he wishes to mount higher, as the American poet so beautifully describes, "by invisible stairs ascending and scaling the heavens;" but let the govind-kite or Indian jackdaw annoy him, then, with a rushing noise like that of a fierce wind, he stoops with a grace truly grand and beautiful. Oft when clambering along a rocky precipice, picking every footstep with studious care, and daring not to lift my eyes for fear of making a false step, have my ears been assailed by the furious rush of the lammergeyer, and a feeling that if he only touched me with his pinions I would have rolled into the yawning abyss below. Although often seen feeding on carrion and putrid animals, especially near European stations, in the solitude of his native mountains he hunts with great intrepidity. Natives have told me that the young of bears, ibex, wild and tame sheep and goats, are often carried away by the bearded-vulture; but I have not seen an animal larger than a marmot in its talons. A red or cinnamon-coloured powder is plentifully distributed among the feathers of the neck and breast of young and adult individuals, and would seem to be composed of soil containing iron, which they obtain from dusting themselves like other birds—a habit much indulged in by the denizens of rocky, bare mountains, from the bear and the ibex down to the mountain-finch.

The Indian vulture (*Gyps indicus*) is gregarious, so far that they generally roost in societies, but hunt singly; its long bill, coupled with the pale cinereous-brown plumage, distinguish it from the Bengal vulture (*G. bengalensis*), which has a white back. The Pondicherry vulture (*Octogyps calvus*) is again at once recognised by its red head and legs, and general smaller dimensions. The largest of the bare-headed species is the great tawny vulture (*Gyps fulvus*), which attains sometimes a weight of 20 lbs. All these species are by no means uncommon on the Western Himalayas.

CHAPTER V.

Excursion to the Chor Mountain—Scenery—Geology—River Gerrie—Fish—Pea-fowl—Jungle-fowl—Bush-quail—Hares—Magpies—Jay—Leeches—Rhododendron in flower—Bees—Habits and Haunts of the Monal, Cheer, Plach, and Kalij Pheasants—Red-legged Partridge—Spring flowers—Musk Deer—White-cheeked Weasel—Pine Marten—Skylark—Birds—Red Fox—Hyena and Leopards—A Himalayan Trapper—Red Honey-sucker—Parrakeets of the region—Wounded Vulture.

On the 7th of March 1851 I started with Young and Bowden on a long-meditated excursion to the Chor mountain and more interior Himalayan ranges. We formed a small exploring-party, equipped with every requisite for securing good sport, to which I added my auxiliaries for preparing and preserving collections.

There is something in the life of the Himalayan sportsman peculiarly captivating. Unrestrained freedom is his; he obeys no man's mandates; and his thoughts and actions receive no guidance save the dictates of his own mind.

It was a fine crisp morning when we started; the cock was crowing on his roost; and long before the inhabitants of our home were stirring, the last man of our thirty followers might have been seen, toiling along the rough path leading to the little village of Narg, situated some ten or twelve miles eastward of Dugshai. The general appearance of the scenery differed only in a slight degree from what has been already described. The bare parts of the mountains were now covered with the rich green carpet of spring, whilst their hollows and sheltered parts were clad with a profusion of tree and bush, which skirted the sides and bottoms of the ravines. High up appeared the long-leaved pine, a little farther down the Himalayan oak ; apricot and peach were again succeeded by the pomegranate and barberry, etc., in the warmer regions below.

The cooling breeze of the mountain-top formed an agreeable contrast to the close and feverish atmosphere of the ravines. In our scramble over hill and dale, we had not time to examine the geological formation. Abundance of argillaceous and mica schists appeared in rough crumbling masses in the ridges and valleys, especially around the village of Narg, where they were encrusted with a white substance afterwards discovered to be impure carbonate of soda. The long-bearded wheat was in ear, while tall walnut-trees almost hid the native dwellings, over which the convolvulus, cucumber, and melon, were twining their tendrils. We found the inhabitants, as usual, very civil and obliging—a character for which the Paharees are celebrated. In manner simple, they are frugal, honest, industrious, and enduring. They love their native hills, and seldom care to visit India, or mingle with the northern tribes. They assimilate to the Rajpoots in their religion. Although in former days they displayed warlike propensities, when urged on by their chiefs, the influence of British rule has moulded them to more peaceful pursuits, which our steadfast ally, the late rajah of Puteala, greatly tended to maintain. The soil of the mountains is exceedingly productive, and requires little culture.

On the following morning we were up at daybreak, and after the tent and baggage had been packed on the backs of coolies, each took his gun, and away we went, beating the jungle *en route.* Soon the clear piping call of the kalij pheasant was heard among the dense wood, as one after another rose before our dogs; while, now and then, a black partridge dashed past us. Vigors's and the red-billed jays sent forth their harsh calls, in concert with the ringing clang of the crested bulbul, the rough chirp of the red-backed shrike, or the wild scream of the rose-coloured parrakeet.

Between the reports of our guns and the barking of the dogs, we had upset the interior economy of the jungle, for every bird in the district and hill-side seemed roused and alarmed. They had evidently not been accustomed to such rude and noisy molestations.

The hamlet of Philora is situate on the banks of the river Gerrie. Here we encamped, and viewed the mighty mountain-stream, now flooded by the melting snow of the higher ranges, roaring and surging some hundreds of feet below us, its banks either clad with profusion of trees and shrubs, or stretching gently up into cultivated terraces, where here and there might be seen a solitary gable-roofed hamlet, with the never-failing tree to shade its inmates from the heat of mid-day.

After a savoury repast on pheasants and partridges, we descended towards the river, for the purpose of exploring the neighbourhood. Great was our chagrin on observing a musk-deer, perched on a projecting cliff some forty feet above us. The little creature stood and gazed at us with apparent unconcern, when a rustle was heard close by, and a native, crawling out of the bush, knelt, and taking a steady aim with his long matchlock, sent a bullet against the rock, about an inch above the animal's back.

The formations in the neighbourhood were composed chiefly of mica-slate, while, along the course of the river, several veins of gneiss appeared, and masses of limestone, in the shape of boulders, strewed its course.

The following day we crossed the swollen river, which delayed the passage of our baggage for several hours. It was a strange sight to witness our copper-coloured followers toiling across the rapids, with our goods and chattels on their heads, some immersed even to the arm-pits; but they braved it manfully. An hour's march brought us to the little village of Thor, situated on a gentle incline some 200 feet above the level of the river, and surrounded by small fields raised one above the other.

We pitched our tent under the spreading boughs of a banyan-tree, and breakfasted on fish, which the natives catch in the river by means of nets. All were evidently a species of mullet, and several weighed about 1½ lbs. each. Besides the masseer, we were told that three other different kinds of fish are plentiful in the river, and there are doubtless many more.

In the jungle along the banks we found abundance of pea-fowl, and I observed two white-cheeked weasels*—one with a black partridge in its mouth. I managed to bag a brace of jungle-fowl (*Gallus bankiva*). These birds, in habits and general appearance, bear a close resemblance to varieties of the domestic bird, especially the hen and young. The jungle-fowl flies with great rapidity; it is generally met with in small flocks, in dense covers by the side of fields or ravines. Its cackle is like that of the tame bird, from which it does not seem to differ in any material degree. Probably many of the former wander from the villages, and take to the wild life of their congeners.

We were up at daybreak on the 10th. My friends enjoyed themselves among the kalij pheasants and jungle

* Known likewise as the yellow-throated marten (*M. flavigula*).

fowl, while I sought wilder tracts, in quest of rarer game. Now and then, among the prickly shrubs by the margins of the fields, a covey of ten or twenty bush-quail (*Perdicula asiatica*) sprang up with a whirring noise; a black partridge or a kalij pheasant would shoot across the valley. A Himalayan hare (*Lepus macrotus*) was killed. This species is larger than the black-necked hare (*L. nigricollis*) of the Indian plains. It is confined to the lesser ranges and sub-Himalayan valleys, and though generally distributed does not seem to be abundant anywhere. Its flesh is more savoury than that of the other species, but in this respect neither can compare with the hare of Europe. The mountain-hare is distinguished from the other by its longer ears, more slender legs, and small feet. The under surface of the tail is rufous.

In wooded situations, all over this district of the western ranges, the traveller is struck with the characteristic and elegant long-tailed jay (*Calocitta sinensis*, Linn.) This graceful creature attracts attention not only by the brilliancy of its plumage, but the loud, harsh screams it utters as the traveller approaches—now jerking up its long tail, after the manner of the magpie, now garrulously chattering, as though reproaching him for intruding on its haunts. The moping owl, the chetah, or its more dangerous enemy the tiger-cat, it seldom passes without uttering a volley of abuse. It is usually seen singly, or at most in pairs. The body is about a foot in length, the tail nearly 18 inches, bill and legs bright red; forehead, cheeks, side of neck, throat and breast, black; back part of neck white; back, wings, and tail, sky-blue, deepening towards the rump; tail composed of twelve feathers, graduating in pairs. The ends of the two longest have their edges turned inwards. Coleopterous insects constitute its favourite food; but I have often seen it eating a species of wild apple (the *Feronia elephantum*), abundant in the lesser ranges. This fruit often rots on the trees, and when in that condition affords the means of subsistence to many other birds, especially the crested bulbul, and the various sorts of parrakeets. On the southern ranges of Cashmere there is a species of jay very closely allied to the above. It will be noticed hereafter.

Besides the wandering pie (*Dendrocitta rufa*), its ally the red-vented pie (*D. sinensis*) affects the same situations, and although not so domestic in habits, and less often met with in the neighbourhood of dwellings, is plentiful in copses and jungles. In habits it is similar to its congener, and feeds likewise on insects and fruit.

Although the common European jay has been shot on the mountains of Afghanistan, I have never heard of it being met with on the Western Himalayas. It is evidently replaced there by a common species, called the black-throated jay (*Garrulus lanceolatus*, Vig.)

I killed on the river a large black-headed kingfisher, which was unfortunately carried away by the current before I could note further particulars than that it was of large size, a general ash colour, with a black hood.*

On the 11th of March, after a long day's journey, we gained a high ridge, overlooking a beautiful valley teeming with rich fields of spring wheat and barley. The hum of bees among the flowers of the mulberry and apricot, in the quiet stillness of a delightful evening, added to the cooling sensations of a bathe in the neighbouring brook, and a sumptuous repast, formed of the partridges and pheasants, made us feel a rare degree of contentment and repose, for we had rambled all day over the grassy hill-sides, pursuing the black partridges

* Probably the large black and white kingfisher (*Ceryle guttata*).

wherever their luckless call attracted us, until, tired and hungry, we returned to the tent.

The houses in this part of the country are generally gable-roofed ; and there are numbers of little towers, which, we were told, were once on a time places of defence, when the tribes quarrelled about the appropriation of the mountain-streams for the purpose of irrigation. A six-pounder would have levelled them with the ground, yet a native informed us that these diminutive fortresses had withstood many a bloody siege. We passed a Paharee marriage-party, about 200 men and women, dressed in the gayest and brightest attire—red turbans, and every variety of colour in the rest of their toilette. The bridegroom was not visible, but the bride, a girl of about ten years of age, was seated in a box, carried on the shoulders of four men. A marriage among the hill-men is always a very grand event, and costs many years' savings.

Our dogs becoming suddenly ineffective from some derangement of their breathing, I examined their nostrils, and found them filled with large distended leeches (*Hæmopsis paludum*). These abound in the pools and damp grass.

On the following morning, as we toiled up the steep ascent above our previous night's encampment, it was a beautiful sight to behold the hill-sides covered with a scarlet rhododendron (*R. barbatum*) in full blossom ; and when we gained the ridge a still grander scene burst upon our view. The lights and shadows thrown across the great valleys, while northward the Chor mountain, monarch of all around, stood out in impressive grandeur, its gloomy sides diversified by pine-forests, and towards the summit with patches of snow. We gained, at noon, the village of Naira, and pitched our tent close by. The natives of this district seemed to be paler and handsomer than the hill-men around Dugshai. Many of the young women were fair and beautiful. Here we observed beehives in the walls of the houses, and were informed that when their owners wished to take the honey they did so by beating drums behind the hives, until the bees were fairly frightened away, when the outer apertures were closed. This method was practically illustrated to us by a villager beating on a tom-tom with a violence sufficient to have terrified a much less sentient animal than the bee.

Next day we mounted a ridge leading towards the Chor mountain through forests of oak, deodar, and pine. On the way were observed several monal pheasants (*Lophophorus impeyanus*), but beyond a transient glimpse of them as they flashed down the vast ravines, amid a blaze of dazzling reflections from their gorgeous plumage, we were unable to get within even rifle distance of them.

Several red-legged partridges (*Caccabis chukar*) were killed on the bare rocky places. In little sheltered nooks I gathered two sorts of primroses, which I subsequently discovered to be the *Primula purpurea* and *obtusifolia* of Royle. The British bracken was plentiful. We were much struck with the magnificence of the forest-trees, which attain vast size at these altitudes.

The height of the Chor is 10,688 feet above the level of the sea, and is composed chiefly of mica-schist and clay-slate, with intrusive dykes or veins of granite. Boulders of the same rock were abundant on the valleys. The summit of the mountain is composed entirely of granite. Gneiss was also often met with on the ridges. Both are, however, large-grained and coarse, the quartz predominating. Sometimes great veins of quartz are observed, containing nodules and crystals of hornblende, especially in the ridge above the village of Churass, where we pitched the tent and commenced our labours. Daily, at cock-crow, each started on his own beat, and returned in the afternoon bringing with him the spoils of the day.

The most interesting denizens of these wilds are the various species of pheasants. Foremost of all stands the impeyan, or monal. This splendid bird, once so abundant in the Western Himalayas, is now, comparatively speaking, restricted to certain localities in the wooded slopes of the higher ranges. Whole tracts of forests, once dazzling with the gorgeous forms of these birds, are now without a single specimen; however, it will be long before it is extirpated, for its haunts are high up among the craggy rocks where few ordinary sportsmen venture. No words can convey an accurate idea of the brilliancy of this bird's plumage,* and that of several of its congeners—indeed, many of the best-executed drawings fall short on this point. However, those in Mr. Gould's *Birds of Asia,* and his *Century* may be allowed the first rank.

The average weight of an adult male monal is nearly 6 lbs.;† that of the female about 5 lbs.; the young of the first year about 3 lbs. The favourite haunts of this species are in the deepest solitude of the forest, or among the bamboo and dense jungle which clothe the sides and bottoms of the valleys.

It is found along the line of the Himalayas, from 6000 to 8000 or 10,000 feet, but is partial to localities.

The monal is strictly alpine in its haunts, and prefers the

* Hundreds are sold at Stevens' sale-rooms. They are bought chiefly to adorn ladies' bonnets!

† Jerdon, in his admirable work on the birds of India, published in 1864, gives the weight 4½ lbs. Surely, unless his data were obtained at a different season of the year, there must be some mistake, as our conclusions were drawn from many adult males weighed on the spot.

cooler regions of the middle ranges to the forests bordering on the plains of India.

Its favourite food consists of acorns, earth-nuts, bulbs, wild strawberry, currants, etc. They may be met with in scattered flocks, singly, or in pairs.

The breeding-season commences about April, when the wailing cry of the males resounds through the mountain, and might be mistaken for that of any of the larger falcons. The female monal lays four to six eggs, very similar in colouring to those of the turkey. The young bird has the dark brown plumage of the female until the autumnal moult. It has certain names in different localities—for instance, about Mussouree and Simla it is known by the name *Monal;* to the eastward it is called *Ratteah Cowan*, and *Monalee*. The male is the *Lont* and the female the *Ham* of the Cashmerians, who adorn their mosques with the brilliant feathers of the male.

The plach pheasant, known by the local names Pukras, Coclass (*Pucrasia macrolopha*), is less plentiful, and does not appear so generally distributed as the monal.

There are, besides, two or three other species very closely allied, but the above is the most common. Its distribution does not yet seem clearly defined, but from all accounts it is most abundant in the western ranges, and rare towards the eastward. In Nepal it is probably replaced by another species, and again, in the woods and forests of Cashmere, I have frequently observed (though never shot) a species which may turn out to be new.

The male plach is 24 inches in length; the head is glossy-green, except the crown feathers, which are ash-brown. They are long and tapering on the side of the neck, where there is a large white spot. The breast, middle of the belly, and tail are dark chestnut, the latter tipped with white; the rest of the body light ash, with a streak of black down the middle of each feather. The tail is pointed, and dark chestnut, verging into black towards the tips, which are slightly edged with dirty white.

The tail-coverts are long and tapering and ash-coloured. The female is less in size, and her plumage is not so gaudy, but is still beautifully variegated with brown, chestnut, and yellow. The call of the plach is composed of a few cackles, or low chattering sounds, which are emitted when on wing.

In the early morning, and at dusk, the harsh crow of the cock is heard among the dense boughs of the pine and deodar, where it frequently secretes itself after being flushed. It is generally met with in pairs or solitary. These birds fly with great rapidity, and although partial to the more alpine regions, I have met with individuals on the pine-clad tops of the ranges in the neighbourhood of Dugshai.

During one of our morning rambles through a wood of stunted oak, I was startled by a covey of light-brown pheasants, which, on our approach, rose, uttered a series of plaintive calls, and dispersed themselves in the dense cover. We searched in vain for them for upwards of an hour. At length I discovered one on a branch within a few yards of me, and Young killed another close by. The specimens proved to be a male and female of the cheer-pheasant (*Phasianus wallichii*), one of the most elegant species to be met with in the Himalayas. It is likewise known by the local names of *Booinchil* and *Herrel*. The male measures about 18 inches, exclusive of the tail, which varies from 20 to 26 inches in length. The naked skin around the eye is bright red. The iris is light brown. The tail is composed of eighteen feathers, which graduate in pairs, and are broadly barred with pale yellow, or dusky brown and olive blotches.

The female is smaller, and has not the magnificent tail of the male—which he displays to most advantage when walking or on wing.

The cheer frequents the lower and middle regions, and is seldom found at very high elevations. It delights in grassy situations, among stunted oak, or such-like, and is generally met with in flocks of from six to twenty. The moment they are disturbed they separate and secrete themselves among the grass, or in the foliage of trees, whence I believe they have been knocked down with sticks.

The female forms her nest of grass in low brushwood, and lays from nine to fourteen eggs of a dull white.

The young are hatched about the beginning or middle of June.

The flight of the cheer is heavy, and not strong, and it seldom perches on trees, unless when disturbed.

Cheer-shooting, like all other sport in the Himalayas, is followed out with most success in autumn. The cheer seems hitherto to have been found only in the north-western Himalayas; possibly its cunning and stealthy habits may cause it to be overlooked in many situations.

The kalij (*Euplocomus albocristatus*) is the most common and widely distributed of the Himalayan pheasants. There is a congener, with white markings on the crest and back, found on the eastern ranges, Sikhim, etc. Mr. Blyth considers it a distinct species, and has named it *E. melanotus*. I am not prepared to dispute the decision of so good an authority. I must, however, remark that I have seen many old males of the *E. albocristatus* with very little white on the crown and back. The kalij pheasant ("*Merghee kookera*" of the natives) is plentiful along the great valleys, called *Dhoons*, bordering on the plains of India, up to elevations of from

6000 to 8000 feet. It prefers, however, the more southern ranges, and is seldom met with in the remote interior.

In habits domestic, and (unlike any of its allies) often met with in the vicinity of villages and fields, its favourite haunts are, low underwood and ravines covered with dense jungle. The kalij, except when disturbed, seldom takes to wing, although its flight is strong and powerful. When rising it utters a loud plaintive cry, which is continued until it gains a place of safety; it is not gregarious, and seldom more than three are seen together. It runs with great rapidity; during incubation the males are very pugnacious; an adult male weighs about 3 lbs., the female about 2½ lbs. Young birds of the first year seldom exceed 1½ lbs., and their plumage resembles that of the female until the moulting-season. The egg is white, and about the size of the bantam's. A nest may contain from nine to twelve, and even more eggs, which are hatched about the end of May. Grubs, insects, seeds, shoots and leaves of trees, constitute the favourite food of the kalij.

The white-necked weasel, the lammergeyer, golden and spotted eagles, etc., prey on this species, whose loud and prolonged cry often betrays its presence to one or other of its enemies.

Like the domestic fowl, this bird, and most of its congeners, are fond of basking on sunny banks, and shuffling the earth about them; on such occasions they fall an easy prey.

The red-legged partridge, better known in the East by the name of "Chukore," has a wide distribution. It does not differ in any well-marked particular from the Greek partridge* of South-east Europe, and shows how easily "species can be

* *Perdix græca*; there is a variety in the island of Crete having the throat rufous.

made," inasmuch as authors have formed the diagnosis entirely from the size of the band on the neck and the intensity of the white on the throat. I have examined various Turkish specimens, and found even these peculiarities not constant. These races form one species, extending from South-east Europe and Syria, across Central Asia and the northern boundaries of Hindostan, where it is not very plentiful, the most advanced of its posts being the low ranges of the Punjaub. The species seems to abound in Chinese Tartary and the sources of the Oxus. Lieutenant Wood, in his journey* to the latter country, mentions taking part in a hunting expedition, when the party bagged 500 chukore by running them down with beaters and dogs.

The chukore prefers barren mountains to the rich and luxuriant vegetation of the more southern ranges; bare stony ridges clad with low scrub are its favourite haunts. It is usually met with in coveys. Although the breeding season commences early, and the young are hatched in July, and rapidly attain the size of the parents, they are seldom able to fly before the middle of September. The nest is composed of dried grass, and is placed in bushy places; the eggs are white, and vary in number from nine to twelve. During incubation the male remains near the nest, and may be heard all day piping his loud call—"*cuc cuc*," resembling that of the domestic fowl. The Cashmerians call the bird "kau-kau" on account of its call. Although not actually a denizen of the valley, it is not uncommon on the surrounding mountains. The chukore is a handsome bird, and to the sportsman affords better diversion than perhaps any of the Himalayan partridges. Its rapid flight, and the trying nature of the situations frequented by it, demand the hunter's best energies. On the

* *Voyage up the Indus to the Source of the Oxus, by Kabul and Badakshan.*

Indian frontier their numbers are never so great as to recompense one who expects good shooting at little bodily exertion; but the sportsman prepared for a rough scramble over rock and fell cannot betake himself to a better and more stirring amusement than shooting chukore on the lower Himalayan ranges.

On the 17th of March the snow still lay thick and hard in the sheltered parts of the Chor mountains, especially among the oak and pine forests; while in the more open glades, among the stunted bamboo jungles, we had to flounder knee-deep through beds of rotten melting snow, around the margin of which peeped up the beautiful pink and purple primroses—the advanced guards of spring; and no great distance down the mountain the apricot and apple-trees were in full bloom. The difference in the temperature of the two regions was well marked—above, an arctic winter was but just ending; below, spring had fairly set in. We observed among the snow foot-trail of bears and large deer—either the Cashmere or Duvaucell's deer (*Cervus cashmerensis* or *duvaucellii*); and the sharp-pointed and characteristic footprints of the musk-deer (*Moschus moschiferus*) were plentiful. I wounded one, but the little creature escaped and hid itself in the impervious bamboo jungle. The custouree, as it is called, frequents the lower and forest ranges, as high as the stunted birch on the limits of arboreal vegetation, and confines of snow, from 10,000 to 12,000 feet above the sea-level. There it often remains until driven down by the approaching winter, for beneath the naked boughs and pale trunks of the birch it delights to dwell, nibbling a scanty fare from the moss-clad bank, or along the sward still damp with snow-water. Seldom is its solitude disturbed, for to these situations the leopard rarely ascends; and save the startling call of the cuckoo, there is nought to disquiet it in this bare inhospitable region.

In the forest it is easily traced by the heaps of dung on its runs, for it is partial to localities, and both in habits and general appearance has a great affinity to the hare. Sometimes I have found it by following up its trail through the copse across the grassy glade into a little dell, where the indifferent custouree might have been seen feeding within a few yards. In districts where it is not often hunted it is by no means timid, and will seldom run away at the report of a gun. On that account it forms an easy prey to the chetah and other leopards. The lammergeyer destroys the young, but seldom if ever attacks the adult. The mode of its progression is remarkable, and comprises a series of spasmodic leaps, while now and then it stops to reconnoitre, or, walking a few feet, resumes these fantastic movements. In thick cover it secretes itself like a hare. Although killed in numbers for its much-coveted scent, the musk-deer is by no means uncommon. The musk is most sought after during the rutting season in autumn. I have repeatedly examined the contents of bags at other seasons, but, except a rank offensive odour from the dark pigmentary substance contained in them, I could not discover a trace of musk. It is said that unless the musk-bag is removed before the body cools the scent evaporates. The market-value of each bag is from £1 to £1 : 10s. There is considerable diversity in the colour of the musk-deer. So much is this the case, that a casual observer, seeing only skins, would be apt to conclude that there is more than one species; but after closely observing these variations, I have been led to the conclusion that they are attributable to age or season, and the nature of the localities. Indeed, two skins are seldom found exactly alike. Individuals partial to dense forests and jungle have the upper parts dark, with black splashes on the back and hips, and the under parts white, or dirty white. Some are yellowish-white all over the upper parts, with the belly and inner sides of the thighs white. This variety I have compared with a specimen of the white-bellied musk-deer (*Moschus leucogaster*, Hodg.),* in the India House Museum, London, and been unable to discern any well-marked distinction. A brown-black variety is common. Not a few have white spots arranged longitudinally on the upper parts; doubtless these are immature animals, inasmuch as all the males so marked had short teeth. When the nature of the climate and country on the Tibetan slopes of the Himalayas are compared with the dense forests and covers of the Cashmere ranges, it is not to be wondered at that regions differing so much in their climate and vegetable products should to some extent influence the external colouring of the animals. In illustration of this, the raven of Ladakh is larger than the same bird in the torrid heat of the Northern Punjaub; and yet the most scrupulous critic cannot venture to separate them. The canine tooth of the musk-deer is from 2 to 3 inches in length, and is rudimentary in the female. The use of these long canines is not very apparent, considering they are confined to the males. Some assert they are employed in digging up roots of plants. I have seen a wounded musk attempt to use them when caught. The ears of females are often found slit, attributable no doubt to the canines of the male during sexual intercourse. The female gestates six months. Seldom more than one spotted fawn is dropped, which remains only a short time with the parent. The overwhelming avalanche entombs many unwary musk-deer; and among its enemies is the yellow-throated or white-cheeked marten, which is said to prey on the young of this species and the barking-deer. The

* *Journal As. Soc. Bengal*, vol. viii.

above weasel is plentiful on the lesser ranges, and may be often seen hunting around the villages in quest of poultry, partridges, etc., or their eggs, on which it chiefly subsists. A tamed specimen in my possession followed me like a dog, and delighted in the name of "Kecky." It was in the habit of constantly uttering a low chuckle, which was prolonged into a harsh scream when the little creature was irritated. In habits it is exceedingly playful, and always detests confinement in a cage. It usually took up its quarters on my bed; and occasionally, in the morning and evening, made excursions into the hedges and thickets in quest of rats, mice, lizards, and snakes, which it despatched with the utmost rapidity, seizing them by the neck. An egg was always considered a great delicacy, and Kecky would run up a wall or leap several feet from the ground to obtain his prize. It nibbled a little hole at one end, and sucked the interior therefrom. When dropping from a height the feet were expanded like the Felinæ; and it delighted in prowling, like them, after its prey, spending hours in attempts to capture jackdaws and sparrows on the Persian lilac-trees, none of which it ever succeeded in catching. On the ground it progressed by a succession of leaps, by which means it captured its prey. The yellow-throated marten is subject to seasonal changes in the colour of its fur. During winter this marten is more hoary on the upper parts; whereas in midsummer the head, neck, and back are jet black, and the throat, breast, and lower parts yellowish-white. The pine marten (*M. martes*) does not apparently affect the Western Himalayas, but its skins are brought to India from Afghanistan.

My specimens of the song-lark (*Alauda triborhyncha*, Hodg.) of the lower region did not scarcely differ from the sky-lark of Europe. One distinction would appear to be, with reference to the former, that it seldom mounts so high or remains so long on wing; it is a summer visitor only, possibly migrating to the lowland valleys in winter. I took a nest and four eggs on the Dugshai hill in May. The eggs were exactly similar to those of the skylark.

The pagoda thrush (*Acridotheres pagodarum*) is probably the bird referred to in Lalla Rookh:—

> "Mecca's blue sacred pigeon, and the *thrush*
> *Of Hindostan*, whose holy warblings gush
> At evening from the tall pagoda's top."

Making allowances for the glowing imagery of the poet, the song of this bird is sweet, and not without melody, and resembles a good deal that of the common paradise grackle, with which it is often found associated. It is more a native of Hindostan than the Himalayas, and is only met with on the lower region during the hot months. I have frequently seen it feeding on the tender shoots of the long-leaved pine, but insects seem to constitute its favourite food.—The spotted-winged starling (*Saraglossa spiloptera*) is evidently a native of the hills; although not common, as many as half-a-dozen may be seen at one time among the woods and jungles of the lower hills during the hot months. In winter it may possibly retire to the hot Himalayan valleys.

The two species of kestrel are common about Dugshai; the lesser kestrel (*Tinnunculus cenchris*) is the most abundant, and may be seen in numbers hovering over the sides of the mountains and the little terraced fields in quest of beetles and large insects. Independent of size, the latter is distinguished from the other by the light colour of its claws, which are black in the common kestrel. During the fine clear evenings which precede the monsoon, when the vultures are often seen soaring at great heights, I observed in their company a very large thick-billed heron-like bird which I supposed was the adjutant (*Ardea argala*). It disappeared before the rains set in.

The cinnamon-coloured sparrow (*Passer cinnamomeus*) is often seen among the pine-woods of Kussoulee, and in the jungles along the lower hills.—The gaura finch (*Melophus melanicterus*) frequents fields and cultivated localities.—The common house-martin of the Neilgherries and Southern India is identical with *Chelidon urbica* of Europe. On the Lower Himalayas and Cashmere ranges a bird appears in spring very closely allied to the above, but all I have shot (amounting to three) differed in one or two particulars,—chiefly in being smaller; the axillary feathers were *brown* instead of grayish-white, and their tails were even. Mr. Gould has named it the *Chelidon cashmeriensis*.* This martin migrates to the the Punjaub during winter.

The golden stachyris (*Stachyris chrysea*) is a little wren-like warbler usually seen among the foliage of fruit-trees, about the size of a willow-wren; iris is red.—The verditer fly-catcher (*Niltava melanops*) appears in spring, and is one of the most common flycatchers. Its habits and haunts are similar to the most typical species, perching on prominent situations, from whence it makes excursions in quest of insects. The luteous-coloured finch (*Leiothrix luteus*) is common in the valleys about Dugshai. I have seen it in the plains in winter.

The blue rock-thrush (*Petrocincla cyanea*). This is the *P. pandoo* of Colonel Sykes, and may be said to be universally distributed over South-eastern Europe and the temperate and torrid parts of Asia. By some it is supposed to be the bird alluded to in Scripture, "the sparrow that sitteth alone upon

* *Proc. Z. S.* 1858, p. 356.

the house-top." The difference in plumage between sexes and young birds caused much confusion with the earlier Indian naturalists. Specimens likewise from the Himalayas have been found to have longer bills than individuals from other countries, and accordingly Mr. Blyth named the latter *P. longirostris*, but no one conversant with the Indian and Himalayan bird in nature will allow the above distinction to remain as specific. The blue rock-thrush frequents wild unfrequented situations; now and then I have seen a solitary individual perched erect like a thrush on the roof-top. It is not common anywhere; and, although familiar with its appearance at different seasons of the year, I had not an opportunity until long after leaving Asia of listening to its melodious note. The European form is indigenous to the island of Malta, where, among the shattered rocks that strew the coast, this fair songster may be seen sallying forth in the bright clear morn, singing, as he flutters from pinnacle to cliff, whilst the rocks and caverns resound with his pleasing strains.—The Himalaya owl (*Athene cuculoides*) is common in the woods and jungle, and is diurnal in its habits so far that I killed one at mid-day with a rat in its talons; however, the bird is most often seen at dusk. Its favourite food consists of mice, shrews, and large coleopterous insects. The pretty pigmy owlet (*Athene brodiei*) is often found in bushes. This diminutive little creature is little more than half the size of the last. Its call is measured, and composed of two notes frequently repeated. Its egg is white, and generally laid in the hollow of a tree, without any preparation whatever.

The red fox (*Vulpes montanus*) is generally distributed over the lower and middle regions of the Himalayas, up even to the limits of frost. Although often seen during the day, its depredations are chiefly at night, when it prowls about houses after poultry, and in the jungles, when it preys on kalij pheasants and other birds. This handsome species is readily recognised by the rufous on the back and pale fulvous on the legs. The little Bengal fox and the jackall are met with in the valleys of the lesser ranges, but do not range far into the interior. The hyena preys extensively on poultry, and often carries away dogs from the stations. A friend shot a very large hyena close to his house at midnight, after repeated attempts to capture the animal, which had cleared out several poultry-yards and killed many dogs. Such depredations are usually put down to the leopard, but it rarely ventures so near the habitations of man. The name *chetah* is applied in a very extended sense to all the leopards. The leopard is generally distributed over the lesser ranges, but is constantly wandering from place to place, like the tiger, which is occasionally met with in the sub-Himalayan valleys.

We recrossed the Gerrie on the 26th of March. The day was charming, and the scenery of that beautiful and sylvan description so characteristic of many sub-Himalayan valleys. At our feet rolled the river, dashing furiously over its rough limestone bed, and gradually becoming less turbulent, until, settling down to a quiet yet mighty flood, it moved steadily onward through the valley, the sides of which were clad with the gayest attire of spring. The oak, plane, wild apple, apricot, etc., sent forth their various shades of green. Many were in blossom, and the deep purple of the pomegranate's petals added a richness to all around. Above us rose a hill covered with profusion of bush and tree, where we had spent the day hunting kalij pheasants and peafowl, and now, tired and weary, were enjoying the evening around the log-fire, while a barking-deer clamoured loud in the jungle close by, as if in defiant reproach for a young buck which had fallen to my gun.

Night-jars (the whip-poor-will of Central Asia) sent forth an occasional "*twu-u-o*," as they flitted noiselessly past us, when, through a gap in the jungle, we observed a stalwart native approaching. He had a matchlock on his shoulder, and was dressed in gray home-spun flannel. His appearance and habit were characteristic of the Himalayan shickaree; the long flowing beard, ample turban, short tunic fastened round the waist by a belt of light-brown sambar-skin, to which the powder-horn and pouches were attached, capacious breeches ending at the knees, from which the limbs were encircled with flannel bandages to the ankle, while on his feet were sandals made of grass, and several pairs ready for use were attached to his girdle. He was one of those houseless wanderers similar to the trapper or leatherstocking of Fenimore Cooper, who made his livelihood by tracking the wild denizens of the mountain and forest. He had heard of our arrival on the Chor, and came to offer his services and show us where bears and deer were plentiful. Although an old man, he was still wiry and active, and like all whose lives have been constantly spent in the dangerous excitement of the cragsman's, he had intense pleasure in recounting his past exploits, especially ibex-hunting in Kuloo, and the days when, in the service of a British officer, he had led him to places where the "burrel and ibex were plentiful as sheep."

This was my first introduction to one of a race with whom many of my subsequent adventures were intimately associated; he was the type of a set of as fine manly fellows as one could meet anywhere—men whose lives have been spent among the dizzy crags and towering mountain-tops; early taught to court difficulties and dangers, they fear no hardships, and are insensible to fatigue. With such the young Englishman gratifies his love of adventure, as with pole he picks his way across the dizzy height, to where yon ibex stands perched on the brink of a yawning gulf; his rifle laid across the rock, with a steady hand and fixed eye he marks the fatal spot; scarcely done when the leaden messenger is on its unerring course, and the noble quarry is seen rolling and bounding down the precipice. It is with such reminiscences I connect the Himalayan shickaree.

The jungles along the banks of the Gerrie are stocked with barking-deer, but although we saw many daily they were too shy, and could not be got at from the denseness of the jungle. Young brought me a specimen of that beautiful sunbird called the red honeysucker or goulparah creeper (*Nectarinia goulpariensis*); it is not uncommon in the more sheltered parts. The note of the male is sweet and varied. In habits, like the sunbirds in general, they resemble the humming-birds, of which they are the Eastern representatives.

We spent a day in Thor Valley among the game, and I observed footprints of wild pigs in great abundance. A herd of large monkeys, with fawn-coloured bodies, black faces, and white cheeks, were seen in a wood. The three species of parrakeet are found here feeding on the buds and tender shoots of trees; the rose-ringed and plum-headed have been mentioned before; the slate-headed (*Palæornis schisticeps*) is only met with in the mountains, and never affects the plains of India. It is usually seen in flocks, and during the harvest-season commits depredations among the wheat and barley. Each of the three species is readily distinguished on wing—the tail of the rose-ringed is a *uniform green*, that of the plum-headed has the tip *white*, the other has the extremity *yellow*. We came on a wounded tawny vulture by the side of a pond; one of the poor animal's legs was terribly mutilated, yet with great courage he repelled the attacks of our dogs by means of his bill and wings, and even seized my loading-rod and held it so firmly in his beak that it was only with great difficulty he could be made let go his hold. The excursion having come to a close, I reviewed the produce of my labours, and arranged the large collection of skins; whilst my friend, no less pleased, produced the game-register, in which was recorded the death of 1 barking-deer, 6 hares, 1 monal pheasant, 5 cheer pheasants, 1 plach and 32 kalij pheasants, besides 58 black partridges, 12 red-legged partridges, 1 gray partridge, 3 bush quail, 6 jungle-fowl, and 4 peafowl. "We should have done better," said Young; "let us hope the autumn will bring good luck." As the sequel shows, his anticipation proved true.

CHAPTER VI.

Second Excursion to the Chor Mountain—Leopards and Tiger-cats—Monkeys—Royal Falcon, Daurian Swallow, Himalayan Siskin and Goldfinch—Monal Pheasant Shooting—Wood-partridge—Small Birds—Nutcracker—Black Bears—Green Woodpecker—Golden Eagle—Climatic Influence on size of Birds—Sporting-bag—Redheaded Bullfinch—Flame-coloured Flycatchers—Paradise Flycatcher—Thrushes—Fish-owl—Red-starts—Lark-finch—Brown Water-ousel.

WE started on our second excursion to the Chor on the 24th of September. The crops were cut, and the autumnal tint was beginning to show on the leaves of the forest. In the corn-fields about Thor we picked up a few common quail, and one of the black-bellied species (*Coturnix coromandelica*), which occasionally wanders up the valleys. Peafowl, pheasants, and partridges were plentiful. We pushed on, however, for the monal-shooting had been reported excellent; and we were full of hope, and anxious to engage in the sport.

Among the feline family frequenting this region of the mountains the most common is the leopard. There seems, however, to be some variety in the colour and size of the individuals occasionally to be seen on the Dugshai ranges. One variety is said to have fewer spots and a smaller head than the other. I give the latter assertion entirely on the authority of native sportsmen, who are often deceived by appearances. They describe no less than five distinct species:—1. A fawn-coloured animal without spots, called "chankoo," inhabits the mountains about the sources of the Ganges. 2. The panther (*F. pardus*); lower and forest regions. 3. The leopard (*F. leopardus ?*)—"dheer hay" of the natives; affects the same situations as the last. 4. The white leopard or ounce, and called the "burrel hay;" found at high altitudes, near the persistent snow-region. 5. The small leopard, above named, "goral hay," is so called from its partiality to feeding on the goral, or Himalayan chamois. A most indefatigable and discerning sportsman, Mr. Wilson of Mussouree, has made a similar observation.*

I believe the *Felidæ* of the Himalayas have been by no means well studied; certainly, if there are not more species, those at present known are subject to great variety. The striped and spotted jungle-cats of these regions are numerous. Of the former I have only seen Horsfield's tiger-cat (*F. horsfieldii*), a very handsome and beautiful species, often met with in the lower jungles, where it preys on small quadrupeds and birds. From a distance it is like a diminutive leopard. The Bengal cat (*F. bengalensis*) is plentiful in the sub-Himalayan jungles. It is difficult to say whether the colouring of the generality of the domestic variety met with in the same situation differs in any degree from their wild congeners. Possibly they may interbreed.

The Lungoor monkey (*Semnopithecus schistaceus*) is usually seen in herds in pine and oak forests. The highest point at the sanatorium of Simla is called "Jacko," from the number of this species which were met with in that locality. The animal is common in the Chor forests, and similar situations on the western ranges. It is dark-slatey above; below, pale-yellow; tail long and tufted; hair on the crown of the head short and diverging. There is considerable variety of

* *Indian Sporting Review* for September 1848.

colouring; the young incline to brown, and the old become more or less hoary. The bunder (*Macacus rhesus*) is the most common. It is distinguished from its compeers by the crown of the head being dusky brown; body inclining to ash; face naked and dusky red. It is easily domesticated and taught a variety of tricks. The Entellus monkey (*Semnopithecus entellus*) is ash-gray on the upper parts; darker on the shoulders and lower part of the back; tail grayish-brown; hands with a slight shade of black; body slight; limbs long and slender; tail lengthened. This species has been mistaken for the Lungoor, and *vice versa*. The entellus is found on the lesser ranges and India, whereas the other is partial to forests at high elevations. There is, however, great variety in the colouring of the Himalayan quadrumana, and, like the last family, their natural history is by no means perfect.

I killed the shaheen, or royal falcon (*Falco peregrinator*), in the centre of the cantonments of Dugshai while it was stooping on a Himalayan pipit, and observed it once or twice on wing afterwards. The bird is by no means common, and much in request for hawking. I saw it among the falcons belonging to the late Rajah of Puteala.

The Daurian or red-rumped swallow (*Hirundo daurica*) is plentifully distributed over the lower regions in summer, but migrates to the plains of India during the cold months. It has much the appearance of the chimney-swallow, which, although common in Cashmere and neighbouring ranges, does not seem to frequent the mountains about Dugshai. The red-rumped swallow builds on the under surfaces of jutting rocks. Its nest is oblong, and has usually two or three openings. The Himalayan goldfinch (*Carduelis caniceps*) at first sight bears a striking resemblance to the European species, but differs in wanting the black on the hind head. The song is fully as rich as the other. Many are caught on the hills, and imported to India. Another congener to a well-known European bird is the Himalayan siskin (*Carduelis spinoides*). It likewise differs in some well-marked particulars. The plumage of the male resembles the female of the former and the pine-siskin of North America. The bill is stouter, and the whole appearance of the little creature is less elegant. Its call-note is not so loud or joyous, but in habits and haunts they are very much alike.

There is a rich and picturesque beauty at this season in the little red patches of "batu" growing around the villages or along the terraced sides of the valleys, looking from a distance as if red sand was strewn on the soil. The mountain-sides were covered with long yellow grass, among which the blue flowers of the aconite were conspicuous, while the little rice-kates teemed with a rich harvest, and showed there was plenty in the land for man and beast.

Lammergeyers were common, and generally observed circling around the mountain-tops in quest of small quadrupeds and young partridges. A pair attracted us from our beaten path to climb a steep ascent, expecting to find their eyrie, which turned out only an ancient roosting-place strewn with bones of sheep which had evidently been carried from the European stations more than ten miles distant.

The pine and oak forests of the Chor were reached on the sixth day, when, to our intense delight, we soon found the pheasants far outnumbered previous expectations, for the ravines resounded with their loud screams, and the higher we went and the deeper we penetrated into the dense forests the more plentiful they became. The cool days, cold, even frosty nights, added increased vigour to our exertions. Our table actually groaned with game, and if there is one gastronomic remembrance of those days more agreeable than another, it is the delight we felt on returning at nightfall with a hunter's appetite to enjoy the monal cutlets which our excellent Bengal cook prepared in what he called "his own way." We found the monal most plentiful in the little openings in the forest, where they were feeding on the seeds of wild balsams and various sorts of earthnuts. The above was the most common species next to the plach; a very few cheer were observed, for the region was too high for them and the kalij pheasants. My companion killed a wood-partridge (*Arboricola torqueola*), the only one I have seen in its native haunts. It is rare on the Chor mountain, but it is by no means so in some situations near Mussouree. The buntetur, as it is called by the natives, frequents the depths of the forest, and is usually met single or in pairs. Besides game, I managed to add to my collection several new and little-known birds. The thick boughs of the pine offered excellent retreats for many interesting sorts. The Himalayan golden-crested wren I shot in company with the black-crested titmouse (*Parus melanolophus*), which somewhat resembles the marsh-tit of Europe. It is usually seen in flocks, and sometimes associated with another pretty species the gray-backed tit (*Parus dichrous*), which is known by its brick-red iris; the forehead and under the ear-coverts a dirty white; upper parts grayish blue; breast, belly, and vent ochrey white. The male is crested. I believe this is the first record of this species having been seen on the western ranges; it is not rare in Nepal. One of the most beautiful is the yellow-cheeked ox-eye (*Parus xanthogenys*), which is like the English bird in some respects; it has still, however, a closer ally in the Eastern Himalayas. The Himalayan nuthatch (*Sitta himalayana*) is the most common species of a genus which furnishes several very closely-allied forms. Moving noiselessly up the trunks of the pines a creeper (*Certhia himalayana*) is recognised. Differing only in very slight degree from the British bird; and seen sporting from the extremity of one spreading bough to another, in true flycatcher style, is the restless little speckled flycatcher (*Hemicheledon fuliginosa*). The nutcracker (*Nucifraga hemispila*) is oftener heard than seen; its harsh call resounds through the forest, and awakes the echoes of the glen. It is a solitary bird, and delights to lurk among the tops of the forest-trees.

The adult plach pheasant (males in particular) are very wild and wary. We shot many females and yearling birds, but only succeeded in procuring three specimens of old males. I shot a pied variety of the monal, with white feathers among the wing-coverts. A few seemingly adult male birds retained the brown-coloured feathers of the first year among the gaudy blue wing-coverts, but the young of both sexes showed no disposition to change their sombre garb. I conclude, therefore, they retain the plumage of the female until the second year. Many of the two sorts were seen feeding on the wild currant and gooseberry. One morning we happened to get into a narrow defile leading towards the summit of the mountain, profusely covered with ferns, balsams, dwarf-bamboo jungle, and long dank vegetation, through which we could scarcely pick our way, much less see the great numbers of monal pheasants which were continually rising around us. I had just discharged my gun at a flock of upwards of twenty monal which rose in front of us, when within one hundred yards were two black bears (*Ursus tibetanus*) ascending a service-tree in quest of fruit; but they caught sight of us, and were off long before we could draw shot and load with ball. My companion, in spite of the uncertain footing and obstacles, killed ten monal in an hour. In the depths of these solitudes, creeping up the trunks of ancient pines, or flying wildly across the valleys, uttering its loud scream as it lights on the side of a tree, is often seen the beautiful green woodpecker (*Picus squamatus*). I was crossing a deep ravine one morning, when a golden eagle sprang from a rock with a kalij pheasant in his grasp. It was the first occasion of my meeting with that noble bird in Asia. I well remember how he mounted into the sky with his prey, casting a defiant look downwar at us; but our Eley's cartridge reached him, and he f..ll lifeless, with his quarry in his talons. It was a young bird o. .nat or the previous year, with a good deal of white on the tail; weighed 8 lbs.; total length was 2 feet 8 inches; and between tips of wings 6 feet 4 inches. The golden eagle is not common on the Himalayas. I saw several woodcocks (*Scolopax rusticola*), and one or two solitary snipes (*Gallinago solitaria*), in the shaded situations and more secluded valleys of the Chor. It is wonderful how much climate and situation influence the size and general appearance of individual species. I do not think naturalists are sufficiently alive to this. For instance, the black partridge of the plains of India is not so heavy or so well plumed as the bird of the Himalayas. Even the kalij pheasant met with in the sub-Himalayan jungles is decidedly smaller than the same species found in the forests of the middle region. The differences in such-like cases are very striking, and no field-naturalist can overlook the effects of these great modifiers of natural objects. It would be well, however, if indoor students bestowed more attention, and made a somewhat more liberal allowance when determining specific distinctions.

One forenoon I saw a bearded-vulture stoop on a monal, perhaps a wounded bird, and bear it off in his talons with the greatest ease. I doubt, however, unless when the monal is taken by surprise, if the vulture is equal to it in rapidity of flight.

After eleven days' uninterrupted happiness, we bade farewell to the Chor and its splendid scenery. The grand object of my visit was gained : I had made myself acquainted with the habits and haunts of its most interesting denizens.

The well-known bullfinch of Europe is represented on the Himalaya by a set of extremely beautiful and interesting congeners. Two very characteristic species are the orange-coloured (*Pyrrhula aurantia*) and red-headed bullfinch (*P. erythrocephala*). The former will be noticed hereafter; the latter is not uncommon in shady groves and woods of the lower and middle regions; about 6 inches in length, head, neck, and breast reddish-yellow, becoming fainter towards the belly; the vent and rump white; back bluish-ash; quills and tail glossy black. The female differs from the male in wanting the red colour on the breast, and resembles the female of the European bullfinch; also the colouring on the head is less clear. The flammeous flycatcher (*Pericrocotus flammeus*) represents a genus of beautiful birds. The males differ very much from the females in colouring. While red is the prevailing hue of the former, the same parts are yellow in the other sex. The crimson-rumped flycatcher has been already mentioned. There are besides various other species, such as the rose-coloured (*P. roseus*), found in Continental India; the short-billed flycatcher (*P. brevirostris*), a native of the Eastern Himalaya; and the black and scarlet thrush (*P. speciosus*) of Latham, skins of which I have seen from the Western Himalaya, but never had the good fortune to meet with this beautiful bird. The flammeous flycatcher frequents woods and forests. I have seen flocks at elevations of from 8000 to

9000 feet, flitting among the pine-tops and frolicking with each other, or sporting about in quest of insects, the deep red of the males contrasting with the like brilliant yellow of the females. Their call is loud.

In oak-forests, feeding on the fallen acorns, were flocks of missel-thrushes (*Turdus viscivorus*). This species performs an up-and-down migration on the western ranges, being found at high elevations in summer, and in the more sheltered situations of the valleys during winter. My specimens, procured on the Chor, and subsequently in Cashmere and Ladakh, agreed in every particular with the bird of Britain, being only a little larger. The black-throated thrush (*Turdus atrogularis*) is generally distributed over the woods and cultivated tracts of these ranges; both in habits and haunts it bears a close resemblance to the last species. It is subject to great variety—so much so, that unless we are familiar with these changes, nothing would be easier than to mistake different individuals for distinct species. The changes appear to me to affect young birds chiefly, whereas situation doubtless has much to do, inasmuch as the species is found on the plains of India and the alpine regions of the Himalayas. The black-throat is wanting in some varieties, and there are several well-marked similarities to what has been called the red-necked thrush (*Turdus ruficollis*), which Mr. Hodgson considers a distinct species; the latter I have not seen.

We were startled one night by the unpleasant laugh of the fish-owl (*Ketupa ceylonensis*); no sound grates harsher on the ear, or is more calculated to bring back recollections of hobgoblins, than the loud hollow voice of this fine bird, nor is it less startling to creep through the bush and come suddenly on an individual moping at mid-day on a branch overhead, flashing his large orange eyes full on your face, as with outstretched wings he snaps his bill, or hissing defiance makes straight off to the nearest cover, pursued by crested bulbuls, jays, etc. This species is not often seen, as its mid-day haunts are in impassable parts of the jungle.

The hill-blackbird or blue water-thrush (*Myiophonus temminckii*) is cne of the most beautiful and common tenants of the Himalayan streams. It builds its nest on the cliff over the mountain torrent; during incubation the male may be seen sallying forth, sporting from cliff to cliff, his melodious note sounding sweetly among the roaring of the troubled waters. The song of this species has a resemblance to that of the blackbird, but is softer. The blue of the body is more intense on the breast, and forms a gaudy halo across the forehead. Another fair denizen of the mountain stream is the white-capped redstart (*Ruticilla leucocephala*) which must not be confounded with the chestnut-bellied or Guldenstadt's redstart (*R. erythrogastra*) a native of the more Alpine regions. The first is distinguished from the other by having the basal portion of the wing quills black.

Associated with the white-capped redstart is frequently observed another and smaller species, the plumbeous or sooty redstart (*Ruticilla fuliginosa*), a diminutive little creature seen hopping around the waterfall, vibrating its tail, which it spreads out like a fan. It is not more than five inches in length. On bare situations and sheepfolds the sober-coloured mountain lark-finch (*Leucosticte nemoricola*, Blyth) is common. Like the British "snow-flake" they may be seen in compact flocks flying from place to place. They congregate often to the number of 300 or 400 on the lesser ranges during winter, and ascend even to the limits of forest in summer. Its call resembles that of the linnet.

The brown water-ousel (*Cinclus asiaticus*) is very generally distributed on the streams of the lower and middle regions, its habits and haunts closely resemble the European dipper (likewise found on the Cashmere mountains) from which it differs only in colour—being a snuff-brown.

CHAPTER VII.

Hill Stations as Sanitaria—Departure for the Plains—Indian Encampment and Marching—Sand Grouse—Antelope—Birds of Passage—Wild Animals — Sediment carried down by the Indian Rivers — Chenab — Great White Heron — Little Cormorant—Quail, Snipes, their Migrations—Black-winged Falcon—Jhelum —Battle-field of Chillianwallah — Rawul Pindee—Munikyala Tope and Coins—Scenery—The Goral or Himalayan Chamois- - Climate—Flora—Geology—European Birds — Hot Months—Raven—Black Ibis—Bald-headed Eagle.

THE naturalist may continue his out-door studies on the Sub-Himalayan ranges until the middle of June, when the monsoon sets in, and renders travelling very difficult, and often impossible. At times it rains uninterruptedly for days. Vapour-charged clouds often envelope the mountain-tops, while a few hundred feet below the sun is shining brightly; it is like walking out of the densest London fog into an Italian sky. This is particularly evident at the sanitarium of Simla, and even on the lower hill stations. All are evidently too high for invalids; in fact, we have overdone our good intentions in sending them from the torrid plains to the region of clouds and storms; a lower elevation is clearly indicated, where the temperature is more equable all the year, and the weakly removed from injurious influences of the humid atmosphere of midsummer.

Rapid movements consequent on march are against making anything like close observations regarding the natural history of a country, nor is the midnight tramp along a dusty road at all likely to form a pleasant prelude to an excursion in the heat of mid-day, in a climate which requires that all journeys be performed before sunrise. Nomadic life in a marching regiment in India has its attractions nevertheless, and those who are content to follow out the routine will find, on the score of health, that there are few more salutary states of existence—the constant changing scene, the varied novelty of every day, and regular habits, have a wonderful effect on man and beast. The pale face becomes bronzed, and the climate-worn soldier plucks up, and after a few weeks' steady marching, and away from the debilitating grog-shops, the men look as if they could do anything, or go anywhere.

An Indian camp breaking up would form a fine subject for the painter. Suppose the hour 3 A.M. No sooner does the bugle sound than the quiet of the preceding hours is broken, and the noise of wooden mallets and the bellowing of camels soon arouse us from our slumbers. Tents are observed falling as if by magic, the white rows of canvas streets disappear one after another, louder and louder roar the camels amid the hum and discord of human voices. The turbaned native and red-coated soldier are seen mingling in inextricable confusion. By the light of the camp fires, the camels' gaunt figures, or an occasional elephant laden with tents and heavy baggage, defile past one after another; the dark forms of officers, just turned out of bed, cluster around the blazing straw fires. Again the bugle sends forth its shrill and deep-toned call "to arms," when all rush through the gloom, the band strikes up a lively air, and headed by two native torch-bearers to light us on our pathless way, in ten minutes the regiment is once more on its orderly march, while nothing remains but the dying embers of the fires, a lagging native, or broken-down camel, to mark the scene so full of busy excitement half-an-hour before.

We left Dugshai in the beginning of November, and after a few days spent at Kalka preparing for the march, started for Rawul Pindee, in the northern Punjaub, by way of Loodiana and Lahore. At Kalka I had a morning with the Rajah of Puteala's falconer, and several gos and chippuck falcons (*Falco badius*) were flown at black and gray partridges. The sport was not exciting, I believe chiefly on account of the birds having been badly trained. As soon as a partridge rose, the hawk was slipped; and if he caught the bird, it was generally just as the latter was about to drop into the cover.

The European short-eared owl is not uncommon in the jungle; one shot at Kalka had a palm squirrel in its craw. The painted or lesser sand-grouse (*Pterocles fasciatus*) differs in its habits from the other species met with in India, by preferring jungles to the open country. Its flight resembles the night-jar's, and its haunts are similar. It is easily known from the others by the white and black band on the forehead, which is wanting in the female; the latter is larger, and, instead of the broad band on the breast, the lower parts are marked with transverse lines. This species is not gregarious. The large "black breast" (*P. arenarius*) is at once distinguished by its size and even tail from the "pin-tailed grouse" (*P. exustus*), which is by far the most common; both are met with in flocks in fields and waste places. Their flight is strong; and although their flesh is tough and unsavoury, they are much sought after by European sportsmen. I have been informed that another species is sometimes seen on the north-west frontier of the Punjaub, possibly the large pin-tail (*P. alchata*), which is said to be plentiful in Afghanistan and westward. In the woods and jungles one can scarcely miss observing the beautiful orange-backed woodpecker (*Brachypternus aurantius*); its brilliant yellow back is conspicuous at all times.

At Morindah, a halting-place, there was a fine tope of mango in the middle of a desert plain; here we encamped for three days, in consequence of the sudden death of one of our officers, whom we buried at the foot of one of the trees in this wild untenanted waste. A small travellers' bungalow was the only human habitation within many miles.

Almost every morning, at and before daybreak, large flocks of geese chiefly (*Anser indicus*) and ducks were observed migrating southwards. There were great numbers of peafowl in the sugar-cane fields, but the natives preserve them with so much care that it is considered next to sacrilege to molest them in any way. In the wheat-fields near Loodiana we bagged abundance of pin-tailed grouse; and among the sand hillocks, covered with bent, three houbara bustards were shot. In the more level places, where a thick-leaved shrub abounded, hares were plentiful. The Bengal fox and the jackal were common. I saw a hyena, and killed a fine specimen of the gray ichneumon (*Herpestes griseus*) or moongus. The male is much larger than the female; they breed in captivity. Wherever irrigation appeared, or there was stagnant water, the spur-winged lapwing and the yellow-headed wagtail were common.

It is scarcely possible to estimate the amount of sediment borne down by the great rivers of India. What vast changes must take place even in a century in the bottom and configuration of the Indus! we can clearly trace its past changes in Scinde, and in the Punjaub, inasmuch as the ancient beds are six miles distant from where the rivers now flow.* That their channels must be constantly changing, we have only to look at their excessively impregnated waters, almost like pea-soup, boiling and eddying along their muddy banks and shoals, which render the navigation so uncertain and difficult. Thus, like the Nile, they are constantly changing their channels, taking up what they had deposited long since, and forming fresh channels where the river had run ages before. I was forcibly impressed with the truth of this in having been shown a village on a bank of ancient river alluvium, near the field of Aliwal, that six years before was upwards of a quarter of a mile inland, whilst at the time of our visit the greater portion had been washed away, and the remainder of the houses abandoned by the inhabitants.

The country between Ferozepoor and Lahore is for the most part cultivated, and covered with fields of wheat and groves of date, mango, acacia, peepul, etc. The famous old Mussulman city of Kussor is worth a visit, were it only to examine its fallen grandeur. Among its old temples, ruined walls, and broken aqueduct, are to be traced the remains of a once important town, which the great Runjeet Singh levelled with the ground when employed in consolidating the Kalsa dynasty. The Chenab river at Wezeerabad has little of the majesty and appearance observed in its course through the Himâlayas; the roaring mountain torrent is transformed into a muddy river, whose banks are often almost level with the plain, especially in the neighbourhood of the city above mentioned, where annual inundations leave great swamps in which wild-fowl congregate during winter. There, wading in shallows I observed the great white heron (*Egretta alba*), a

* See an interesting paper on the ancient and present channels of the Ganges by Mr. Ferguson in *Quarterly Journal Geol. Society for* 1863.

handsome bird, and easily distinguished by its large size and snow-white plumage. The lesser cormorant or dwarf shag (*Graculus sinensis*) frequents the rivers and marshes of the Punjaub, and is easily distinguished from the other cormorants by its smaller size. I found abundance of mallard, teal, pin-tailed ducks, egrets, the Indian rail, greater bittern, and the handsome little black-bellied tern, so common on the Indus.

Proceeding northwards from Wezeerabad, we entered a district more or less uncultivated, and often covered for miles with tall scrubby jungle, where the sportsman might pick up a few quail at almost any season of the year, and by beating the bushes make a fair bag of gray and black partridges and hares. From the great numbers of quail met with in the fields during the ripening of the grain, and their sudden disappearance afterwards, it is generally supposed they migrate, and in certain situations this may doubtless be the case; but I am inclined to believe that in general they disperse themselves over the jungles of the north-west, and congregate when the wheat and barley are beginning to ripen. A few snipes are found at all seasons on the marshes of upper Bengal, but the majority come and go with considerable regularity. In the Punjaub they are plentiful from December to February, and at the same season are said to visit the lakes of Cashmere. September and October are their months in the Deccan, and I believe in Southern India they come earlier; their migrations, however, are not well-defined. The black-winged falcon (*Elanus melanopterus*) is generally dispersed over the country; few rapacious birds have such a wide geographical distribution as this pretty little hawk, which is found in Asia, Africa, and south-eastern Europe.

Proceeding towards the city of Jhelum, the country has very much the same appearance as has just been detailed.

Thick, bushy jungle alternates with large open spaces, which are cultivated, or overgrown with grass. The Sewalik range and the Peer Pingal stand forth in their still grandeur, the former only a few miles distant, the latter seen bounding the horizon, capped with a broad covering of snow. We passed the little villages of Koree and Russool. The latter stands conspicuous on a spur which runs from the Himalayas into the plain, and ends in the jungle of Chillianwallah, so memorable in Indian annals. Two years had not sufficed to obliterate all traces of the sad struggle, for the first memorial we encountered was the graveyard, a little square, not 30 yards either way: there, in rows, lay fifty-three officers and several hundred men. It is said to have been the spot where the commander of the forces stood during the action, the ill-fated hillock over which rolled the round shot which called forth the ill-judged order for an advance. On our left, at a little distance, was the village, and in front and between us stretched tall and bushy thickets, intersected by little green patches. In this ambuscade the cannon and matchlock men of the Sikh army were hidden, and through this labyrinth-like jungle, with its numerous devious twinings, our unsuspecting troops wound their way until they arrived at the cannon's mouth, when volley after volley of grape swept through their ranks, followed by thousands of matchlock bullets from the lurking foes behind the guns. We were shown over the field by a Sikh belonging to the village of Chillian. He minutely and, I afterwards discovered, correctly described the positions of the various British regiments, and spoke with considerable fervour of the bravery of his countrymen on that occasion, and how the "Lal Kotees" (the red coats) were obliged to retire. As I picked my way through the masses of bush and brake, grim and ghastly relics were observed strewing the ground; several human skulls bore deep sabre-cuts, and in one secluded spot we came on an entire skeleton. It has been asserted that all the British were buried, so that the bones we saw bleaching on the field were possibly those of the enemy.

A nobler picture of filial and heroic devotion is not enrolled in history than the death of the younger Pennycuick, who, on seeing his brave old father fall while leading on the brigade, rushed forward to save him from the Sikh tulwar, and fell himself, fighting *pro patre patriaque.* There was no lack of courage on that fatal day amongst the officers and men of the British army.

An officer who shared in the fight informed us that the night after the battle was one of awful suspense, for nearly half the British force lay dead or wounded in the jungle, and at the mercy of a cruel and relentless enemy. Peace to the ashes of the noble fellows cradled together on the field on which they fell! History records what the peaceful naturalist even cannot pass unnoticed, and in the wild jungle the white obelisk will mark the spot, and many a British soldier will point to the little graveyard, and say, "There lie the brave men who fell on the field of Chillianwallah!"

After a pleasant march of nearly two months' duration, we arrived at Rawul Pindee, which is situated on a slightly undulating plain about 24 miles from the Himalayas. The country around is intersected and much broken up by ravines and watercourses; and the surface is covered with kankur, a calcareous concretionary deposit now in course of formation, mostly in nodules, but here and there forming masses of considerable thickness.

Sixteen miles from Rawul Pindee stands the remarkable round mound called Maunikyala tope, which is composed of blocks of stone forming a dome 70 feet in height, with an opening on the top, by which one of Runjeet Singh's generals descended, and found a vase containing many ancient coins. Their antiquity, however, was found not so great as had been formerly ascribed to the tope, which was thought to have been built by Alexander the Great to mark one of his victories. The coins show the usual devices to be met with on those found in the northern Punjaub. Several were procured by us from the natives, who have, unfortunately, a way of not only telling lies with reference to the localities where they are found, but, as we discovered, had counterfeited several. All the coins we saw were of copper, and of the exact figure of the old native piece of Hindostan. On one side was a "male figure with crossed legs," on the other, "a man riding on an elephant"—a figure with an arm akimbo and the other extended, "and with a spear or sceptre in his hand."

The absence of wood about Rawul Pindee, and the general uncultivated and barren appearance of the country, afford few natural history materials, compared with the fertile and densely-covered slopes of the Himalayas; nevertheless, there are attractions sufficient to repay an ardent student. Let him follow down the dubious windings of the Hummok river from its sources in the Sewalik range to where it joins the Swan —a river of fair dimensions which empties itself into the Indus on the west, near Kala-Bagh. Among the pools and deeper parts of the Hummok, the migrating waterfowl repair in the cold months; and a few miles from the native city of Rawul Pindee, in a low marshy flat, he will find at the same season many European birds not observed in other portions of the continent southwards.

Along the base of the Himalayas, in the dense jungles, an occasional tiger prowls; the leopard is not uncommon; while the game birds named about Dugshai are there also plentiful. Among the lesser ranges bordering the plains, and to an elevation of 8000 or 9000 feet, barking-deer are common; and on the more secluded and craggy mountains, the goral or chamois of the Himalayas may be occasionally seen sporting among the pine-clad precipices. This little antelope is gregarious, feeding in scattered herds, so that when the loud hissing call of alarm is uttered by one individual, the others, one by one, take it up; and if you were on a prominent position at the time, you might see from ten to twenty gorals in different parts of the hill bounding across the precipices. The goral is rather higher than the barking-deer, and more compact and agile in appearance. Its coat is dark brown above, neck and throat white. Both sexes have short black horns curving backwards, and ringed towards their base. The young are born in May or June. The immediate neighbourhood of Rawul Pindee is far from inviting. A few acacia or Persian lilacs are planted round the villages, and also set off the otherwise dismal appearance of the Englishmen's houses. The barren, stony wastes, level in some places, slightly elevated into low hills or plateaus in other situations, are covered with low scrub, and the wild oleander and olive are not uncommon. Among the few northern forms of plants I searched in vain for the dandelion, mentioned by Sir A. Burns in his travels as a "common weed." I think he must have been mistaken both as to its frequency and that of the "chickweed" and "plantago," neither of which I have seen on the cis-Indus portion of the Punjaub or even in the valley of Peshawur. The change, however, in the vegetation of the northern Punjaub, compared with the low countries, is very striking, The peach, plum, apple, pear, quince, mulberry, etc., grow in gardens. The chief geological feature about Rawul Pindee is a tertiary sandstone, common to this part of the country and the lower Himalayan ranges; it has evidently been much disintegrated and denuded in the plain, and here and there abuts in the form of large bare masses on the sides of ravines or irregular hogs-backs and rugged prominences observable south-west of Rawul Pindee. The great depth of the alluvium of the surrounding country, especially towards the Himalayas, may in part result from the disintegration of the sandstone, which is friable and easily broken up.

In Afghanistan, or even in Kohaut, one of the trans-Indus districts, the wild raspberry and blackberry are common. At Gundamuk, in the former country, Burns discovered white daisies, clover, and forests of pine. Even at Rawul Pindee the fauna more resembles that of Northern Europe and Asia than the south. It is, as it were, on the confines of two great regions, which differ in their fauna and flora, and partakes more or less of both. The migrations of its birds are therefore very interesting, as thereby we are enabled to trace the goings and comings of many species, and find out the habitats and distribution of individuals, whose existence before was limited to the districts they frequented. Take, for instance, the *common European jackdaw*, which may be seen in flocks in winter in the northern frontier of the Punjaub, associated with the *Cornish chough* and the *rook*. The first two come from Cashmere, where I have found them in great abundance during the summer; but the rook, if ever seen in Cashmere, is only a cold-weather visitor. I believe it comes from the west, inasmuch as it is said to be common in Afghanistan. It appears at Rawul Pindee in flocks about the beginning of September, and disappears entirely in March. I believe it is found in winter as far south as Lahore. The hooded-crow has been brought from Northern Afghanistan, and is mentioned by Lieutenant Wood in his travels as common in Kunduz, but it is not found in Cashmere or in the Punjaub. Besides these British birds, the *chimney swallow* makes its appearance in October and leaves again for the straw-built sheds of Cashmere, where it breeds and spends the summer months. The *white-rumped martin** and *sand martin* are both likewise migratory, and repair to Cashmere and Ladakh in summer The *black* and *alpine swifts* remain longer, and may be seen careering about during the summer evenings, especially after a shower of rain. The *ring-dove* is a resident on the sub-Himalaya. The *common starling* is plentiful in the north as elsewhere in Hindostan. The lapwing (*Vanellus cristatus*) arrives in flocks in the beginning of November, and departs for the west early in spring; its summer residence I have not been enabled to find out, but I imagine it must be common in certain parts of Persia and Afghanistan. The *common* and *jack snipe*, with a few painted snipe, appear in the Rawul Pindee in February and March, when I have procured as many as thirty couple at a time.

On the 11th of December I shot several barred-headed geese, and also the gray-lag, which had evidently just arrived from the north with *mallard, teal,* etc., as they were very tame, and allowed me to approach within easy shooting distance. Nearly all the water-fowl met with in the rivers and marshes of the north-west come from the Tartarian lakes, where they may be found breeding. At the commencement of the cold months great flocks are seen steering their course southwards to the Punjaub rivers. I have seen large flocks of the greater and pintailed grouse flying southwards in September, October, and November, and flocks of cranes, of up-

* This is the *Chelidon cashmeriensis* referred to before. It is at least a distinct race, if not a different species, from *C. urbica* of Europe.

wards of half-a-mile in length, may be observed pursuing the same course; their loud gabblings, and those of ducks and geese, and the harsh "guggle" of the sand-grouse, are often heard overhead at night. It is a busy time in the bird-world when the cold months are setting in on the north-western frontier of British India.

In May, as soon as the hot weather appears, nearly all the birds of the North-western Provinces retire to their various summer quarters, and only a few permanent residents remain. The raven, Indian jackdaw, govind kite, and sparrow, are about the chief. The raven hunts about houses, or sits gaping and croaking on the roof-tops at mid-day in a temperature of 130° Fahrenheit and upwards, whilst his more knowing companion, the Indian jackdaw, seeks the shade of the Persian lilac or the castor-oil plant. The kite is seen soaring aloft over barracks and bazaars, or indeed anywhere at all likely to supply refuse. Sparrows* breed in June and July among the thatch of our verandahs, and the Indian roller in the chimney-top. After a sultry day it is usual to see the wire-tailed swallow skimming over the plains, and by the side of pools and streams a solitary green sandpiper (*Totanus ochropus*) is not rare. I have also shot the brown-backed heron (*Ardeola leucoptera*) in such situations. The black ibis (*G. papillosus*), with its red crown, is seen flying, along with the rooks and European jackdaws, during the cold months; and besides, on the marshes about, the great and little bitterns, with the spotted rail, are not uncommon. Of the other European birds may be noticed the short-eared owl, moor buzzard, the pale harrier (*Circus swainsonii*), the cormorant, ruff, and smew, all coming and departing with the winter months.

* This is *P. domesticus;* the Spanish sparrow *P. salicarius* is found in Kohaut, on the west frontier of the Punjaub.

The bald-headed eagle of Asia (*H. macei*) pays cold-weather visits to the inland marshes. I took its eggs as early as the 12th of December; the nest was built on an old peepul-tree near the Rawul Pindee bog. I had then several opportunities of observing the extraordinary rapid stoop of this fine eagle; the noise of its wings, and the wild scream as it darted obliquely downwards on a flock of mallard and teal (none of which, however, did it manage to capture on that occasion), brought to recollection Wilson's and Audubon's descriptions of its American ally. The handsome little chicquera falcon is plentiful in the acacia "topes." The crested lark and green wagtail (*M. viridis*), with the blue-black head in the breeding season, are both exceedingly common. The last, as before noticed, is subject to seasonal changes of plumage, which have occasioned much confusion, and led to errors in nomenclature.

CHAPTER VIII.

Excursion to the Salt Mountains of the Punjaub—Wild Sheep—Ravine Deer—Geology—Ornithology—Scenery.

DURING the months of March and April the climate of the Northern Punjaub is delightful. If the heat at mid-day is oppressive, the morning and evening are always cool and pleasant. Having despatched our tent and baggage to Ranouthera, a village 32 miles south of Rawul Pindee, on the 21st March 1853, we started very early, and rode through an almost barren country, intersected by ravines and water-courses—now floundering through a stagnant pool, now cantering on a level space, covered with pebbles or rough and hard kankur. This substance, already mentioned, is extensively distributed over the Northern Punjaub, either as a surface deposit, or in heaps along the sides of river-beds and ravines. It is usually met with in the form of tufaceous nodules, but not unfrequently also in large irregularly-shaped concrete masses. When broken up and mixed with brick-dust and lime, it forms a durable cement. It is also used in road-making, and even building purposes. Professor Ansted is disposed to consider the kankur referable to the drift period.* I have, however, observed a similar deposit in course of formation on the surface, and throughout the alluvium of rivers and streams both in the Punjaub and banks of the Nile in Egypt and Nubia.†

* Professor Ansted's analysis is as follows :—72 per cent carbonate of lime, 15 per cent silica, 18 per cent allumina.

† *Proc. Geol. Soc. of London*, 1863, p. 8.

Long before day-dawn the well-known call of the spur-winged lapwing (*Lobivanellus goensis*) was heard. This unsettled water-sprite often flies about at night, startling the unwary with its cry of *Did dee doo it, did did did dee doo it.* Like the European lapwing, it assails all who intrude on its haunts. The horny spurs on the wings I have never seen used either as a means of attack or defence. When morning dawned we found ourselves on the banks of the Swan, one of several streams which rise at the foot of the Himalayas, and, coursing westward, empty themselves into the Indus. Many of these tributaries are completely dried up in summer, and present only a series of pools and stagnant ponds, with broad pebbly beds. They are very different, however, during the rainy season, when, after a storm, the rush of water from the slopes around is frequently sudden and furious. On one occasion, during a terrific thunderstorm which took place in February near Rawul Pindee, three soldiers were bathing in one of these pools, when the flood overwhelmed them so suddenly that they were carried away by its violence. One poor fellow was drowned, and on recovering his body, a few days afterwards, it was found to be horribly disfigured by a small species of crab which abounds in the rivers and streams of the Punjaub. The fish called masseer is prized by Europeans more for the sport it affords than as an article of food, being frequently caught by the rod and fly; however, in the more rapid parts of the Punjaub rivers throughout these mountain-courses, it attains not only a very large size,* but its flesh is firm and savoury. It is said to spawn in the deep ponds above mentioned, where it is occasionally caught. We observed a flock of cranes in the shallow waters of the Swan. The crane migrates to Central Asia in May. Journeying on, we

* Individuals 30 to 40 lbs. in weight have been captured.

passed little villages, surrounded by high walls of mud, clusters of camel-thorn, and fields of wheat and barley, with here and there a banyan-tree, despoiled by the elephant-drivers, who cut down its broad leaves for fodder,—now a clump of mulberry, now a ravine or a tract of waste and arid plain. Such are the natural features of this and great portions of the Northern Punjaub. Among the low brushwood that covers the sides of ravines and hollows, flocks of the striated babbler (*Malacocircus caudatus*) were observed chirping and chattering in a low note, or fluttering from bush to bush with their characteristic, feeble, and unsteady flight. The blue rock-pigeon abounds in ravines; and in the fields and hedgerows the Senegal dove (*Columba senegalensis*) is generally seen either singly or in pairs. On the side of a steep ravine I killed a fine specimen of the spotted eagle, which is not rare in the district.

The black-throated wheatear (*Saxicola atrogularis*) is common; its favourite food is a small white worm, which it digs out of the sun-baked soil. Flocks of the crested lark (*Galerida cristata*) were scattered over the desert plains, as plentifully as in the southern provinces. With the exception of an isabel tinge of plumage, so characteristic of larks and chats frequenting dry and arid wastes, there is no difference between this bird and the crested lark of Europe and North Africa.

March 22.—To Fureed, about twelve miles. It blew strongly during the greater part of the night, and day dawned in the usual Indian style, followed by a grilling hot forenoon. The first half of our march was very similar to that of the previous day, until we debouched on a vast plain, cultivated here and there. In the distance, running from east to west, the salt range was seen, but so far away that in the hazy atmosphere of mid-day we could do little more than define its outline. Green bee-eaters covered the surrounding country, flitting swallow-like after their winged prey. It is extremely common all over India and westward to north-western Africa. The Indian specimens show some variety which I have not noticed in those of Egypt. Numbers of a small white-rumped martin were often noticed. No specimens, however, were procured; and although I then supposed the species to be identical with the European martin, I hesitate now in coming to that conclusion, in consequence of skins procured by me on the frontier of Cashmere having been considered to be different from the *Chelidon urbica.* Around the villages—for what native village would be complete without them?—were govind kites, Indian jackdaws, and the noisy mina birds. In the fields and sandy wastes were numbers of a pipit, usually gregarious in the cold months, and often seen associating with the crested lark previously named. This species is larger than the *Anthus agilis*, Sykes, to which its plumage bears a resemblance. Its total length is 7½ inches; the markings on the throat and breast are more numerous, with a slight tinge of rufous on the latter; inner surface of the wings dirty white.

March 23.—To Bone, fifteen miles. In order to escape the heat of mid-day, we started very early, and marched the first few miles by moonlight. The route led by narrow foot-paths through stony ravines and cotton-fields. When day dawned, we found ourselves toiling up a rather broad valley, and soon had the mortification of discovering that the guides had lost their way, and our three hours' travelling had been to no purpose; we soon, however, got on the right track, and entered on a fine open district, thickly covered with fields of green wheat, and by noon arrived at the town of Chukkowal, during a Sikh festival, and just as one of their priests (*goroo*) was about to address a large assembly in a tent pitched under a copse of peepul and other trees. Here we spent the hottest portion of the day watching the busy scene. Pilgrims, fakirs, and dirty beggars from all parts of the country were pushing onwards towards the tent, whilst many were bathing in the neighbouring tank;—the heat and dust, the continued hubbub of human voices, the cawing, chattering, and chirpings of impertinent jackdaws, bulbuls, and rose-winged parrakeets, among the branches overhead, rendered our stay anything but agreeable, and made us only too glad when the afternoon came, and we were able to quit the scene. The red-vented bulbul (*Pycnonotus bengalensis*) is generally distributed over the Punjaub. The lesser yellow-vented bulbul (*P. leucotis*), although not so plentiful, is by no means rare, and both were often seen on the same tree.

The inhabitants of this part of the Punjaub, known as the Scind Sagour Doab, are chiefly Mussulmen. They are a fine hardy race, with long flowing beards and large turbans. The women (such as we were permitted to see) wore capacious peg-tops, their hair knotted behind, while a loose jacket and a piece of red cloth over the head completed their eccentric-looking costume.

We often noticed the pale harrier (*Circus swainsonii*), which is pretty generally distributed over Asia, Africa, and Southern Europe, evidently replacing its very close ally, *C. cyaneus*, in certain portions of these continents; the latter species being partial to their more northern regions. He who aims at uniting the meagre distinctions which are often made to separate species may, in this instance, consider how much of the little that divide the pale and dull chested hen harriers are the result of climate, food, and such like; but until we care less for making new species, and think more of applying ourselves to the study of animals in nature rather than in the cabinet, there is no prospect that any great strides will be made in the discovery of laws which shall regulate the varieties and geographical distribution of species.

The Asiatic pigeon (*Turtur humilis*) is somewhat common in the Punjaub. The gay Indian roller sported before us, now perched on the stump of a decayed tree, anon pursuing its corkscrew-like flight through the hazy atmosphere. This roller is replaced in Eastern India by a very close ally (*C. affinis*). The palm-squirrel (*Sciurus palmarum*) is common in every grove. A fox, differing in some respects from the Bengal fox (in the lower parts, which are white in the latter, being in this species black), was not uncommon in the ravines and around the villages.*

The pied wagtail (*Motacilla luzoniensis*) was plentiful at this season. Perhaps, if more was known of the general distribution of this species and the pied wagtail of Western India (*M. dukhunensis*), also the well-known European bird, the slight differences in plumage would scarcely permit us to separate them.

March 24.—Kuller Kahar, 8 miles. We started early, and performed the greater part of the march by moonlight, and at day-break reached the side of a steep ravine overlooking a beautiful valley, composed chiefly of reddish and gray sandstones, cultivated in several places, and with a large lake several miles in length occupying its centre. Flocks of wild fowl covered the surface of the lake, and the pink and white plumage of the flamingo added greatly to the beauty of the landscape.

The wandering pie (*Dendrocitta vagabunda*) was observed. I do not think I have ever seen more than two of these birds

* This fox agrees with descriptions of *Vulpes pusillus*, Blyth.—*Jour. As. Soc. Ben.* 1854.

together. Its habits are like those of the British magpie. The pied stonechat (*Saxicola picata*) was common. The Indian robin, so generally distributed over most parts of Hindostan, is seen here in almost every village and field. Although differing altogether in the colour of its plumage from the European robin, there is a great similarity in their habits. It frisks before the door and picks up the crumbs, jerking its tail as it hops along. How often have associations of home been brought to mind by seeing this pretty little warbler pursuing its gambols before the door of an Eastern bungalow! Although its song is far from unmusical, it wants the melody of the northern bird.

The Indian porcupine (*Hystrix leucurus*) is found among the low scrub and bush. As an article of food, its flesh is much sought after by Europeans as well as natives.

The Salt Range extends from the Himalayas across the Punjaub in about a straight line to the Suliman Mountains on their west flank, and is composed of low hills intersected by narrow ravines or prominent ridges, for the most part devoid of vegetation. Limestones, saliferous red and gray sandstones, would appear to form the chief geological formations which, according to Professor Fleming, belong to the carboniferous period.* The plateaus, excepting where extensive denudation has taken place, are covered with rounded pebbles, mostly formed from the breaking up of the limestone beds. Salt is found in veins in various situations, more especially among the sandstone and marl beds in the neighbourhood of Kuller Kahar, where there are extensive salt-mines. The barren and sun-burnt appearance of these mountains strikes the traveller; indeed it is chiefly on that account that they become a safe retreat to the wild sheep, for, except in the cultivated

* *Quart. Jour. Geol. Soc.* 1853 and 1862: also *Jour. As. Soc. Ben.* 1853, etc.

districts, their dreary and desolate wastes are seldom disturbed by man.

The Houriar (*Caprovis vignei*) extends along the eastern spurs of the Salt Mountains, but becomes less common as we proceed eastwards, and, I believe, is seldom met with on the ranges beyond the town of Jhelum, or southwards of the Beas River. Accordingly, in British India it is confined to the north and western portions of the Punjaub, including the Suliman chain, where it is known by the name of *Kuch.* It is also a denizen of the mountains around Peshawur, including the Khyber Pass, Hindu Koh, and Kaffiristan. The *shapoo* or *shalmar** of Ladakh, if not identical, is certainly very closely allied; its differences are slight, and, I opine, such as might result in a great measure from the marked diversity of climate, food, etc., of the two regions. This species is no doubt the *Sha* of Tibet described by Vigne,† and possibly the wild sheep of western Afghanistan, Persia, the Caucasus, Armenian and Corsican mountains, is the same species, altered mayhap by climate and other external agencies. I have not been enabled to fix with certainty the eastern limits of the Shapoo, but as far as all my inquiries have yet extended it would seem that, commencing at Ladakh, it proceeds westward towards the Indus, into the regions where the houriar is found, and probably when we are enabled to explore these regions we shall find out the relation between what has been supposed distinct, but which I am much inclined to consider one and the same animal. There is considerable variation with regard to the shape and curvature of horns in

* "Habits of some of the Mammalia of India and Himalayas" (*Proc. Zool. Soc.* 1858, p. 521). The name *Shalmar* I give on the authority of an English officer who had shot the animal in Ladakh.

† *Travels in Cashmir*, etc. vol. ii. 280.

several specimens I have examined from the Salt Range and Ladakh, as well as in size of the animal. For example, the rams' horns of the Ladakh sheep were larger, and had the upper surface rounded, with the tops turned more inward; whilst the houriar had the upper surface of the horn flat: that of the female seemed in no way different from the shapoo, and the skins of both houriar and shapoo were similarly coloured. The above peculiarity is certainly striking, but too much value must not be placed on the horn as a means of distinction. Every one at all conversant with the wild goats and sheep of the Himalayas, knows that these organs are subject to considerable variety in individuals of the same species. The upper parts of the houriar of the Salt Mountains are fawn-colour, the belly and inner side of the thighs pure white. The male has long black hair extending down the dewlap. The horn resembles certain varieties of the domestic animal, but perhaps rises higher and curves more backward; it often measures from 25 to 30 inches over the curvature, and from 8 to 12 inches around the base; that of the female is small, and seldom exceeds 6 inches in length.

On the 25th of March we ascended the side of a steep ravine covered with brushwood, and gained a broad and partly-cultivated plateau, where our beaters flushed several coveys of the red-legged or chukore partridge, and a smaller species called by the natives "sisi." The former is by no means common on the range, or indeed in any part of the Punjaub, although a few are met with on the plains along the skirts of the Himalayas; its favourite haunts are on those mountains where it extends northward to the Altai ranges. The average weight of an adult male is about one and a half pounds. It is found likewise in Persia and Afghanistan. Mr. Vigne mentions having seen "red-legged partridges" in Kurdistan, but does not identify species. The red-leg of south-eastern Europe (*C. græca*) does not appear to differ in any well-marked degree from the above, inasmuch as several specimens obtained by me in the market of Constantinople, when attentively compared with *C. chukar* from the Himalayas, showed only a slight difference in the intensity of the white of the throat and the rufous of the ear coverts, which did not even appear to be constant. When we are enabled to trace a bird over a continent, and find that we change climate and enter on a country widely different in its physical aspects, it is surely not extravagant to expect that there will be some change in the colour of its external coverings, or even the size of the animal.

The sisi (*Ammoperdix bonhami*), or bastard chukore, as it is known to Europeans, is much smaller than the last. The male measures in the flesh about 10 inches, the female about 9½ inches. The iris is hazel, bill brownish-yellow, lighter on the legs. Its existence has been known to naturalists for several years, but all the specimens were brought from Afghanistan, where it abounds in sandy wastes and barren mountains. The sisi is not found in Ladakh, nor on the ranges to the south and east; and I think, with the Salt and Suliman chains, and probably the mountains around the forbidden Khyber Pass, we define its limits eastward and in British India. A species, closely allied both in size and plumage (*A. heyii*), I procured in rocky and barren gorges on the banks of the Nile in Nubia. It is a native likewise of Palestine and Syria. The sisi often associates with the chukore, to which in habits it bears a close resemblance; the call-note, however, is very different. The pretty little redbreast (*Muscicapa parva*) is very much like the robin of Europe; and, although less familiar, has many points in common. It affects hedges and dense jungle, and is usually seen solitary. This little robin has a wide Asiatic distribution, and even extends westward to south-western Europe.

On the 27th of March we pitched our little tent close to the village of Norpoor, and were not settled before its kotwal (*Anglice* mayor) arrived to offer his services in procuring supplies, bringing with him a rupee, which, according to the usual Indian custom, he held out for our acceptance. Our friend, however, appeared somewhat dubious as to our social position, and if we were acquainted with the etiquette which expects that gentle-folks should on such occasions merely touch the offered gift and then make a salaam of satisfaction to the host. As each of us touched the coin, our Sikh friend squeezed it spasmodically, and even closed his fingers over it, grinning most benignly when he found out that we were respectable young gentlemen, and above accepting his present—a discovery our shady jungle attire was certainly not calculated to further. I spent the day among the hot ravines, searching after wild sheep. The reflection from the sand and limestone was excessive; and we suffered much from want of water, which was only procurable from red muddy pools in the worn-out bottoms of water-courses. After much fagging and occasional snap-shots at wild sheep and ravine deer, which we startled in the narrow lanes between the marl-heaps, I at length espied two of the former under the shadow of an acacia, and, by dint of much knee and hand travelling, managed to crawl unobserved within 50 yards, when, neglectful of the old adage, "that a bird in the hand is worth two in the bush," I sought a nearer approach in hopes of procuring both; but, by so doing, had the mortification to find out that the ram had caught a glimpse of me, for he sprang to his feet, and, sending forth a loud whistle, disappeared with his companion among the tortuous lanes. This mishap was one of many such like, from which, as my experience increased, I was taught "never to lose a good opportunity in hopes of obtaining a better"—an advice I recommend in all its bearings to every young hunter.

The gray-capped bunting (*Emberiza caniceps*), the bearded vulture, and the blue water-thrush, before seen only on the Himalayas, were here occasionally observed. The bearded vulture feeds sumptuously at this season on the young houriar, which are dropped in March. The raven is common, but rather smaller than the bird of Tibet and Europe.* The Indian carrion crow (*Corvus culminatus*) was not seen on the Salt range, nor about Rawul Pindee, where, however, the rook is plentiful during the cold months. Now and then the pied woodpecker (*P. himalayanus*) was observed on the acacia and other trees; its similarity to the greater spotted woodpecker of Europe and Western Asia, is striking; the differences lie chiefly in a less brilliant state of plumage. Again, in China there is the *Picus cabanisi*, and on the ranges of Nepal another species, *P. majoroides;* all these are perhaps capable of being brought into one species did we only know the range and limits of each in Asia. The hare (*L. nigricollis*) is not common.

We pitched our tent in the most retired spot we could discover, far distant from the villages, and in the centre of the salt district, where the houriar repair at dusk to lick the salt-

* The raven of Tibet has been called *C. tibetanus* by Mr. Hodgson (*An. and Mag. Nat. Hist.* iii. p. 203), for the reason that it "is somewhat larger than *C. corax.*"

encrusted rocks. The streams and wells in the neighbourhood being more or less tainted with salt, we found great difficulty in procuring a sufficiency of fresh water for our wants. One morning, early, while clambering across a steep ridge, I suddenly came on a Sikh sitting under a ledge of rock, where he had passed the night; he was *minus* his nose and right hand, which he said were cut off during the reign of Runjeet Singh, as a punishment for having murdered his brother. When told that now-a-days his life would be forfeited for such a crime, he, with a sly shrug of his shoulder and twinkle of his little black eye, turned and moved down the ravine, muttering something about the difficulties attendant on such proceedings under the British rule, and no doubt bent on salt-stealing, for which he had come, whilst I pushed up the slope, and, gaining the top of the spur, had a magnificent view of the Indus on one side and the Hydaspes on the other flank, tracing their windings for many a mile, in spite of the heavy atmosphere which hung over the plains below. The heat at mid-day, especially when reflected from the sides of the red ravines, was very powerful. Of wild sheep we saw many, but the cover was scanty, and the animals always on the alert; if a herd was feeding in a ravine, an old ram was sure to be on the outlook on some near eminence, and as soon as he apprehended danger, would send forth a loud whistle, when the whole set off at full speed. There are few ruminants in which the senses of sight and smell are more highly developed; natives allege that their smell is feeble or wanting, but I doubt if this animal is behind any of its compeers in that respect. By European sportsmen it is frequently called the "deer sheep," and from the circumstance that although its eye, hair, gait, and bleat are decidedly ovine, it has the infra-orbital apertures of the deer, together with the gracefully-formed limbs and fleetness of that animal. The hair is thick, and approaches nearer to the wool of sheep than the pleage of deer. The bay-backed shrike (*Lanius hardwickii*) was plentiful in bushy places, and flaunting in numbers among the yellow flowers of the acacia; the pretty little purple honey-sucker (*Nectarinia mahrattensis*) was often seen in pairs, now commencing to build their nests, the soft songs of the males sounding sweetly. Surrounded by gnarled acacias, grass, and rubbish, were frequently noticed ruined buildings, evidently of ancient date. Graveyards were seen often, but mostly in secluded and out-of-the-way places, showing that large parts of the district now unfrequented had at one time been densely populated. One of these buildings, more entire than the rest, is to be seen near the village of Jubba; it is quadrangular in shape, low and flat-roofed, with a small, narrow, and arched doorway, not four feet in height, opening into separate compartments on each side of the square; these are generally occupied by itinerant fakirs. The graves appear to differ from those of the present race in having a club-shaped erect stone at the head, and one rough and unhewn at the feet, and sometimes another in the middle. The style of architecture and antiquated appearance of these remains speak of a far-back period in the history of the Punjaub. A native hunter who accompanied me stated that he had often seen tigers, leopards,* the hyena, wolf, and a few black buck, besides an occasional black bear† (*Helarctos tibetanus*), which

* I have only seen one species of leopard in the Punjaub, and that was killed close to the Himalayas; it was the true *Felis leopardus* of Temminck (*Monogr.* i. p. 92).

† See A. L. Adams, *Proc. Zool. Soc.* for 1858. A variety of this species is said to frequent the lower Himalayas near the plains.

probably finds its way across from the Lower Himalaya. However, the black bear of the Southern Provinces (*U. labiatus*) is not found in the Punjaub.

March 30.—Although the scenery of these mountains is generally devoid of beauty, one will come occasionally on little spots by no means wanting in natural attractions. This morning we rose at daybreak, and after an hour's toil across a very stony plain covered with briars and thorns, arrived at the brink of a broad ravine, the sides of which were covered with a dense and luxuriant vegetation. The peepul, camelthorn, mulberry, and wild fig, formed small shady groves in which the fakirs had built their little temples, surrounded by gardens which rose in terraces along the steep slopes, where tobacco and the red and white opium-poppy were growing. On a prominence jutting into the ravine stood one of these shrines, which at a distance looked like a miniature castle, and far down among tangled briars and bushes rolled a clear stream, whilst numbers of peafowl in all their native elegance and beauty were sauntering in front of the temple or perched on the tops of trees—their wild cries resounding through the glen, and now and then one darted past us in all his gorgeous shades of plumage refulgent in the morning sun. It was an enchanting scene, but as the heat increased every hour, we hurried across the ravine, and on gaining the opposite plateau discovered a herd of houriar, headed as usual by two of the largest rams standing sentry by the prostrate herd. The open nature of the ground, however, prevented a near approach, and obliged me to discharge my rifle at a long range, which was no sooner done than all were up and flying with the wind, excepting one of the rams who lagged behind with a broken leg. This poor animal escaped, although pursued by us under a burning sun for many a mile up hill and down dale. When once disturbed, it is seldom the houriar rests for the remainder of that day, but keeps constantly on the move, selecting the ridges and most prominent points. The old are said to be untameable, but when caught young it is easily domesticated, and will herd with tame goats and sheep. The rams, however, are very pugnacious, and are often unmanageable. They fight in the same manner as the domestic sheep. When driving a jungle in search of wild pigs I observed a fine specimen of the great wild cat. It is common in the Punjaub, and hunts among the ravines and around the villages at night. In a hollow we were suddenly startled by observing large blood-stains, and in one spot decided traces of a struggle, with the foot-prints of a tiger. The villagers informed us that their cattle, goats, and sheep were frequently carried away by an old tiger which had confined his depredations to the domestic animals of two villages for several months. This would appear frequently the case with old males of many quadrupeds. The leopard seldom attacks cattle, and confines its plunderings to sheep, goats, and village dogs. The black partridge is not general in these parts, the country not being sufficiently cultivated; moreover, I do not think the chukore and this species ever frequent the same locality, although the former and the gray partridge are often found on the same hillside. Flocks of the wood-pigeon (*Columba palumbus*) were common in the fields. All the Indian specimens I have examined had the neck-patch clay-coloured and rather smaller than that of the European bird. I believe the same has also been noted with reference to Chinese specimens. It would be interesting to follow this permanent race towards the west, and see where the one ends and the other commences.

On the 2d of April, after several hot and sultry days with a close and murky state of the atmosphere, a hail-storm took place and lasted for nearly half-an-hour. Many of the hail-stones were as large as sparrows' eggs.

The geological formations and mineral features of the salt range are undoubtedly very interesting, but there was no time to examine them with care. Above the village of Kotela I wandered over a rugged steep composed of limestone, picking up fossils at almost every step, chiefly bivalve and large spiral univalve shells, Terebratula, and several species of *Galerites* and other Echinodermata, until attracted by a lake on which a flock of flamingoes were resting; their tall gaunt forms looked like balls of pink and white suspended over the shallow waters; each bird had its head under its wing, and was supported on one leg. I rudely disturbed their slumbers, for, resting my rifle on the wall of an enclosure overlooking the lake, I fired into the denser part of the flock, and when the frightened host had fled, and the ball had skipped and bounded far beyond, one small pink and white object floated alone on the placid surface, but it was unfortunately borne by the gentle breeze into deeper waters from beyond our reach. The average length of many specimens procured in the flesh was 5 feet 7½ inches from the bill to the extremity of the middle toe, and between the tips of the wings 5 feet 10 inches. Weight about 5 pounds.

A smaller race is sometimes met with in separate flocks. The plumage varies with age and sex. The young are dark on the back, and pink on the wings, with the rest of the body nearly pure white. The female is a delicate pink all over; the plumage of the male is brightest during the breeding season.

Behind the village of Kotela a mountain rises, perhaps one of the highest of the range; its summit is clothed with the long-leaved pine (*Pinus longifolia*) and other plants which grow on the Himalayas at altitudes of 4000 or 5000 feet. When toiling up the steep side of the mountain I was struck, on nearing the top, to notice the sudden transition from a desert to a region of verdure, and so abruptly defined that in the course of a few minutes, from clambering among decayed and burnt-up vegetation, we were wandering among long tangled grass; in fact, a flora peculiar to the temperate altitudes of the great chains northward. This little fragment, tipping as it were the summit of the mountain, might be called a "botanical outlyer," with reference to the Himalayan and Suliman chains north and west, as the nearest hill-top capable of producing a similar flora is at least from 60 to 80 miles distant.

The wild pig is plentifully distributed over all the range; wherever low dense jungle exists there it secretes itself during the day to issue forth at night and feed in the fields. In many situations whole crops of grain have been destroyed by them. When passing through a wheat-field I observed the ground covered with masticated pellets, wholly composed of the tops of wheat and barley, which they chew merely to obtain the juicy portion. Although the natives attempt to frighten them away by making loud noises, like the Himalayan black bear they soon get accustomed to the sounds, and care little for any disturbance unless in their immediate vicinity. The houriar feeds also mostly at night, repairing at daybreak to the hill-sides and inaccessible places under rocks; indeed, such appears to be the case with many wild quadrupeds whose feeding-grounds are subject to be invaded by man.

The ravine or Bennett's* deer, better known to Indian sportsman as the "chinckara" (*Antilope bennettii*), is somewhat common on the salt range, and most parts of the Punjaub,

* Sykes' Dukhun Mammalia, *Proc. Zool. Society*, 1831, p. 104.

but does not affect the Himalayas. The horns of the male seldom exceed 18 inches in length ; the females are smooth and usually 4 inches. The ravine deer is met with singly, but now and then from six to twelve may be seen together. The secretion from the infra-orbital sinus of one killed by me on the Salt range and rubbed on the surface of the horn, gave the latter a polished appearance, which even in the dead animal lasted for weeks ; possibly the use of this substance may be to preserve the horn from decay. With the smaller species having permanent horns, this might be the case ; but in large antlered deer, and such like, with deciduous horns, the probability is great that the animal could scarcely accomplish the task. I have, however, often noticed deer and antelope rubbing their foreheads and horns on the bark of trees ; indeed, this is a common occupation with deer when chewing the cud in the forest during the heat of the day, or when the fur is being shed.

The ravines in the district of Jubba have a peculiar appearance. Viewed from a height, they present a series of worn and angular-shaped hillocks, intersected by narrow defiles, by no means inviting to the traveller, for not a blade of grass is visible, and the disintegrated red sandstone and marl suggest the idea of sleeping volcanic embers, which we found, during the heat of mid-day, had more than a mere resemblance. I do not think I have ever witnessed a scene so perfect in its desolation. However, we determined to descend in spite of the stewing heat, and reflection from the hillocks on each side. Whilst threading our way among a series of narrow lanes, we came on a young houriar just dropped, and evidently abandoned by its mother on seeing us approach. Several herds of rams (which separate from the ewes during the breeding season) were observed dashing across ravines, offering a snap-shot occasionally. As we anticipated, the heat by noon became excessive, and our thirst intolerable. No water could be procured save what was strongly impregnated with salt. At last, exhausted, I gave in, and must have been verging on a *coup de soleil,* as my senses began to leave me, and I felt that both eyesight and hearing were rapidly failing, accompanied by a loud buzzing sound in both ears. In this condition I lay stretched on one of the red banks, whilst the shickaree set off in search of a spring. I think I may have remained for nearly half-an-hour in this condition when I was roused by the voice of a native, and looking up, beheld a half-naked man carrying a basin of milk, and platter full of cakes, which he at once begged I would accept. This good Samaritan had seen my distress from his grass-built hut on the top of a neighbouring hill, where he resided for the purpose of guarding a vein of salt. Never can I forget the kindness of the poor fellow, who, unsolicited, came to my aid at a time his services were so sorely needed. Whilst we remained in this part of the district a young man paid us a visit. He was employed in the Salt Revenue Department. He seemed a regular Robinson Crusoe, having spent many years among these hot ravines, almost without a human creature to bear him company. He informed us that he seldom saw a white face from one year's end to another, and during the hot months was obliged to turn night into day when visiting his various posts on the surrounding hills. He was an example of a race of Englishmen born and brought up in India without the shadow of an idea of anything beyond Hindostan and its European society, and even the smallest portion of thought on these points, for in his manners he had most in common with the native, whose language he spoke more fluently than his own. He allowed that his present occupation was considered one of the most unhealthy in the district, but that he expected to be soon promoted and sent to another part of the range, where he would have a better nouse to shelter him from the blazing sun. He felt somewhat concerned about the state of his health, in consequence of a fever which had twice nearly finished him; and judging from his wan and worn face, there seemed just cause for the poor fellow's anxiety; but, like many others, he stuck to his post until the fever came again, when, as I subsequently learned, his feeble strength gave way, and he left his bones among the haunts of the houriar. Young, during the day's ramble, found two lambkins and bagged two rams. Our little herd of houriar, now consisting of two males and two females, soon took kindly to tame goats, and frisked around their foster-mothers as they would have done with their own. The goats also became attached to them, excepting one old dame, which refused to suckle her foundling, and required to be held during the process. It was delightful to watch the lambs rushing towards the goats on our approach, and bleating whenever they found they had strayed beyond a safe distance. For several days all seemed to thrive, when they began to pine away and die one after another, with a discharge from the nostrils and cough, which I found by dissection to arise from the well-known disease pleuro-pneumonia, so fatal to the domestic animal; arising in this case, in all probability, from the want of the maternal heat at night, when the temperature was low, even to nearly freezing-point.

The blue rock-thrush is not a rare tenant of the rocky parts, which it enlivens with its joyous song. All I have examined in the Punjaub and lower Himalayan ranges were of the short-billed variety; the long-billed variety,* it would

* *Journ. As. Soc.* xvi. 150. Mr. Blyth has since adopted the view here

appear, is confined to the higher and more northern chains. The geographical range of these two varieties has not, however, been definitely settled. This species is a cosmopolite in so far as it is widely distributed over the warmer parts of Europe, Asia, and North Africa, and, like the generality of birds with an extensive geographical distribution, is subject to variety. The rock-thrush is everywhere a wild and wary bird, and not easily approached.

The pale-chested harrier, and moor buzzard, were often noticed to pounce on our dead and wounded quail; their chief food, however, appeared to consist of lizards and a short-tailed field-mouse (*Arvicola*), which is very common in cultivated districts.

Several flocks of the black-breasted sand-grouse were observed at daybreak and dusk, drinking at ponds and tanks. The rufous-rumped or Daurian swallow, and the wire-tailed species, were plentiful in the ravines. The "tooty," or roseate finch (*Carpodacus erythrinus*), was seen in flocks feeding on the unripe Mulberries; also the Malabar grosbeak (*Munia malabarica*) frequented the hedges, where its sweet, plaintive twitter was often heard. This little creature is so tame that you may approach a flock within a few yards; numbers are caught in nets and kept in confinement.

Although many of the birds of the Kuller Kahar Lake had by the 12th April, taken their departure for the cooler regions of Tartary to breed, a large number still remained, and afforded us two days of uninterrupted excitement in procuring specimens. For several days previous to our arrival the weather had been very hot, and the day haze denser than usual. The latter may in part be owing to exhalations from

taken, indeed it requires to be proved that what he names *P. affinis* (*J. A. S.* xii. 177) is not another variety of this widely-distributed species.

the soil, but from the circumstances and localities where it is often observed, there can be little doubt that some unexplained electric or other condition is also connected with its phenomena. I have seen it in the desert of Scinde and lower regions of the Himalayas, but not in the rainless tracts of Ladakh and Tibet. A thunder-storm seems to disperse the fog, and leaves the atmosphere more or less clear for a day or two afterwards. On the night of our arrival at the lake we were awoke by a furious storm which nearly blew our little tent away; the roar of the thunder and the brilliancy of the lightning were perfectly appalling, whilst the rain fell in torrents. The whole did not last above an hour, and left behind the usual cool and exhilarating weather, so grateful to man and beast after days or weeks of feverish heat. I well remember the enchanting scene on the bright sunny morning following, as groups of red and white flamingoes in long lines stretched along the shallows of the lake, and flocks of ducks and other aquatic birds lined the margins, or crowded in dense masses in the deeper parts; whilst from the jungle-clad hill on the right loud wailings of peafowl, kept by the fakirs of the temple on its summit, resounded across the valley, and the green bee-eater, the usual successor of a storm, sailed around the copse under which we were encamped, pursuing with the black Indian king-crow the countless insects which come forth on these occasions, especially white ants, which appear to afford a staple article of food for bee-eaters, shrikes, and the large insectivorous birds.

Flocks of long-legged plovers (*Himantopus candidus*) were seen on the lake. It is a common bird on the weedy pools of the Punjaub during the winter months. Specimens may often be found with the legs bent and deformed, to which this species seems subject; also some well-marked and permanent discrepancies as to colour and size. Here, again, is a species common to the three great continents of the Old World, having several varieties, as its numerous synonyms might indicate. European birds—viz. the cinereous godwit, green sandpiper, and water-rail, are generally distributed over the lakes and fens of the Punjaub during the winter. The lark-toed and pied wagtails are plentiful; the former is usually seen perched on tufts of rush or grass in wet places. The little brown-coloured lapwing (*Vanellus leucurus*) I did not observe elsewhere; it is certainly rare in most parts of India, and most probably migratory in the Punjaub. I have been informed that it is common in Afghanistan, where, according to Mr. Blyth, it is known by the name of chizi. In habits it more closely resembles sandpipers, frequenting the margins of pools, along which it runs at great speed. A small brown sand-martin was often seen during the excursion. I took it at first for the bank-swallow (*H. riparia*), but I am doubtful if met with in N.W India. It differed also from the short-tailed swallow; and the only other small martin at all likely to agree with it is the Nepal species (*Cotyle subsoccata*, Hodg.),* with which I have not been able to compare my specimens. We returned to Rawul Pindee by a somewhat different route, more to the north and east; the weather was excessively hot until mid-day, when, for upwards of a week, a thunder-storm took place almost daily at noon; always ending in a clear and brilliant afternoon, when we enjoyed magnificent views of the great Himalayan chain from the Bimbur Pass to Attock on the Indus. Near the village of

* Gray's *Zool. Misc.* 1844, p. 82. The similarity, however, is so close between these three, that, beyond a shade of plumage, there is no appreciable distinction.

Bone we came on a party of natives sifting the soil for gold; it is found in minute particles among dark-coloured earth on the sides of hillocks and in dried-up watercourses. Boys were employed pouring water on the soil, which, on percolating through a perforated box, was removed and then carefully examined. The workers informed us that they scarcely found sufficient to repay their labour. On the rugged footpaths among the barren ravines are round cairns of stone similar to the "chaits" of Ladakh, and solitary graves, called "ragheers" by the natives, were also common on the side of the road and pathway, surrounded by heaps of stones, white pebbles, rags of various colours, pieces of wood, cotton, etc., the offerings of passers-by, who invariably leave some token of respect, and, following them, Young and myself had always been in the habit of adding a stone to these cairns, even as our forefathers were wont on the bleak hill-sides of old Scotland.* "I will add a stone to your cairn," says the old Celtic proverb.

By the middle of April the mulberry was ripe, and the village trees laden with the delicious fruit, which, in point of flavour, equals the celebrated mulberry of Cashmere. Our route for some days led through fields of grain, then rapidly coming to maturity, or across ravines, where we were now and then interrupted by streams which had become swollen by the daily thunder-storms. The Persian lilac was in full bloom, an abundant spring harvest approached, and everything promised well for the industrious people who had settled down to our rule. If they would only make comparisons, they would find out that they now enjoy double the com-

* *Curri mi clach er do cuirn*—I will add a stone to your cairn; *i.e.* I will do homage to your memory when you are dead.

fort, security, and independence they experienced under the sovereignty of the Sikhs.

In every wheat-field boys were employed frightening thousands of the brown-headed bunting (*Euspiza luteola*, Sparm.),* and rose-coloured pastor (*Pastor roseus*). Great flocks of these birds were seen scouring across the country, and settling on the ears of grain. Both species commit havoc among the crops at that season, and chiefly by pushing down the ears of wheat; consequently large patches are prostrated in the same manner as when laid low by wind. The brown-headed bunting is only common during harvest, and may possibly come from Afghanistan, where it is said to be plentiful from April to autumn. The other species is generally distributed over the Punjaub at all seasons. A species of lizard is common in the ravines and arid plains of the North-western Provinces: its burrows are made on the open country, and it may be usually seen basking in the sun at their entrances. It is about a foot in length, blunt-headed, tail obtuse at the tip, and body covered with large and broad scales. The blue-throated warbler was occasionally observed. Its habits resemble the redbreasts and redstarts; possibly it might hold an intermediate position. The black-bellied lark-finch (*Pyrrhulauda grisea*) is a common tenant of the waste and barren tracts, and as usual is seen squatting on the ground—a habit I have noticed to be common, although in a much less degree, with larks in general, especially when they anticipate danger, and before taking to wing. The European heron† was seen wading in pools; whilst the gull-billed tern (*Sterna anglica*), in

* Cat. Birds of East Indian Company's Museum, by Dr. Horsfield, vol. ii. 487.

† Wilson's *American Ornith.* pl. 72, f. 6. I am not aware of any changes in the plumage of this great cosmopolite.

scattered numbers, flew wildly northwards, not settling anywhere, and evidently on the way to the cooler regions of Central Asia to rear its young.

Within ten miles of Rawul Pindee we found our horses waiting, and scampered across the burning plain, sorry indeed to return to the monotony of cantonment life. My keen hunting friend complained of his indifferent luck in not having procured more wild sheep. For my part, I had no cause to feel dissatisfied.

CHAPTER IX.

Start for Cashmere and Ladakh—Incidents on the way to Murree—Black Bear, variety of—Changes of Temperature—Beauty of Scenery—Native Surgery Discovery of a New Species of Bullfinch—Native Tyranny and Extortion —Birds—Scenery—Traces of Glacial Phenomena—Dogs—Scenery at Uri—Magnificent View—Birds—Antiquities—Deodar Cedar—Noushera—First Peep at the Happy Valley—Ornithology of the Jhelum—Serinuggur—Goulab Singh—His Mode of Governing—Wretchedness of the Inhabitants—Shawl Manufactures—City Lake—Turkish Bath—Boatmen—Heronry—Chinese Jacana.

ACCOMPANIED by Young, we left Rawul Pindee on the 24th of March, and rode straight for the mountains, intending to gain the Murree Sanitarium or the lower ranges at dusk. However, our hopes were doomed not to be realised, although the morning was promising, and the fresh relays of horses at different points indicated a rapid journey. Murree is only occupied during summer; its distance from Rawul Pindee is 36 miles. It is situate on a ridge, at an elevation of from 7500 to 8000 feet above the level of the sea, and at the time referred to was only being formed, and consequently little more than the barracks and a few cottages had been built. We breakfasted at Salgram with our two friends Morrison and Salkeld. The latter has since enrolled his name with many others in the memorable phalanx of Indian heroes who fell before the walls of Delhi. After commencing the ascent over a road by no means easy, the coming storm began to show itself by dark masses of clouds and distant thunder and lightning. At last down it poured, and with such violence that the footpath for long distances formed the bed of torrents reaching to the knees of our horses. At last matters got desperate, and we were fairly overcome by the difficulties, which increased with a pelting hurricane, and drove us to seek shelter in two deserted huts on the mountain-side, where, with our drenched servants and baggage, we spent a cheerless night, to wake on the following morning and find matters in much the same or even worse condition than on the previous day. But there was no help for it; so, mounting our horses, we floundered up the mountain-side, and arrived at Murree at dusk. On the following morning several inches of snow lay round the hill-top, and the neighbouring ranges were covered; whilst the great Peer Pinjal chain, on the verge of the Cashmere Valley, seemed completely robed in a mantle of snow. The thermometer stood at 42° at 9 A.M. The scenery of this little mountain retreat during summer is peculiarly beautiful. All the fruit-trees grow in great luxuriance, and most vegetables and plants of the temperate zone thrive admirably. Here are collected all the military invalids for the stations on the north-west frontier of the Punjaub, and whoever can manage to escape from the heat of the plains. During a walk about the empty cottages we traced footprints of a black bear that had passed across the road, and saw several kalij pheasants and a troup of entellus monkeys in a pine-wood close to the barrack. The black bear of the lower ranges of the Himalayas does not seem to differ in any very appreciable extent from that of the middle region; only I have noticed that the former are seldom so large, and all I have examined had the fur on the paws and snout rust-coloured instead of white. This peculiarity, however, may not be regular; at all events, the distinctions cannot be called specific. Our course for the Jhelum River lay in a north-eastern direction, and we had to descend several thousand feet, which took nearly two days to accomplish, owing to the state of the weather and footpaths. We were struck with the change of temperature on arrival at the banks of the river, where at six P.M. the thermometer stood at 70° Fahrenheit in the shade, and mosquitoes were troublesome. The valley of the Jhelum at the ford presented a very wild and imposing appearance. The great river, swollen by the late rains, rolled in a mighty flood down an enormous ravine, the sides of which rose up to several thousand feet, forming long "horsebacks," and clothed with grass or patches of oak and forest trees, whilst here and there a little flat-roofed native house, hidden among the vegetation, with its terraced fields, indicated the presence of man. In twenty-four hours we had descended from an arctic temperature to an almost tropical, and through what delightful scenery! None but those who have wandered over mountains like the Himalayas can form an idea of the beauty and magnificence of the region we are now considering. To the naturalist the attractions gather so fast that he can barely make himself acquainted with the most familiar objects. I noticed the wandering pie, the chimney swallow, and Alpine swift; two species of a beautiful hyacinth, blue and white, and a tiger lily, were in flower. The long-leaved pine, the rough and smooth-leaved oak and wild barberry, were the common trees and shrubs. We were escorted for the greater part of the day's march by a Sepoy from the last halting-place. He had been in Rungeet Singh's army, and fought against the English in the Sutluj campaign. He spoke highly of the bravery of the Europeans, but laughed at the native troops, unless backed up by the white men. The river was running strong and rapid, but by means of powerful oars in the bow and stern of the flat-bottomed boat, we managed to gain the opposite side without much difficulty. The course of the Jhelum in this district forms nearly a triangle; proceeding westwards in the first instance to Mazufurabad, it then suddenly nearly doubles on itself, and runs in a southerly direction. Our route lay across the triangle thus formed in a north-eastern course. The Jhelum divides the British from the territory of the Cashmere ruler, whose little mud forts are seen at almost every little village on the way. The farmers were loud in their complaints of the tyranny of the Maharājah Goulab Singh, and kept continually extolling the rule of the English on the other side of the river; but when we advised them to go across and squat on the opposite hill-sides, they said they could not endure to leave the old huts and homes of their fathers. At one of the hamlets on the way I was asked to give my advice with reference to a broken arm, and was struck with the good native surgery, as far as apparatus went, which consisted of a hollow piece of ash-bark, lined with fine moss, and placed one on each side of the limb. It had been put on fresh from the tree, and became hard after having been fitted to the inequalities of the arm. A more effectual splint could not have been adjusted. We passed a night at the little fort of Dunna and on the following morning, in pelting rain, pursued our course down ravines and over ridges. By the side of a little graveyard we observed a cypress very like that of Europe; the fir, spruce, oaks, poplar, ash, elm, etc., covered sheltered portions of the ridges and along the lower parts of the valleys. We saw a barking-deer, and in a little ash-wood I shot the beautiful orange-coloured bullfinch (*Pyrrhula aurantiaca*), which, until then, had been quite unknown to naturalists. The male is brilliant orange, and very different from the red-headed bullfinch mentioned with the birds of

Dugshai. This valuable addition to the ornithology of the Himalayas has been since figured by Mr. Gould in his magnificent work on the *Birds of Asia.*

A tulip, with white petals tinged with rose-colour, is very common all over the ranges at this season, and in damp situations the slate-coloured primrose, whilst ivy clung fast to the old pine-trees, of which more than three species were observed. On gaining the top of a ridge, we espied the little fort of Chacar on another opposite, and after a very toilsome descent across a broad valley, and a rough clamber up-hill, we got to the little stronghold at dusk, to find the commandant, a gray-bearded Sikh, waiting our arrival in the verandah of his house, and, as usual, surrounded by his minions accoutred with sword and shield.

After the usual Oriental preliminary forms of recognition, we were told that the Maharajah's order was, that every European visiting his country was to be considered his guest, and on no account to be allowed to pay for provisions. We soon found, however, that this munificence was at the expense of the poor villagers, for our next-door neighbour exclaimed from his roof-top that he had been ordered to supply us with fowls; another, that eggs had been demanded from him; and a third was to furnish us with wood. In vain we protested and offered to pay for everything; but the Sikh soldier who catered for us would not hear of such an arrangement; however, on our departure, he was not above receiving any amount of "backshesh" on his own account. What could not be done in justice and in public, we accomplished unknown to these myrmidons, so that the natives were no losers by our presence.

The tyranny of the late Goulab Singh was then beyond belief; proofs of which were seen everywhere in the deserted villages and ruined houses on our route. Extortion was the order of the day; from the ruler down to his sepoy, all aimed at robbing the cultivator of the soil of whatever they could lay their hands on. Nor are matters much changed for the better since his death. We sat long in the verandah of a little hut waiting the arrival of our baggage; night fell, and still no appearance of the servants and porters; at last a torch appeared, and coolie after coolie arrived in a long line toiling under the weight of their burdens. A few minutes before we had indulged in very strong language with reference to their delay; but when we saw them bending under the large leather baskets our hearts failed us, and, instead of a reprimand, we praised them for their hard day's work. Poor simple souls! a little firewood and a dry corner in a shed close by were all they required, and in a few minutes they were singing over their little fires, and busily employed cooking their wheaten cakes (*chupattees*). Each coolie is provided with a walking-pole, and a T-shaped piece of wood, on the horizontal part of which he rests his load without setting it down. With the pole they guide their footsteps over the dangerous and difficult parts. Their dress is composed of home-spun gray flannel, with grass shoes, such as are generally worn by the poor people of the western ranges. The coolie of the hills is a stout and robust fellow, very different in appearance from the listless and apathetic native of the valley of Cashmere.

We were astonished to observe numbers of open graves, and on inquiry found that it is the custom merely to cover the top of the grave with wood and earth, so that after a time the former decays, and the scant covering falls down on the coffin.

On the 2d of April we continued our route towards the

Jhelum by a narrow footpath which leads down the Chacar Hill in a N.E. direction to the river, then turns suddenly eastward along the left bank on to the valley of Cashmere. On the march to Hutier (about seven miles) we shot a few chukore and black partridges; the latter were heard calling in every field, even in the immediate vicinity of the houses. The black-throated bunting (*Emberiza cioides*) is common on the banks of the river; in habits it bears a great resemblance to the yellow bunting, and also resembles it both in figure and call. Allied to this species is the gray-capped bunting (*E. stewarti*, Blyth); its throat is black likewise, but the male has a gray head, a black streak through the eye, and a rufous band across the chest. We had not time to examine the geology of this interesting day's journey. The strata, however, seemed now to be composed entirely of mica-schist and syenitic granite, with a few boulders of the latter strewed along the bed of the river.

The scenery was truly beautiful, and could scarcely be seen to greater advantage. Every turn of the river disclosed a fresh picture; on the hill-sides overhead were green fields of spring-wheat—the varied shades produced by the trees of the jungle—among others, the apricot was seen in full blossom—the roaring river below; while on the furthest mountain-tops the snow still lingered. The valley of the Jhelum here varies in breadth; in some situations it is fully two miles, but the greatest breadth of the stream is not much more than a stone-throw. Landslips are common along its banks, and not a few are of large extent; masses of alluvium form plateaus, from 100 to 250 feet above the level of the river; these are cultivated and turned into terrace-fields, which rise like the seats of an amphitheatre. There is no difficulty in irrigating the fields from the hill-sides, which abound with streams where the wearied traveller can refresh himself by a grateful bathe—of all remedies the most sovereign to a frame overheated and taxed by hard walking.

The native dog of this district has a great resemblance to the pointer, and doubtless was introduced from India. Mr. Vigne* makes a similar remark with reference to the dogs of the Rajawur district, south of the valley of Cashmere, where a formidable breed is also found, having the external appearances of the shepherd's dog, but much larger. A closely-allied form, not differing in any way from the Scotch collie, is common all over the cultivated regions of the Western Himalayas, and even westward to the sources of the Oxus, as observed by Lieutenant Wood. This uniformity is in favour of the view that the shepherd's dog forms almost a permanent race, which may have been one of the original varieties.

The gray wood-shrike (*Tephrodornis pondiceriana*) is a common tenant about the farm-houses. It resembles the Indian gray shrike, but is very much smaller.

Uri Fort is placed on a projection composed of vast accumulations of alluvium and gravel, which must have either been deposited by the Jhelum in that situation during far back geological periods or the result of ancient glaciers. Here the Jhelum bursts through a barrier of primary rocks with considerable violence, and rapidly widens out into a broad and more placid river.

The scenery around this is exceedingly beautiful; either by following the river onwards through the narrow boisterous course, with its banks clad with a variety of soft and hard wood trees, towards Cashmere, or in the direction of the stream, across hill-sides covered with long grass and clusters of pine.

* Vigne's *Travels in Cashmere*, vol. i. p. 231.

The banks of the influent rivulets are hidden by profusion of apricot, barberry, mulberry, wood-apple, and other fruit-trees. Large boulders of granite strew the bottoms of the valleys, some carried down by landslips, but others evidently deposited by either fluviatile or glacial forces far exceeding in extent and intensity anything of the sort now going on.

As usual, the walnut-tree shades every hamlet. The fruit is much used by the natives; the wild olive and pomegranate are also common.

Indian corn, wheat, cucumbers, melons, etc., are cultivated. The first is reaped in autumn, when the black bears and pigs repair at night and commit great havoc in the fields and gardens, so as to necessitate watchmen sitting on raised platforms in the middle of the fields and keeping up a constant noise by screaming and beating drums. It is, however, seldom, with every care, that these unwelcome intruders are kept off, for in spite of every means had recourse to, both bears and pigs manage to destroy whole fields of Indian corn. During the summer, when insect life is in full vigour, the noise made by crickets and their allies, especially at night, is almost deafening. A constant wailing cry, possibly of one of the owls or night-jars, was heard at dusk. So persistent was the doleful *wa-wa*, that I do not think we often missed hearing the sound at night throughout the journey to Cashmere.

Proceeding from Uri to the next halting-place, Noushera, the traveller passes through as beautiful scenery as can be seen anywhere. Let him choose any season of the year, there can be only one feeling uppermost, and that is of wonder and astonishment at the grandeur and surpassing beauty around him. Before the river had appeared to him a mighty flood, moving steadily onwards through a broad valley; now—

"Between two meeting hills it bursts away
Where rocks and woods o'erhang the turbid stream;
There, gathering triple force, rapid and deep,
It boils, and wheels, and foams, and thunders through."

We descend from the alluvial plateau and cross a stream, mount the opposite bank, and are soon lost among the profusion of tree and shrub which clothe the mountains to the river's brink. Pursuing the little footpath along the left bank, now wandering through forests of the noble deodar,* anon under the leaves of the wild cherry, the mulberry, wood-apple, or chestnut; whilst mountain-wards, like a huge wall, the schistose rocks rise hundreds of feet above him. If it is spring he will mark the beautiful "forget-me-not" on the pathway, or the gaudy tiger-lily, with its broad, smooth, sagittate leaves. In the gaps of the forest the eye wanders up many a solitary pine-clad glen, where the snow lags long in sheltered portions. Above the wail of the forest the roar of the troubled waters deadens almost every other sound, save the shrill pipe of the blue water-thrush, or the chirp of the chestnut bellied redstart, as they sport among the rocks. The wild rose is seen mingling its beautiful flowers with those of the pomegranate, whilst the ivy and many other graceful creepers twine around the trees and adorn the bosky cover. In such situations, among the mulberry-trees laden with their luscious fruit, you may come on a black bear feeding. He will not tarry when he sees man; but if suddenly surprised and hard pressed, often shows fight, and attempts to hug his victim by rearing on his hind legs, offering at the same time a good aim to the cool-headed sportsman. The right bank of the river rises upwards into wood-

* "The deodar has not been seen east of Nepal." By some the old familiar cedar of Lebanon is considered an unusual variety of the Himalayan deodar. (See Hooker's *Him. Journal.*)

less mountains, bare or covered with grass. Nearly half-way between Uri and Noushera, in a wild-looking jungle, surrounded by pine, and nearly overgrown with rank vegetation and weeds, are the remains of one of the ancient Cashmere temples. It is built of the green basalt of the Peer Pinjal range. Like the generality of the old ruined temples in the valley, its architecture is said to be Gothic, with gables having "pediments of high pitch and trefoil arches," the whole decidedly of Hindoo character, in imitation of the later Roman buildings. This would assign them a period beginning with the Parthian conquest of Syria, between 250 B.C. and 850 A.D.* There is another within a few miles of Noushera, if anything more perfect, and built of granite. Many of the cedars have been cut down and floated to the plains of the Punjaub. One feels sorry at witnessing the fall of a majestic tree, whose growth has extended perhaps over half-a-dozen centuries; and never did I feel that to a greater extent than on my return from Cashmere, where some of the noblest monarchs of the Uri glen were lying prostrate on the river's bank. Before Goulab Singh discovered the value of his cedar-forests, it was customary for the charcoal-burners to set fire to the trunks, and hollow out large caverns, which generally ended in the death of the tree and waste of much valuable wood. During this day's journey, we often met gangs of pilgrims proceeding to or from the sacred shrines in Cashmere. We came on a group of gipsy-looking men and women, who informed us they had been travelling constantly for six months from Agmeer, in Central India, and were on their way to the shrine of Umernath, among the Northern Cashmere ranges. A few of the young women were exceedingly beautiful, and

* "Essay on the Hindu History of Kashmir."—*Trans. of Asiatic Society*, vol. xv. by H. H. Wilson, A.M., Professor of Sanscrit in the University of Oxford.

the light sunburnt faces and dark flashing eyes of all of them were very characteristic of the race in general.

The hamlet and ruined fort at Noushera is situated on a flat almost level with the Jhelum, which here sweeps downwards at great force. Gable-roofed houses now begin to take the place of the little flat-roofed hovels, and give an almost English appearance to the Cashmere landscape.

At Noushera I met with the gray wagtail (*Motacilla boarula*) for the first time. The leaden-ash redstart is likewise common. I procured also several specimens of the yellow-billed jay (*Calocitta flavirostris*), which differs from the red-billed species, mentioned before, and which is plentiful in the lesser ranges towards Murree, by the duller cast of plumage, the bright yellow bill, and the white on the hind-head being narrower, and having a broad band of black below it. I shot my specimens in spring, so there could be no question as to their being adult birds. Perhaps, however, the yellow-billed jay has scarcely a claim to be considered other than a local variety of the Himalayan bird. The Siskin (*Carduelis spinoides*) is common in the forest, and generally seen in flocks. The cuckoo we heard daily at that season. It is common in every wood.

Associated with the black-crested tit (*Parus melanolophus*, Vigors) I shot the pretty little red-headed species (*P. erythrocephalus*). It is a little larger than the golden-crested wren. There is a genus of warblers mostly common to the Himalayas, to which the name *Abrornis* has been given by the great Himalayan ornithologist Mr. Hodgson, who has described several species, of which one or two are common in the woods and forests about Cashmere; but from the very close connection of several recorded species, I have not been able to identify my specimens.

Holding a north-east course along the bank of the river, through forests of deodar, or woods of mulberry and fruit-trees, together with the hazel-like fothergille (*Fothergilla involucrata*), we entered a little valley surrounded by mountains and pine-forests, with beautiful fields of green turf; gable-roofed hamlets, built of logs and thatched with straw, were hid among a profusion of arboreal vegetation. At the northern extremity the Jhelum was seen gliding placidly round a corner towards a gap in the west, where it suddenly begins its furious downward course to Uri—a distance of fully sixteen miles. Shoals and little islets of alluvium have been formed at the above point, and possibly most of the deposits of this little nook have been obtained from the river during former conditions. Although it rained constantly during our stay at Noushera, we could not help admiring this little corner of Cashmere; it was as it were a prelude to the splendid panorama which burst on our view on the following morning, when, after crossing the valley and mounting the summit of the little pass above Baramala, we had the first glimpse of the Vale of Cashmere. There it lay in all its beauty, with the Jhelum twisting through its grassy glades, the Wulur Lake in the distance, and the great Pinjal ranges, covered with snow, surrounding the valley on all sides. The lofty Haramuk, greatest amongst the rock-giants, raised its granite top 13,400 feet above the level of the sea. The town of Baramala is placed on the right bank of the river, and occupies the most-west point of the valley. It is composed of a few hundred log-built houses, its streets are filthy beyond description, and the poor half-clad natives, in their long robes and turbans, looked pictures of human misery in that cold, wet, April morn. The weather was too unsettled and rainy to allow us to proceed to the capital overland, we consequently embarked in covered boats, and were pulled up the river by natives. The banks of the Jhelum are not above a few feet in height anywhere in its course through the valley of Cashmere, and in many places almost level with the surrounding country, which during the inundation is overflowed in many places. The grass was just appearing in the glades, where herds of lean, half-starved sheep, horses, and cattle were pasturing. The fine bald-headed eagle was often seen on the banks, and formed a prominent ornament in the landscape. We strolled gun in hand along the bank, and by the sides of fens and marshes where the last of the winter visitors yet tarried, such as flocks of mallard, teal, red-headed pochards, and curlews. A large fox, named by the natives "shawul," to distinguish it from the red-mountain fox (*V. montanus*), was common among the ravines, and on the kirawas or alluvial flats. The jackal seemed also a larger variety than that of the plains of the Punjaub. A male we shot measured 3 feet 6 inches from snout to tail. The native tradition that the valley is the bed of an ancient lake receives corroboration from its geological features. Lines, like the parallel roads of Glen Roy, but not so well defined, are seen in various situations on the sides of the ranges around the basin. The Mussulman tradition has it that Solomon drained the valley by directing a Jin, called Kashuf, to remove the barrier at Baramala. Time would not allow of careful observations on the intricate study which refers to this portion of the history of the valley. It appears to us, however, that if it has ever been a mountain-lake, the barrier had been originally occasioned by glaciers damming up the current at the western end of the basin.

The capital, Serinuggur, is, according to Jacquemont, 5246 feet above the level of the sea. It is built on the river, over which are thrown several wooden bridges. Direct supplies are for the most part conveyed by boats. As the small gondolas glided slowly towards the entrance to this little Venice of Asia, our attention was directed to two human skeletons suspended in cages on the river's bank; these, we were informed, were criminals that had been executed some years before, and were left on these gibbets as a warning to all malefactors. We were not altogether unprepared for such examples of Goulab Singh's mode of rule, having read of his horrible deeds in the days when he was weaving the meshes of the net that ended in capturing Cashmere. One cannot without a shudder recollect that it was he who, at Poonch, under the slopes of the southern Pinjal, had two prisoners flayed alive in his presence, and, not content with that, sent for his son (now the present ruler) in order that he might "take an example" from his father in the art of governing. Such was the ruler of this valley when I had the pleasure of visiting it. A striking difference is worth noticing with reference to the natives of the capital—that is, the healthy and sunburnt faces of the boat people and the pale and bloodless aspects of the men and women who crowd the banks of the river. Many of the fair sex are extremely beautiful, but filth, poverty, and tyranny have made their impressions on the Cashmeree, who for centuries has been subject to tyrannical governments.

With so noble a river, and the natural advantages of situation, it might be supposed that few cities have better opportunities of preserving cleanliness and comfort; but, like all Oriental towns, it vies with the filthiest. Let travellers who have sensitive olfactory organs beware of the streets of Cashmere, and content themselves with admiring all its towns from a respectful distance. We had excellent quarters assigned us, by order of the Maharajah, on the right bank of the river, above the city. I will never forget the morning after our arrival; it had rained almost uninterruptedly, so that, hitherto, everything had been seen to a disadvantage; but now the weather settled, and I was awoke at an early hour by the song of the sky-lark, the mellow note of the bulbul* (*Pycnonotus leucogenys*), and the twitter of the chimney-swallow. It was a lovely spring morning, and so like home, that I could scarcely persuade myself I was not in some beautiful nook in Old England.

The palace or shergur is situate on the left bank below the first log-bridge. It wears a very dungeon-like appearance, which the shining cupola built by the Maharajah Goulab Singh somewhat relieved; withal, the royal domain might with truth have been considered to be in a very shaky condition; its crumbling walls were the abodes of myriads of jackdaws, and its interior only a shade cleaner than the filthy domains around. According to the usual custom, we paid a series of visits to the shawl-manufactories, with which we were much disappointed, more especially for having always understood that the vast numbers of Cashmere shawls imported had been manufactured there, until we inspected every warehouse in the place, when it became clear that the numbers to be seen in London and Paris could never have been made in the shops of Serinuggur—not even in a century according to the means then prosecuted. One magnificent shawl was being made for the Empress of the French in Mookh du Shah's manufactory, and, I believe, at the outside

* The red-vented bulbul, the nightingale of Eastern poetry, is not found in the Valley. Hooker, in the Himalayan journals, mentions hearing the song of the nightingale in Sikkim, but I can find no record of the *Luscinia philomela* having been met with by ornithologists on the Himalaya ranges nor British India; possibly the song of the *Copsychus saularis* may have been mistaken for that of the other.

not more than ten of any value were in hand from one end of the city to the other. It is said that the water of the lake gives a softness to the Cashmere shawls which cannot be obtained elsewhere. This may be doubted, as I have been given to understand that those made in the looms at Amritser in the Punjaub equal any from the Valley.

One evening, on our return from the lake, the report of a cannon from the palace startled us, and raised a thousand echoes along the margin of the still waters. It was a royal salute of one gun for the heir-apparent, who had just returned from visiting his sire at Jamoo—one of the frontier forts. It is a beautiful sight to see the boats, propelled by little hand-paddles, shooting along the river or up the canal and across the city lake, the oarmen keeping time to a lively chaunt which they sing, sometimes with great pathos and some artistic skill. The inundation takes place with the melting of the snow in April and May, when the banks are overflown in many places.

There are several species of fish in the river, the most common being a sort of carp usually called the Himalayan trout. It has two long string-like appendages projecting on each side of the mouth. Young caught several with a hook bated with dough,—the largest did not exceed 3 lbs. in weight. The flesh is soft, very pale, and almost tasteless.

The Turkish bath is in repute among the better classes; but all I saw were so excessively filthy; and had attendants so dirty, that we cut short our visits after the first ablution.

A Cashmere boatman would consider his establishment incomplete without an Afghan lark (*Melanocorypha torquata*). This bird is said to frequent the Valley in winter. The sweet notes of these songsters issuing from the boats as they pass up and down the river were very enchanting. The common heron is plentiful, and a heronry is preserved in the Shalimar gardens. Their plumes go to deck the imperial head-dress. Towards sunset the rough cricket-like chirpings of thousands of a species of hedge-warblers were heard all over the lake; and so loud as almost to drown every other sound.

The beautiful pheasant-like bird seen squatting on the broad leaves of the lotus (*Nelumbium speciosum*) and marsh marigold (*Caltha palustris*) is the Chinese jacana (*Parra sinensis*). Its flight is not strong, and composed of many flaps; the call is rough, like that of the water-hen. The curved tail-feathers, the brilliant yellow patch on the hind part of the neck, shining brown of the back, white wings, more or less tinged with black, will at once serve to distinguish it.

CHAPTER X.

Excursion to the Northern Pinjal—Ancient Temples—Earthquakes—Geology—Bear and Deer Shooting—Adaptation of Sight to Long Distances—Snow Pheasants—The Last of a Royal Line—The Isabella or Brown Himalayan Bear—Shooting—Shikaree turns an Æsthetic—Splendid View—Scenery of the Valleys—Cashmere Stag—Large Deer in general—Hunting Bears and Deer—Beauty and Grandeur of the Northern Pinjal—Climate of the Ranges—Judging Distances—Pilgam, its Neighbourhood—Rapid Changes of Climate and Vegetation—European Water-ousel—Flora and Fauna—Return to the Valley—Silkworm—Sylvan Scenery—Birds—Ruins of Martund Islamabad—Atsibul and its Beauties—European Plants—Southern Pinjal—Native Misery—Scenery—The Red Weasel—Ringdove—Thunderstorm.

We left Serinuggur on the 14th of April for the purpose of exploring the valleys and ranges on the north side, and hunting large game. Our party was now increased by the addition of our friend Captain Halkett, who had preceded us to Cashmere. We tracked up the river to the village of Pampur, celebrated for the superior quality of its saffron. The banks of the Jhelum were fringed with willows, walnut, and chunars. These and the long-withdrawing meadows looked beautiful exceedingly. We visited the pretty little temple at Pandreton—another of the ancient Hindoo ruins similar to those seen between Uri and Noushera. It is situated in a pond; the building is a square chapel, with "trefoil arches," and made of the neighbouring mountain limestone. There is a gigantic sitting figure cut in the same rock on the hill-side, and a little farther on an enormous pillar, evidently the fragment of an idol. The two last are also possibly of Hindoo origin, and were overthrown mayhap by earthquakes,* or the Mahomedan invaders. I recommend the traveller to mount the grass-clad kirawah, behind Pampur, any clear day, and he will not only have a magnificent view, but by running his eye along the sides of the range northwards, he will observe the old water-lines already noticed; nowhere are the latter more distinct than on the faces of the limestone ridges in this part of the valley. It is while calmly viewing the vast amphitheatre around him that the geologist will realise the magnitude of the force which upheaved the great Himalayan chain. The basin of the primeval lake may have been originally a fissure, scooped out afterwards by glaciers, which at some far-back period were more extensive than at present, as their moraines testify. These may be seen at almost all the debouches of the valleys which enter Cashmere.

The mountains forming the northern barrier of the valley belong chiefly to the carboniferous series, and contain abundance of molluscs and other marine animals, but beds belonging to older formations, as well as mesozoic rocks, are met with on the surrounding ranges,† and nummulitic limestone on the slopes of the Peer Pinjal.

On the 15th of April we marched northwards from Pampur, through its saffron-beds, which at that season were covered with the wild white and red tulips, the saffron-plants not having appeared above ground; then, directing our footsteps towards

* Cashmere has always been subject to severe earthquakes. It is on that account the houses are built of wood.

† See interesting papers on this subject by Captain Godwin Austen and Mr. Davidson in the *Proc. of the Geological Society of London* for February 1866.

the mountains, we arrived at the little village of Lidur, situated at the foot of a long straggling limestone ridge covered with wood and bush. There is a small tank close to the village containing Himalayan trout, which I attempted to capture, but had to desist on account of having been informed that the animals were sacred, and if I killed one I should be certain to incur the displeasure of some departed saint.

The thermometer stood at 76° in our tent during the day at Pampur. We found, however, on the hill-side above, that the temperature that night was very different, and made us glad to sleep under blankets. Before daybreak each of our party, accompanied by his shickaree, struck off in divers directions. I followed up a wooded spur, with a valley on each side, and had not gone far before the loud bellowing of the Cashmere stags was heard in various parts of the thick cover, and a herd of eight was seen in a jungle on the opposite ridge. To cut them off was our only chance; so, on hands and knees I scrambled through tangled bush and brake for upwards of an hour, when, most unexpectedly, I came upon a hind, and delivered the contents of my rifle on her at ten yards. Although desperately wounded, I could not discover the animal from the extreme density of the underwood and difficulty of finding our way through it. On gaining the top of the ridge a brown bear was seen in a valley some distance off, but I was too much disappointed at my failure to go in pursuit, and returning to the tent, found Halkett exulting over a very large bear he had killed in the neighbourhood. The animal measured 7½ feet in length, height 3 feet 5 inches; around the chest 58½ inches; the thickest part of the fore-legs was 24 inches, and the thigh 37 inches in circumference. I mention the dimensions of this individual, as they are the largest of several hundred I have examined. One afternoon, on gaining the grassy top of a very steep mountain, I descried a black bear feeding very intently, and as the wind was favourable, there was no difficulty in stealing within thirty yards. On firing the contents of my first barrel into his body he gave a loud grunt, and, unconscious of the direction from which the shot came, cantered to within a few yards of me, when a second bullet through his loins brought him up, and he stood hesitating for a moment; then coiling himself into a ball, he rolled down the hill-side, bounding from one prominence to another like a huge cricket-ball, until brought to a stand-still on a flat, on which he unrolled himself, and running to the next declivity, rolled to the bottom, when he took to his legs and disappeared from our view in the dense cover. His downward course was marked with blood, but night came on, and rendered farther pursuit perfectly useless. I was not sorry to lose this bear at the onset of my shooting, as I learned the truth of experience and what an old Himalayan shickaree had told me, that a bear will carry away as many bullets as you can send into his hinder quarters, but one behind the shoulder, in the forehead, or breast, will be certain to drop him. The above is a favourite proceeding with the black bear if suddenly frightened, or when he finds himself on a steep mountain and at a great distance from jungle or cover.

On the 18th of April we raised our camp, and proceeded eastward over the mountain of Wunster Wun, where we had been shooting for the two previous days, into a beautiful little valley, about three miles long by a mile or so in breadth. A river, fed by numerous rills from the high ranges on each side, flowed down the middle, and, dividing into many branches, served to irrigate the rice-fields. It is wonderful how the eye adapts itself to seeing objects at long distances. My shickaree would seat himself on a hill-side, and with his hands on each side of his head, so as to concentrate the rays of vision, remain motionless, intently scanning every portion of the distant valley or mountain. At last he would point out a small object, which the telescope showed to be a stag or bear. Having satisfied ourselves as to the direction of the wind and the general demeanour of the animal, whether feeding intently in one direction or nibbling as it walked along, we then commenced our stalk. The beginner must trust to the native shickaree and be guided by him, and if at all expert, he will bring his master within 20 yards of the game. Amongst our men was a well-known hunter called Ebhul Khan, a Khyberee from the famous pass of that name near Peshawur. He had spent many days among the Cashmere mountains, and knew almost every corner in the Northern Pinjal. From age and experience he claimed the consideration and respect of his comrades, who always allowed him to choose the most likely beats. It was surprising how this man outshone us all in finding game. His eagle eye scanned every spot within its range; and often when we were perplexed as to the nature of some minute object a long way off, Ebhul Khan settled the matter at once. This faculty is only to be gained by great experience; but let the young aspirant remember that there is nothing intuitive in it, and that, by dint of patience, perseverance, and practice, he may, with an original good pair of eyes, find all his game for himself. In the woods and jungles of the valley I saw several of the new species of bullfinch discovered at Chacar. Halkett fired at a fine leopard, but the ball just grazed the animal's back. Although nowhere common, the leopard is not rare on the Cashmere mountains, and preys chiefly on musk-deer, sheep, and dogs. Our friend was fortunate in killing another brown bear.

On a range, and close to the melting snow, we came on several flocks of the great snow-pheasant, known to the Cashmerees by the names *gor-ka-gu,* and *kubuk deri.* It is also called "lepia" and "jer monal" in other districts westward. This species seems to frequent the high ranges of Afghanistan, and suitable situations all over the great Himalayan chain. There are three allied species, one of which is possibly only a local variety (*Tetraogallus tibetanus*); the other two are decidedly distinct. One of the latter is said to frequent the Ladakh mountains; it is smaller than the bird we are now describing, and has a band on the front of the neck like the chuckore. The great snow-pheasant delights in high altitudes, and may be said to be partial to the upper region, from whence it is only driven by the rigours of winter. Amidst the dreary desolation of these arctic heights its plaintive whistle is often the only symptom of animated nature. The ash colour of the plumage is so like surrounding objects that I have often found great difficulty in discovering individuals. The call, however, is loud and prolonged, and may serve to fix the position of a flock which otherwise would remain unnoticed. Commencing with a few short calls, the notes get rapidly prolonged, much in these words "*whōō, wĭt whĭt whĭt, wit wit wēēĭt wēēĭt wēē,*" continued at intervals of a few minutes. In hunting the gorkagu the best way is to approach a flock from below, and fire the first shot when they are on the ground, when the chances are, that all will fly downwards, as they almost invariably do when near the mountain's top. In general appearance and gait on the ground, this bird has a resemblance to a large gray goose. Tender leaves and stalks of the alpine primroses, fresh shoots of grass, and other plants, constitute the favourite food of this species. Its flesh is not well-flavoured. I have often seen flocks of snow-pheasants get very much excited on the approach of the lammergeyer, or any other large rapacious bird, and run from one part of the mountain to another, evidently in great fear. Doubtless the golden and imperial eagles often pounce on the young, but they do not seem to attack the adult. The plumage of the snow-pheasants differs considerably in summer and winter, and there is likewise some individual disproportion as to size, both of which are worthy of attention. An adult male is about 29 inches in length, and the breadth from tip to tip of wings. about 40 inches; weight 8½ to 7½ lbs. The legs are armed with short blunt spurs.

It is particularly refreshing, after a few hours spent among the cold and snow of the higher regions, to descend to the region of verdure, among the fragrant wild thyme which grows abundantly on these mountains, along with the iris, crocus, and tiger-lily. After a day's hard work on the mountain-side, searching for *lepiœ*, we were returning homewards through a little belt of birch, when I came on a musk-deer, and shot the little creature as it stood gazing in astonishment at my sudden appearance. The female is of little value, except for its skin, as the flesh is dry and tasteless. During our stay in the little valley of Trahal, we had a visit from Mirza Shah, ex-rajah of Iscardo, one of Goulab Singh's state prisoners: he had been exiled for twelve years, and was living in destitution in a small village close by. The poor fellow seemed completely borne down by sorrow, although only thirty years of age. He was tall, slender, and handsome, and wore a large white turban and blue mantle. Through an interpreter he informed us of the unjust way in which his country was taken from him by Goulab Singh, but his dull eye seemed to brighten up when he recounted the friendly relations that used to subsist between his father and the British government, ending with the Cashmeree's prayer, "that the day might not be distant when the Feringee would rule over valley, and his mountain home restored to him." He looked, however, as if he was not likely to live to see that day. Grateful for our sympathies, he took his way, and soon reappeared with a piece of rock-crystal, which we feigned to think was valuable; and in return Halkett made him a present of a penknife, which he looked on as a courtly gift. How are the mighty fallen! He was the last one of the royal race of Gylfos, who had lorded over Ladakh and Tibet for several centuries.

The isabella, or brown bear of the Himalaya, is an exceedingly stupid and unsuspicious animal in districts where it has not been disturbed. My first encounter with one well exemplifies what may be considered a common occurrence with those who have hunted it in the more secluded valleys. An individual was discovered feeding on the side of a very steep ridge, which was intersected by a succession of deep furrows, so that when the bear was feeding across the declivity it was constantly rising over these inequalities, and dipping into the intervening hollows. The result to us who were stalking the animal was, that we had to wait until it had crossed one ridge before we attempted to pass over another; and so on, until we arrived at the last, when, to my astonishment, on peeping over the eminence I descried bruin's ears within an arm's length, and heard him nibbling and blowing on the grass; so, springing on my feet, I discharged the contents of two barrels in his body. However, he regained his footing, rushed down the slope, and disappeared in the dense jungle at the base. No time was lost in following up his trail, which was evident enough from great splashes of blood, and I had no sooner gained the cover, when, with a loud snort, he advanced towards me, rearing on his hind legs, when I planted another ball in his chest; then, with a yell, he turned, and entering the jungle, was soon lost to view. We traced his footprints from one place to another through tangled bush, until night came on and compelled us to desist. The following morning saw me up before the sun, and on my way towards the scene, with villagers to assist in beating the bush. After several hours' fruitless search, the animal was found lying stiff and dead under a tree. He was wounded in five different places. We removed the skin, but the shickaree was not content until he came into possession of the gall-bladder likewise, the contents of which are much prized as medicine by the hill people. He, moreover, was careful to remove the liver, and assured me that the number of lobes indicated the age of the individual. This piece of anatomical information I had subsequently cause to doubt, as all the adult specimens I examined had exactly eight lobes.

It was fortunate our antagonist was the brown instead of the black bear, inasmuch as had we been brought to close quarters it is highly probable he would have attempted an attack on us.

On the following day we struck our little camp, and moved eastward over a pass covered with thick beds of snow, and had not proceeded any great distance before a very heavy snow-storm came on, in the middle of which we were surprised by a courier appearing with our "home letters," kindly forwarded to us by the British resident at Serinuggur, Major M'Gregor. Among the items of overland news was recorded the death of the poet who has sung so sweetly of the scenes we were visiting. By the time the valley was reached, the snow, which had fallen thickly on the mountain, now accumulated to even several inches, and the little village of Sipoor looked on the 24th of April as if it had been midwinter; and what appeared strange, among the cold and snow all the apricot trees were in full bloom! The thermometer stood at 40° in a neighbouring hamlet, where, among cattle and cackling hens, we spent a sleepless night from the attacks of legions of "cimex" and "pulex," both of which abound in the native dwellings of Cashmere.

One beautiful morning, shortly after sunrise, as my shickaree was seated beside me on a mountain-top, from which a magnificent view of the valley was visible, we had been intently scanning the hill-sides for game, when, suddenly turning towards me, and pointing downwards, he exclaimed, "What could have induced the English to have given that fine valley to Goulab Singh?" He knew the story of how it was purchased by the present ruler at the termination of the Sutluj campaign even better than I did; but the sudden ebullition of affectionate regard for his native land overcame him, and seeing it to such advantage on that bright spring morning, the simple shickaree turned an æsthetic; and no wonder, for before or since I never beheld a lovelier scene: there lay the fine broad valley, far, far down, the Jhelum, twisting through its rich fields covered with grass, and irrigated by numberless mountain torrents,—the rising sun just gilding the tops of its snow-clad barriers, and the smoke rising from hundreds of villages and hamlets, half-hid among profusion of tree and jungle. Verily, well might have the poet sang,—"If there be an Elysium on earth it is this—it is this."

From the Trahal we crossed a range, and entered the Duchinpara, a magnificent offshoot from the Cashmere valley, where it opens out into a broad plain, several miles in breadth, then gradually narrowing and bursting through the Northern Pinjal for upwards of thirty miles, ends among the high ranges on the frontiers of Little Tibet, where spring the infant-rills of its beautiful Lidur—a fine mountain torrent, which, gathering strength as it runs along the valley, becomes nearly as large as the Jhelum itself at Bij Bedra, where the two unite.

The mountains of the Duchinpara are chiefly composed of limestone, and, for the first fifteen or twenty miles, slope gradually into the valley; their sides are clad with dense pine forests, alternating with grassy glades, whilst the bottom and banks of the Lidur are covered with dense jungle, diversified by little villages, hamlets, fields, and groves of apple, walnut, &c. In the secluded depths of its forest the Cashmere stag finds a safe retreat, and the musk-deer, although getting much reduced in numbers, is occasionally met with. A few of the strange goat-antelopes (*Capricornis bubalina*) frequent the more secluded parts, while on the grassy openings round the limits of forest, a brown or black bear may be found. Had the game of the Duchinpara been preserved with even moderate care, there is no place in the world where the sportsman might pursue his pastime with more advantage; but for years, and at all seasons, natives and Europeans have been constantly at the work of extermination, and before long the north "glades and glooms" will be without a single denizen, save on the mountain-tops, where the stag roams secure from the rifle of any but the most expert and adventurous cragsman. The Cashmere deer (*Cervus cashmeriensis*) is known by the native names "bara-singa" (twelve-horned), and "hanglu." It seems to be very closely allied, if not identical with, *Cervus affinis** (Hodg.), and perhaps likewise Wallich's deer (*C. wallichii*), both natives of the forests of Nepa and the Eastern Hima-

* See *Journal As. Soc. of Bengal*, xliii.

layas. What may be the difference between them and the red-deer (*C. elaphus*) I cannot say. The red-deer of the Altai ranges,* and of Amoorland, are said to be identical, and differ only from the European animal in being a little larger. That is not to be wondered at, especially with reference to the Scottish red-deer, which is well known to have been steadily deteriorating as cultivation has intruded on its haunts; neither in size nor in the development of the horn is the animal now what it once was; but the noble heads preserved in the mansions of the aristocracy, or found in bogs or superficial deposits, show that individuals were equal in size to any met with in the present day in Central and Northern Asia. Not only has the curtailing of its freedom been one of the chief causes of the deterioration of the red-deer, but by breeding always from the same stock, and the destruction of adult harts, leaving the propagation of the species entirely to immature animals, a feebler race has been the result, and doubtless, unless measures are taken to counteract these evils, the red-deer will become extinct; for what greater modifiers of animal existence are there than those which change habits or curtail natural tendencies? With all the attention bestowed on the red-deer, and the vast amount of pleasure and occupation it has afforded man for ages, it seems curious that no one has attempted to trace its relations and examine fully into its distribution. This deer appears to have been co-existent with man's earliest history, for among the peat morasses and caverns of Europe we find abundant remains of the elk, rein, and red deers, all of which roamed at one time in vast herds over the British isles; and as primeval history records man's doings, we find him hourly employed in the great

* See Atkinson's *Travels in the Regions of the Upper and Lower Amoor;* and the *Natural History Review* for 1861.

work of extermination which has gone on from age to age, until the animals have become extinct, save in wild and sequestered regions, where his dominant sway has not yet extended.

The Cashmere stag stands about 14 hands in height; the upper parts are a dark brown or liver-colour in summer, becoming more hoary as winter advances. The inner sides of the hips are reddest, and the belly and lower parts white. The male has large massive antlers, which are shed in March, and are not properly developed or free from velvet until the end of October. The most handsome heads have not the most points. The horns that branch gracefully are in greater repute as trophies than those of older individuals, whose antlers are often irregular and badly-shaped. The hind gestates six months, and when the hart is shedding his horns, repairs to the depths of the forest, where she brings forth a single calf, which retains the white spots until the third or fourth year. The pine-covered slopes and jungles of the Duchinpara, and valley of the Scinde river may be considered the head-quarters of this deer. In the secluded depths of these solitudes they lie all day, to issue forth at dusk and feed on the grassy glades, descending even into the valley in winter, where they may be seen around the villages, and are frequently mobbed and killed by means of long bludgeons shod with iron rings. The Cashmere deer is erratic, and seldom remains long in one locality, but wanders from forest to forest according to the weather and season. As summer advances the herds mount to the limits of the forest, and by August are only to be found on the mountain-tops and situations where they are least likely to be annoyed by insects. It is only in the rutting season that the sportsman is certain of success, when, winding his way through the forest, the decayed twigs crackle under foot. There a noble stag, in expectation of meeting a rival or mate, in maddening excitement rushes forward, and before he has time to make good a retreat, receives his death-wound.

In this way many a stag has fallen in the mountains of Cashmere.

The tiger, panther, bears, and wild dogs (*Canis primævus*), are its natural enemies. The first has been killed at Poonch, among the southern ranges, and although I have not been enabled to prove its existence in the Northern Punjaub, there is little doubt but it frequently visits the deer-forests. The native appellative, "sher," is used indiscriminately for all the larger Felinæ, and as the shickarees assert full-grown harts are often killed by the "sher," I conceive tigers must be the depredators, inasmuch as the panther is not a match for an adult, although beyond doubt young deer are frequently killed by them.

It is not uncommon to find shed antlers much gnawed, and as the same has been observed with reference to the red-deer of the Scotch forests, there is some appearance of truth in the assertion that the animal is in the habit of gnawing the cast horn during the formation of the new for the earthy salts it may contain. The natives state, however, that bears are the depredators on such occasions.

There is a large species known as *Cervus duvaucellii.* It frequents the lower ranges of the Eastern Himalaya, and may possibly be likewise found on certain parts of the western chains. It is impossible, however, in the present state of our knowledge of the haunts of Asiatic Cervidæ, to be able to define accurately their distinctions and localities. The sambar (*Rusa equina*) of the Mahrattas is said likewise to frequent the lower region of the Western Himalaya ; also the sambar (*Rusa hippelaphus*), a native of the forests of India. The jari (*Rusa *aristotelis*) or jarrow is a noble animal, from 14 to 15 hands in height, with antlers often a foot in circumference and 4 feet long, is found on the banks of the Jumna and Ganges in their mountain courses. A few stray along the sub-Himalayan valleys, and have been shot and seen near Simla. On the Cashmere ranges, however, its native stag would appear to reign supreme.

Eld's deer (*Cervus eldii*), found in the valley of Muneepoor, Burmah, and Malayan Peninsula, is worthy of note in a list of the antlered deer of Central Asia.

On the 25th of April we continued our hunting excursions. I ascended a mountain behind the village of Sipoor, and came on abundant trail of deer. A black bear was seen scampering towards a wood, and we flushed a woodcock in the forest, and several coveys of chuckore on the bare hill-sides. The Himalayan and yellow-backed woodpecker were common. Young wounded a deer which he lost after a tedious pursuit through the forest; Halkett reported having seen a wild cat (*Felis bengalensis*) of the small striped species. The shickarees picked up several antlers newly shed with their points gnawed, but nothing was bagged that day. On the following morning I crossed the Duchinpara, and ascended the wooded ridge opposite, by the side of a broad grassy opening: traces of deer were plentiful, for, irrespective of footprints, the bark had been peeled off the trees by them, whilst the fresh-ploughed soil in the forest showed that bears had been lately digging for roots. We did not reach the brow of the hill before the report of a rifle in a jungle below drew our attention in that direction, when soon afterwards two harts were seen charging at full speed across the mountain-side towards a belt of forest trees. This unexpected intrusion on our evening's beat obliged us to retreat homewards. When descending by the outskirts of the forest a herd of deer was observed to emerge from the wood, gaze about for a few minutes, then move leisurely down a hollow, where they were lost to view. Following with great caution, we had scarcely dared to peep over the intervening inequalities, when the herd was discovered feeding in a little depression on the hill-side. I saw there was no time to be lost, as they were scattered, and one buck was within twenty yards of me. Accordingly, singling out the largest, I fired, when he rolled down dead. The others, taken by surprise, and not knowing from whence the shot came, rushed furiously towards me, led on by an old hind, in whose chest the contents of my left barrel "found a billet;" staggering, she fell, and rolled down the steep, bumping from rock to rock, until brought up by a jutting shelf far down among the long green bracken. There was no time for hesitation; so, seizing my spare rifle, I planted another bullet behind the shoulder of a young hart, and as the remainder were scampering up the hill-side the last ball was heard to strike the largest with the unmistakeable "thud," and soon the wounded animal became out-distanced by the other two. With all the satisfaction, and even pride, experienced by the hunter on occasions like the above, I will candidly assert that with an ardour and love for the chase equal to most men, I have more than once experienced a sorrowful feeling after the work of destruction was over, and I came to gaze on the noble frame I had deprived of existence. There was no time, however, on the above occasion for reflection, as already the carrion crows and vultures were circling overhead, and the shades of night approaching. Accordingly the carcases were collected together after the shickarees in the most approved Mussulman fashion had cut their throats. Two men were left to protect them during the night from bears and panthers, whilst we returned to the tent; and next day the half-starved natives of the village of Yenaür fared sumptuously on venison. The secretion of the infra-orbital opening is much prized as a remedy for almost all diseases. The largest of the deer measured 13 hands at the shoulder. Young added a she-bear to our day's bag, and seldom a day passed but one or other was fortunate in some way. I killed another stag on the morning of the 28th of April, after a long and exciting stalk across the slippery sides of a very precipitous mountain. It is wonderful how the excitement of the chase carries one over dangerous and difficult places; a break-neck sort of indifference seizes you; you rush on regardless of obstacles, which in cooler moments might cause considerable concern. With the rifle in one hand and pole in the other, the prospect of an ibex before him, where is the hunter that would hesitate at any common obstacle? Mayhap these lines may sometime catch the eye of a Himalayan hunter, and if so, let me bring to his remembrance that significant signal, like the tapping of the woodpecker on the trunk of the pine-tree, used by the Himalayan shickaree to draw his attention when a whisper would attract the game. No noise is better suited, for beyond the woodpecker's tap and the "wailing of the forest," there is oft no other sound that breaks the stillness of these alpine solitudes.

Our tent was moved from village to village whilst we explored the mountain slopes on the right and left, departing at an early hour in the morning to return at dusk. During midday when the game sought the shelter of the forest, my time was usually employed in wandering through the woods in quest of birds. Sometimes when perched on a projecting cliff I have been so overcome by the magnificent beauty and grandeur of the scene around me, that, lost in admiration, I could scarcely confine my observation to any particular spot for three consecutive minutes. In these glens nature appears in all its wildness: the noble pines scattered here and there, or assembled in woods or forests, adorn the hill-sides, whilst the openings are clad in a rich grassy covering; at the bottom dashes a stream, fed and nourished by the melting snow above, its banks are clad in luxuriant vegetation, and fertilised by the debris of the flood; when—

> Along this narrow valley you might see
> The wild deer sporting on the meadow ground,
> And here and there a solitary tree,
> Or mossy stone, or rock with woodbine crowned.
> Oft did the cliffs reverberate the sound
> Of parted fragments tumbling from on high;
> And from the summit of that craggy mound
> The perching eagle oft was heard to cry,
> Or on resounding wings to shoot athwart the sky.
>
> BEATTIE'S *Minstrel.*

As we ascended the Duchinpara the climate and scenery kept constantly changing; it seemed to be retrograding from spring to winter, as the mountains were half-clad with snow, and the temperature and vegetation decreased as we advanced. The fine broad valley was gradually narrowing into a glen with steep and rugged sides. On the 2d of May we reached Pilgam, where the mountain barometer gave an elevation of 8000 feet above the level of the sea. The ascent had been almost imperceptible, and yet we had risen several hundred feet since leaving Sipoor, and except a slight tinge of green on the hill-sides, there was no sign of spring even at that advanced time of the year. We explored the slopes below this village, where my companions killed a bara-singa and black bear. I saw a few hill-foxes (*Vulpes montanus*) and a musk-deer. Now and then large masses of rock were observed to become loosened by the melting of the snow, and roll down the sides of the mountain, carrying destruction before them. Halkett had a narrow escape from one which struck a rifle from the shoulder of his servant. The nights were bitterly cold, and unless in the sun there was a chilling wind that necessitated us moving about. To judge distances exactly, or even with moderate certainty, is only to be gained by much experience and practice in a level country ; it is generally no difficult matter to guess with accuracy any distance within 500 yards, but on mountains, especially in firing across valleys or downwards, unless the hunter is careful, he will experience many a heartache. Across ravines objects generally look nearer than they actually are, and the reverse when below you ; the latter, however, is by no means always the case,—a great deal depends on the nature of the mountain, whether clad with vegetation or barren. In all barren places and mountains objects appear nearer than they really are. At Pilgam, one forenoon, I marked a black bear feeding on a hill-side at what I fancied was 100 yards distant. Adjusting my rifle accordingly, I placed it with great care and fired, when to my astonishment the ball hit a rock half-a-foot above bruin's back. I measured the distance, and found it did not exceed 60 yards! Such pieces of bad luck soon taught me to be more particular in judging distances, and it was not until I had practised a great deal that I could make a moderate computation of any range beyond 50 yards. The scenery about Pilgam is full of noble grandeur, comprising steep and rugged mountains, their summits jutting into rocky pinnacles or beetling crags overgrown with moss and lichen, and often scarped and bare ; lower down the pine diversifies the scenery with its clustering or scattered forests, which the grassy glades and perpendicular banks tend to beautify; the latter undulating downwards into the valleys with almost every variety of woodland and savannah. Northwards from the village runs a glen by which a pathway extends to Ladakh and Little Tibet, and about three miles upwards one of the chief tributaries of the Lidur is seen gushing from below a huge glacier. I followed the stream to this point, in expectation of meeting bears on the way; but from the quantity of snow still covering the mountains and valleys, except a solitary bearded vulture, there were no symptoms of animal life. The mantle of winter was spread over everything; not a blade of grass was above ground, neither had willow or birch ventured to bud. However, a few days suffice to alter nature's aspect altogether. At Pilgam the thermometer stood at 76° F. in our tent on the 4th of May, and the Lidur rose rapidly from the melting of snow on the surrounding mountains. The bare parts became tinged with green, and the walnut-trees were budding. The magical way in which vegetation springs up in these regions is really wonderful. In a single week, from "dismal winter hoar, comes gentle spring in all her ethereal mildness." I remember taking my gun one evening, and as I was strolling along the banks of the Lidur, came on a pretty little "dipper" (*Cinclus aquaticus*) for the first time since leaving Britain. This well-known tenant of the mountain-streams of Great Britain and Northern Europe is rather common in the secluded mountain valleys of Cashmere; but I believe I am the first to record its presence in this portion of central Asia. My specimens from Cashmere resemble that met with in south-eastern Europe, and named by Temminck *C. melanogaster*, which must now stand as a local variety of the other. One of our party assured me that he saw the common European squirrel in a forest near

Pilgam. This may not be unlikely, considering it is a native of Tibet, and skins are imported to the Punjaub from Afghanistan. We soon found out our mistake in coming so far up the Duchinpara, for we had left the good shooting-ground behind. The bears and deer had all moved down the valley. Accordingly, retracing our steps by the left bank of the Lidur, we arrived at the village of Eish Makam, after a march of four hours. Every mile indicated an advance into a more genial region, but the descent was very gradual. That night the temperature rose from 42° to 60°, whilst everything around our new halting-ground betokened the appearance of summer: the chimney swallow twittered from many a straw-built shed; the villages and hamlets half-hid among groves of walnut, apple, pear, apricot, almond, and willow,—all pleasing pictures of rural beauty. The blooming iris decked the little village graveyard and mustjid, and there, as everywhere in the valley of Cashmere, added additional beauty to the loveliness of many a sylvan scene. There are two species of iris—a large-leaved (*Iris longifolia*), with purple and white flowers; and a smaller, with narrow leaves (*Iris nepalensis*). On the fine grassy glades the hoopoe was seen digging its long bill into the soft turf in quest of insects, and oft as its labours seemed nearly over, down would pounce a Drongo shrike to secure the fruits of its toil. The latter is a perfect little tyrant wherever he thinks he can be so with impunity. Even the Indian jackdaw seldom passes his haunts unmolested. What more pleasing sight can there be than, in some delightful evening in summer, to observe flocks of the beautiful crimson flycatcher (*Pericrocotus peregrinus*) pursuing their gambols around the tall walnut-trees of a Cashmere hamlet? Their soft twittering notes and graceful motions have oft excited in me feelings of admiration and pleasure, until the Drongo shrike, or some unwelcome intruder, drove the gorgeous little fairies away.

The mountain-slopes on each side of the valley at Eish Makam are reported to have once been among the best hunting-grounds in Cashmere until the murderous rifle of the Englishman almost annihilated the large game. I beat over one hill-side south of the village, and in the course of the day met with several herds of bara-singa; but the harts were all without horns, and, from shedding their hair, were not in good condition either as trophies or for the table. Two old hinds passed within a few yards of us, and for a few minutes seemed doubtful whether to scamper off or face us. After trotting leisurely into a wood, they turned round, stamped with their fore-feet, and barked in their coughing-like way, and only took to flight when we bellowed after them. My shickaree, evidently more scrupulous of the quantity than the quality of his venison, kept exhorting me to kill one; but my better feelings decided otherwise, and we left them for the autumn. Several monal pheasants were observed. I wounded a young black bear, but owing to the denseness of the ferns growing along the base of the hill we lost its trail. Halkett was more fortunate, and killed a she brown bear and wounded its cub, which he found the following day lying dead at some distance from the spot. Wild rhubarb is exceedingly plentiful on all the exposed parts of the mountains, and when young forms the first food of the brown bear on its exit from its cave in early spring. Nothing can exceed the variety and beauty of the wild flowers of these mountains; to the botanist they are replete with the greatest interest. My time, however, was so occupied with other natural history pursuits that I had not leisure to devote to this enchanting study. I observed two species of humble bees somewhat common along the grassy banks of the Duchinpara. One sort was rather larger than the common British species, but is jet black; the other had the head and lower parts black, the back and loins white, with a red spot close to the sting. In a pine-forest, for the first and last time, I had a glimpse of a rare woodpecker, about the size of the lesser woodpecker. Its head was white, neck and breast bluish-black, and belly and vent red.

By the 10th of May spring had fairly set in, and clothed the woods and jungles along the sides of the valley with their gayest attire. The hawthorn, wild rose, and a lilac (with small flowers and numerous elliptical leaves) were in full blossom, and filled the air with their delightful perfumes; whilst creepers hung in beautiful festoons on tree and shrub. The edolio or black and white crested cuckoo (*Oxylophus melanoleucos*) was heard piping its well-known call, and in the evening, sporting like swallows, and attractive by their loud and wild cry, were flocks of the common European bee-eater. Summer was come, and the long grass and ferns on the mountain-sides showed us the uselessness of seeking for bears in such dense cover. Accordingly, I packed up my rifle, and commenced the ornithology of the district, descending from the excitement of deer-stalking, to the no less agreeable pastime of searching after the little feathered denizens of the woods and glades. Among bushy places a small white-throated warbler, a little less than the cinereous white-throat of Europe, is very common. The jackal's howl was heard every night.

The silk-worm is reared in great numbers in several parts of the valley and its offshoots. At Brar we witnessed cocoons being boiled over a slow fire, when the silk was collected by winding the threads round a wheel worked by the hand, afterwards dried, and made up on reels.

On the 11th of May we moved down the banks of the Lidur, now a fine rapid river, to the pretty village of Mattun, situated in a grove of magnificent chunar and walnut trees, under the umbrageous boughs of which we pitched our little tent, close to a square enclosed tank, which literally swarmed with the so-called Himalayan trout, some to all appearance 2 lbs. in weight.* After the long march and exposure to the rays of a powerful sun, we plunged headlong into the cold and refreshing water of the tank, which is supplied by a stream that rises in the neighbouring mountains. It was delightful to sit under the trees and enjoy tne pleasant afternoon. Sardinian starlings chirped in hundreds overhead among the branches or holes in the trunks of the old trees, where they build, and the sparrows in countless thousands joined in ready chorus among the light-green leaves of the chunars. The above starling is easily recognised by its uniform shining black plumage, and the long and tapering feathers on the neck and collar. The blackbird-like note of the Cashmere song-thrush (*Turdus unicolor*, Tickell) was heard in all directions. A few were building their nests among the chunars around the village. This thrush remains in Cashmere until winter, when it migrates southward to the plains of India, and returns to the mountains in spring. The changes to which its plumage is subject have puzzled naturalists; hence each variety has created for itself a name. I believe the Calcutta thrush (Latham), *Turdus dissimilis* (Blyth), to be one of the varieties, as undoubtedly the *Turdus unicolor* (Gould) is another variety approaching that

* I was unable to determine this species. It is soft-mouthed, and in no particulars does it assimilate the genus *salmo*; the name has arisen from its frequenting brooks; its flesh is soft and almost tasteless.

described by Tickell in 1833.* This plain-dressed but characteristic tenant of the wooded parts of Cashmere represents the song-thrush of Europe. It is less in size, being not larger than the redwing. On leaving Mattun we turned eastward to examine the celebrated ruins of the temple of Martund, situated on a slope near the mountains overlooking the magnificent kirawa of the same name. Again, from this point the geologist will mark the old water-lines across the sides of the mountains, and the shingly conglomerate which abuts in several places. The similarity between Martund and the temples in the Baramula Pass is striking; with the little temple of Pandreton they belong doubtless to one epoch, as shown in Professor Wilson's *Essay on the Ancient History of Cashmere*, or the carefully-compiled descriptions of Mr. Vigne.† Making allowances for the ravages of time and the ruthless hand of the invader, nothing I have seen in the valley testifies to the severity of the earthquakes which have shaken it from time to time more than the yawning gaps and tottering walls of the temple of Martund.

The city of Islamabad is only a few miles distant. It is composed of seven or eight hundred houses, scattered without much regularity and appearance. From the little hill westward of the town the traveller may command a magnificent view of the valley. The chunar-trees here are of gigantic size, and the largest I have seen anywhere. The circumference of one at 4 feet from the ground measured 29 feet. They form a delightful shade around the sacred spring of Annat Nag, which, like the tank at Mattun, is surrounded by a wall, and swarms with Himalayan trout. There are two sulphureous springs in the town, one of which deposits sulphur in small quantity, and has a temperature about ten degrees higher than the spring-water in the neighbourhood.

* See *Jour. As. Soc. Bengal*, ii. 577.

† *Travels in Cashmere*, vol. i.

Islamabad is proverbially famous for its dirtiness, and fewer cities have better natural advantages at command; with abundant water supplies, and every benefit as regards position, yet no one can help being forcibly impressed with the utter disregard for anything approaching order or cleanliness in the inhabitants or their dwellings. It is perhaps too severe to lay this charge altogether on the people of Islamabad, inasmuch as poverty and extortion have had their usual effect on the Cashmerees in general. I always felt relieved of many olfactory discomforts when I found myself clear of their towns, and was once more among the green fields and lovely groves. One of the chief songsters of the valley is the yellow-vented bulbul (*P. leucogenys*). The red-vented species (*P. hæmorrhous*) is common enough in the woods of the lesser ranges southwards, but not in the valley. Among the topmost branches of the tall chunars, fluttering in the sunbeams, but usually in the evening, is the small flycatcher (*Hemichelidon fuliginosa*). Several specimens procured near Islamabad had a good deal of rust-coloured markings on the wings, and resembled the description of *Hemichelidon ferruginea*, Hodg., which is clearly a very close ally.

About three miles in a south-easterly direction stands the old garden of Atsibul, with its beautiful natural fountain gushing from beneath the trap rock. The spring rises with some force for a height of about a foot and a half, and from its volume would indicate considerable pressure. This ancient pleasure-garden of the Mogul emperors is famous in the history of their times. Among its shady avenues the enchanting Nourmahal spent her evenings, and the great Jehangire is said to have repaired to its revigorating baths, the remains of which bear the impress of their former importance. During our visit the garden was stocked with vines, apricots, peaches, plums, apples, pears, etc., all growing in great luxuriance, and surrounded by the most beautiful sylvan scenery to be seen anywhere. I took my gun and strolled through the groves in quest of birds. The fairylike form of the paradise flycatcher flitted from bough to bough, while the cooing of the Oriental pigeon sounded sweetly through the copse, and the blackbird-like chaunt of the Cashmere song-thrush was heard sounding mellowly in the neighbouring groves; but of all that charmed me most was the well-known and familiar voice, "that has no sorrow in its song, no winter in its year;" the remembrance of the budding trees and the green fields and copses of dear old home; and often is it heard in these regions, for the cuckoo calls all over Cashmere and the neighbouring ranges from March to June. In bushy places numbers of red-backed shrikes were seen hunting after beetles; and the roller and oriole, as if doomed to dwell in the midst of alarms, were off on the first symptoms of our approach. The latter has a soft, short note, and may be often seen in the wooded parts of the valley. The common sandpiper was by the side of the brook, emitting its clear plaintive cry, and about on the sandbanks we saw several ring-plover. I shot two pied kingfishers and a black stork on the rivulet near the village of Changos, so famous in the olden times for its pretty dancing-girls. But Changos now-a-days has no such pretensions, although the dark eyes and sunburnt countenances of old and young testify to a race distinct from their neighbours, and with all the appearances of gipsy extraction. It has been asserted that more than one Changos girl entered the zenanas of the Delhi emperors. There are several springs in the neighbourhood of Atsibul. The one at Kokur Nag gushes forth with considerable force, and forms a rivulet of a good size, which ultimately joins the Barengi, a tributary of the Jhelum. In the limestone near the stream there is a vein of iron, which produces small quantities of the metal. After a few miles' journey through a country densely clad with tree, bush, and scrub, chiefly the hazel-like *Fothergilla*, and across several branches of the Jhelum, we arrived at the celebrated fountain of Vernag. This place, although in ruins, bore still the impress of its pristine grandeur, and, even in all its fallen beauty, stood in point of comparison with the wretched edifices built there by Goulab Singh as would its noble founders have ranked with the avaricious and tyrannical Jumoo Rajah. Over the ruined gateway is inscribed in Persian—"This fountain has sprung from the waters of Paradise;" and on the octagonal wall which surrounds the spring is another tablet on which it is recorded that—"This place of unparalleled beauty was raised to the skies by Jehangiere Shah Akbar Shah, in the year 1029" (A.D. 1619). The well sends forth a volume of water of some size; the former abounds with trout. The little hill behind Vernag hides the view towards the east, but in every other direction the fine valley, with its gentle slopes, fields, and crystal streams, gladdens the eye. We ranged through beautiful copses, by smiling hamlets, and across grassy levels, through rice-fields; at others winding up the willow-fringed banks of rivulets, that "chatter, chatter as they flow, to join the brimming river." The gay little kingfisher and the spotted enicurus were seen hunting along the babbling brook-sides. I gathered many well-known English plants, which may have been in part introduced from time to time with the cereals and other grains. The bird's-foot trefoil, the wood strawberry, burnet saxifrage, were all common. Again, white and red clovers clad the grassy banks. A species of burdock, resembling the British; the dandelion, goose-grass, shepherd's purse, were all plentiful; besides the wild thyme, which sent forth its sweetest fragrance. A viburnum, differing in several respects from the English Guelder rose, bloomed sweetly by the sides of streams and in shady places; the wood geranium, with its white variety, was abundant. The meadow grass and ribwort plantain covered the fields, whilst in "humble bowers" the Cashmere bluebell "lurked lowly unseen." There was, however, something wanting to complete the floral picture of home—the "wee, modest crimson-tipped flower" was not there—no "daisy decked the green."

Following up our explorations of the southern portion of the valley, we kept along the base of the Fuťi Pinjal, whose tops were still covered with snow, whilst lower down the dark forest and rich green vegetation clad their prominent ridges and gradually retiring slopes, at the bottom of which great banks of alluvium stretched into the valley. The wheat was springing up, and ready for the deluging rains of the S.E. monsoon, and already masses of cloud were accumulating on the mountain-tops. The rainy season commences about the end of May, when vegetation attains its maximum in the course of a week; the climate is then very relaxing, and it is perhaps the preponderance of wet over dry which is the great objection to the valley being used as a sanitarium during the summer months. Ague is not uncommon, but the other diseases peculiar to India are seldom observed. Small-pox has left its fearful traces on many a cheek; and ophthalmia, the nursling of poverty and filth, is rife among the lower classes. The ignorance of their doctors is in keeping with the wretchedness of everything intellectual in the Cashmerian character, and, as in India, the wandering vagrant or fanatic fakir serves all sanative demands. My small stock of medicines was soon exhausted, for scarcely a day passed without numbers of applicants crowding round me. I often relieved suffering humanity, and with more ample means at disposal might have done substantial good. Many cases of cataract were cured simply by means of a fine sewing needle, slightly bent at the point, and stuck in the end of a piece of wood : the success of such operations proclaimed my presence far and wide. I daresay even now there are Cashmerees who remember my humble efforts, and I will say, with all their faults, gratitude to those who soothe the bodily sufferings is never wanting with them.

I recollect in a subsequent visit to the valley I had been delayed by one of Goulab Singh's minions at the fort of Chacar, near Dunna, from want of coolies to carry my luggage. No persuasion or expostulation availed ; the fellow seemed determined to prevent our progress if possible, or at least to throw obstacles in our way, so that we might not again attempt another journey, and inform others of the difficulties to be encountered. After much useless negotiation, a wretched-looking man made his appearance at the door of the hovel in which I was quartered. He had been wounded in one of the many disastrous raids made by Goulab Singh against the chief of Dardu. This poor fellow's left knee was contracted, and he had long despaired of any relief to his deformity. One could therefore fancy his state of mind when I found that the distortion depended entirely on the simple contraction of his ham-string tendons, and was removed at once by division of the latter, so that in a few minutes the bent limb was made straight. I had the satisfaction afterwards of seeing him walking about. The result of my operation reached the fort, and the next morning I had twenty of the best coolies the governor could procure, all ready to carry myself or baggage anywhere.

The Vishau river is considered by the Cashmerees as the parent of the Jhelum : it rises in the Kosa Nag lake, which is fed by the melting snow and glacier in a hollow or an upland valley of the southern ranges. The river runs through a narrow rocky glen, remarkable for picturesque grandeur. The falls of Arabul are well worth a visit, as few localities in the Cashmere mountains possess such attractive scenery. A pathway leads from the village of Utu to within a short distance of the cataract. Few Englishmen could sit on the grassy banks, and witness the rare mountain beauty of Arabel without a feeling that did Cashmere belong to England, there is no spot among all its lovely scenery better suited for a pic-nic. To one of us it brought back recollections of similar mountain beauties

> "Among the rugged cliffs that guard
> The infant rills of Highland Dee."

I gathered wild asparagus (*A. racemosus*) and rhubarb, thinking to give my companions a treat; but much to our disappointment, although the asparagus looked excellent, it had none of the esculent qualities of the cultivated plant. In damp situations a *forget-me-not*, mouse-eared chickweed, and sheep's sorrel were observed. A broad-leaved dock was plentiful around the village of Hungipoor.

The ring-dove is often seen in the valley, and frequents bushy situations.

I killed a red weasel (*Mustela subhemachalana*) close to the hamlet of Utu, where we found it had destroyed several young chickens and fowls' eggs. Its total length, including tail, was 19 inches ; colour, an uniform light-brown, darker on the back ; nose, mouth, and throat, white ; tail lax and tapering. This handsome little creature is not uncommon in the valley. I have seen several ermine-skins said to have been procured in the Cashmere mountains : it is considered by natives to be somewhat common. The heron is a tenant of the parent streams of the Jhelum. From the hamlets of Hungipoor, in one of the valleys at the southern end of Cashmere, we witnessed a thunder-storm, which, for awful grandeur, I have seldom seen surpassed. The lightning shot in tremendous zig-zags across the mountain-tops. One bolt struck a pinnacle of rock, and remained a globe of fire for upwards of two minutes. Such meteoric phenomena are said not to be uncommon during Himalayan thunder-storms.

CHAPTER XI.

Magnificent View of the Valley of Cashmere—Traces of an Ancient Lake—An Excursion to the Interior of the Futi Pinjal—Fauna of the Northern and Southern Cashmere Ranges—Bears, Deer, Ibex, and Wild Goats partial to Localities—Mode of Fighting pursued by the Wild Goats and Sheep—A Noble Specimen of the Great Goat or Serpent-Eater—Bear—Wild Grandeur of the Scenery—Natural History of the Markhore—The Tare-Goat—Wild Dog—Black-headed Pheasant—Silver Fox—Weather—Monsoon—Ornithology of the Valley—Cashmerian Valley Scenery—Goat Antelope—Snakes—Small Venomous Viper—Water-Snake—Birds—Cross the Wurdwun Pass—Snow-storm—Servant lost—Inhospitable Region—Bear-shooting—Misery of the Natives—Habits of the Isabella Bear—Herd of Ibex—Frightful Accident by an Avalanche—Flying Squirrel—Ibex-hunting—Hermit Bears—Lost in the Forest—Himalayan Ibex—Dangerous Travelling—Steep Mountains—Imperial Rock-pigeon—Distribution of the Brown Bear of the Himalayas, and its Habits—The Black Bear; its Natural History—Return to the Valley—Red Marmot—Scenery and Fauna of the Valley—Serinuggur and the Ruler of Cashmere—View from the Temple of Solomon.

One of the best views of the valley may be had from the top of the little hill behind the village of Shupeyon. The Bimber pass may be seen traversing the Southern or Futi Pinjal, and presenting an appearance as if a great slice had been cut out of the mountain barrier. It is the chief entrance to the valley from India, and seems to have always been the high-road, although that by which we entered is open all the year, even in the depths of winter, when all the others are impracticable. The vast accumulations of gravel and detritus are nowhere better seen than at the mouth of the Bimber pass. The great banks several hundred feet in thickness, with their water-worn pebbles, sand, and clay, together with erratic boulders here and there, all point to a far-back period in the history of the country, when the glaciers now confined to the most upland hollows stretched down into the valley of Cashmere. The view looking up the pass is very striking and grand.

Dense forests of pine clothe the sloping ridges, and stretch far along the windings of the defile. As we are now in the neighbourhood of the Peer Pinjal, I cannot omit a few recollections concerning a hunting excursion I made to this district two years after the events here recorded. The journal of my travels in Cashmere on that occasion was unfortunately lost during my absence in Turkey at the close of the Crimean war. I regret the loss the more, as it contained many valuable natural history notes on the habits of several of the large mammalia of the western mountains. In traversing the forests and mountains of the Futi and Peer Pinjal, one is astonished, after a visit to the northern chains, to find there noble forests without the bara singa, or the numbers of bears he had been accustomed to encounter on the opposite ranges. I could not satisfactorily account for this; the advantages as regards wood cover and food being the same. This partiality on the part of certain animals to localities is not peculiar to the two just mentioned, for I have often travelled over large tracts of the Himalayas of the most inviting character, and scarcely met with a wild creature of any sort. As a rule, the northern slopes are more devoid of animal existence than the southern, from, possibly, being exposed to the boreal blasts, and their floral characters participate in nearly the same differences.

The brown and black bears never associate, and when they

meet, one invariably attacks the other. As far as my observations extend, the black seems always the assailant. However, the ibex and markhore often dispute each other's footing; and I am not aware that they are ever met with on the same ranges. The shickarees all agree that the Cashmere stag flies before the tare and markhore, when the two latter are driven by the rigors of winter to seek food and shelter in the deer forests, for it is seldom they leave the dizzy crags or the mountain-tops unless forced by severity of weather. The pugnacious tendencies of both goats and sheep in the wild state are just as strong as when domesticated. The markhore, tare, ibex, and houriar all charge in much the same fashion as their civilised congeners. I have seen two strange herds meet, and the old males rushed at one another, whilst the hinds and young seemed perfectly indifferent. A native informed me that he had observed two male ibex fighting on the shelf of a rock until one pushed the other over, which fell, shattered to pieces, many hundreds of feet below. Thus the strongest gains the day, and the weakest goes to the wall. The constant warfare for ascendency must act through ages on a race, and provided the victor and the strongest males get possession of the females, the result will be a healthy, vigorous progeny; whereas, as already remarked in the case of the red-deer, by destroying the old stags, we leave the propagation to immature individuals.

In spite of the remonstrances of the natives, and the insalubrious weather of the monsoon months, I started alone, in July 1854, from Serinuggur to hunt the markhore on the summits of the Peer Pinjal. At that season the larger game are casting their winter coats; the deer are without horns, and in bad condition; the bears are safe among the ever-green verdure of their native haunts, and the ibex and markhore, which in spring might have been stalked low down, were now browsing among the clouds on the peaks of the highest mountains. It was the worst time of the year for hunting; and had it not been that my shickaree had gained good information of a herd of tare and markhore on the spurs running towards Zuznar, one of the loftiest peaks of the southern Pinjal, it would have taken a great deal to have induced me to undergo all the fatigue, discomfort, and dangers of a fortnight's bivouac among the clouds. Before or since I never underwent so much arduous bodily exertion; and I may truly say never were zeal and determination more amply rewarded. The first week's occupation was chiefly in following up the trail of a herd of markhore, when one young male and a tare were killed. One day I spied a bear asleep on the decayed branch of a pine on a jutting shelf of rock. I remember, when the bullet hit him, how, bounding upwards, he fell with a tremendous impetus some 400 feet into the bed of the torrent, and was rapidly borne down and landed high and dry on a bank; moreover, just as the echoes of my rifle died away, how, looking upwards, through the misty vapours, I spied a herd of frightened markhore, led on by a noble old male, all dashing at full speed across the crumbling mountain-top. On the three following days we continued on their trail, sleeping under rocks, and were up and after them as soon as day dawned. However, the wily old buck was invariably on the look-out, always guiding his herd to open and inaccessible places, until on the afternoon of the third day, tired and wearied from repeated exertion, and vain attempts to circumvent the vigilant leader, my shickaree was about to clear a spot for the night's bivouac, when we espied the patriarch of the herd on a jutting cliff far above us. Then the old hunter Ajez Khan exclaimed: "We shall have better luck tomorrow;" and his words proved true; for at day-dawn we came on the herd feeding in a hollow above a glacier which sloped gradually down into the valley. Singling out the two largest, I pressed my trusty Westley Richards to my shoulder and fired on the fine old buck; before he had fallen another bullet pierced the second largest male of the herd, and when the smoke cleared away both were seen rolling down the ice-clad slope. How my heart beat with delight, and Ajez Khan hugged and kissed the rifle! with what wild excitement we half-slid half-bounded down the glacier after our quarry, which lay like little black specks on the snow far below us! They had bumped and rolled until brought to a stand-still by a huge boulder on the ice, where we found them just as the sun was setting. In all my Himalayan travels I have never witnessed a scene so wild and grand as that glen; and never shall I forget the circumstances which have fixed its noble magnificence on my memory. The largest trophy measured 11½ hands at the shoulder, and each of his horns was 48½ inches in length, and 3 feet 2 inches between their tips. His long, flowing black beard, dashed with gray, stretched from the chin down the dewlap to his chest, hanging in long straight tresses to his knees. He looked in every respect the very monarch of the glen. The shickarees who crowded to my house in Serinuggur subsequently, to examine the head, alleged that it was without exception the largest that had been seen or killed on the mountains of Cashmere.*

* Young measured a pair of horns in the possession of the present ruler of Cashmere which weighed 20 lbs.; the length of each, 3 feet 7½ inches; between the tips, 3 feet 11 inches; circumference, 11¼ inches. Their points were blunted and worn. The animal must have been larger than the above. The horns were picked up in a snow-drift on the mountains of Dardu.

The markhore (*Capra megaceros*, Hutton) is known in Little Tibet as the *rawacheh* and *tsuh-ra* or *water-goat*. It is undoubtedly the "rass" mentioned by Wood in his journey to the sources of the Oxus. The markhore, signifying serpent-eater, is found on the mountains of Persia, Afghanistan, and, proceeding eastward, is plentiful on the ranges around the Khyber Pass. From Torbela and Little Tibet it wanders down the Suliman range as far as Mitenkote on the Indus, at the junction of the latter and the Sutluj. It is common on the north-western ranges of Cashmere, including Dardu; from thence a few herds are to be met with all along the southern or Futi Pinjal as far as Kishtewar on the Chenaub. I have not heard of its having been found eastward of the river Beas. The northern ranges of Cashmere and Ladakh are apparently without a single individual, perhaps on account of the ibex and wild sheep frequenting these mountains. It is curious to observe the differences as to size and curvature of the horns of individuals from different localities. All the males observed by me on the southern Pinjal had flat horns with few twists. The specimen just mentioned had one perfect and two imperfect turns, while specimens from Peshawur ranges and the Suliman were rounded, straight, and twisted like a corkscrew. A pair of horns in the museum at Kurrachee in Lower Scinde, and said to have been brought from Herat, resembled again the Cashmere specimens. Some horns rise perpendicularly from the head, whilst others diverge backwards and outwards. I have examined the skins of many markhore from different localities, and after allowing for changes consequent on the season of the year, I could not discover any difference worth mentioning. Mr. Blyth and Dr. J. E. Gray consider this species is most likely a variety of the domestic goat, but from all I can learn of its habits and appearance, there is perhaps more cause to consider it the progenitor of the domestic animal than even the ibex.

The markhore is usually found in small herds. Like the ibex, it delights to browse on steep and rocky mountains, ascending and descending with the seasons. In winter, in common with other alpine species, the fur becomes dense from the woolly pileage, which gives a lighter colour to the coat than during midsummer and autumn, when it disappears, and the fur is short and brown. As before stated, the old males have an enormous beard extending from the chin down the lower part of the neck to the chest. That of the females is short, and her horns are flat, and seldom more than 10 inches in length. The tare has much of the habits and appearance of the markhore, and is frequently seen associated with herds of the latter. Shickarees have strange stories of the serpent-eating disposition of the markhore, but apparently without any real cause. I recollect my friend Ajez Khan assuring me that an ammonite he picked up on the mountains had become petrified from having passed through the intestines of a markhore!

Herds of tare (*Capra jemlaica*, Smith) were often observed during my excursion, usually young. The short triangular horns of this species of goat distinguish the males from any of its allies. The tare is plentiful on the mountains by the banks of the Chenaub, in the district of Chamba; it is also found in Lahoul and Kooloo, where it is likewise known by the name of kras. The natives of the southern Cashmere ranges call it jugla. I was told that during severe winters both markhore and tare may be found in the same forests. The former has been killed on the mountains near Uri Fort, on the Jhelum.

A fine rhododendron, with pale pink flowers, grows on the

sheltered sides of the valleys around Zuznar. On bleak situations I met with the only specimen of the black-breasted warbler (*Calliope pectoralis*) I have seen on the Himalaya. It is a solitary bird, and affects the stunted juniper-bushes at high altitudes ; it is about the size of the redstart, which in habits it much resembles. The ram-hun or wild dog (*Canis primævus*) is a native of the Cashmere ranges, and although not to say common, is by no means rare ; but it is so stealthy in its habits that all my attempts to obtain specimens proved abortive. I devoted ten days to the pursuit of a pack, and followed their fresh trail over many dangerous and difficult places ; but they were too knowing, and always kept out of sight. Many native sportsmen, though familiar with its depredations, have never seen the animal. They hunt in packs, and attack the largest deer. Even the Cashmere stag is said to be brought to bay and killed by packs of wild dogs. One was killed by my friend Lieutenant Abbott of the 75th Regiment, near Allahabad Serai, on the Peer Pinjal, and its skin identified with specimens at home. The wild dog seen by Dr. Hooker on the Khasia mountains, and known there by the names kuleam, khas,* may be a different species. Even on the western ranges, I have been told by natives of considerable variety as regards colour and size of wild dogs. In a collection made by Captain Peyton, 87th regiment, on the Karakorum mountains, north of Ladakh, I saw a skin of a wild dog he had procured from the natives, who assured him preyed on the *Ovis ammon* and Tibet antelopes, and that it often killed the tame sheep and goats, and in winter came close to the native villages. The nose was pointed, hair long and thick, the latter containing much woolly pileage ; the general

* Colonel Sykes considers this species identical with the kolsun of the Deccan (*C. dukhunensis*).

colour of the coat was white, with splashes of black on the back and hips; the tail was short and bushy, with the tips of the hairs black. The domestic or pariah dog is often forced to depend on its own exertions, and hunts in packs over large tracts of country on the Indian plains, but not apparently on the Himalayas.

The black-headed or Hastings pheasant (*Ceriornis melanocephala*, Gray) is found on the wooded slopes of the Peer Pinjal. This noble representative of the Phasianidæ is one of the gayest, and at the same time largest, of its family. From the brilliancy of plumage, it has been designated by Europeans the Argus pheasant, but the true Argus is a native of Sumatra and the Malayan peninsula. The most common local name for this species, besides the above, is "jewar." In some parts of the Cashmere ranges, especially in the district we are now investigating, the male is called "sonalu," and the female "selalee." Its close ally, the Sikim horned pheasant (*C. satyra*), has not to my knowledge been met with on the north-western Himalaya. The loud wailing cry of the jewar sounds mournfully along the valleys, and is more often heard at dusk and break of day than at any other time. Oft, in the stillness of an alpine solitude, at my tent-door, by the cheerful log-fire, have I listened to the well-known *wa, wa, wa* of this bird. I believe the jewar is much more common than is generally supposed, for its habits are cunning and stealthy, always preferring the deepest solitudes of the forest, and seldom taking to wing unless when hard pressed. Like other Himalayan forest game-birds, it is fond of secreting itself in dense foliage. The jewar is usually met with in flocks. I have never seen the plach or monal frequenting the same localities with the above species. The two former are common on the high wooded slopes of the northern Pinjal, but the jewar is not found in these situations. One night we were disturbed by the barking of a fox, and at daybreak on the following morning I shot a female and cub of the silver fox (*Vulpes flavescens*), both within a few yards of my resting-place, where they had been devouring the refuse of my previous night's dinner. This species differs in a well-marked degree from the red species of the hills, which was likewise seen on the Peer Pinjal. The silver fox, as we shall see, is also a native of Ladakh and Tibet, where it is said to be common.

To return to the original narrative. On the 21st of May we left Shupeyon during a very heavy fall of rain. I fear, with all the veneration one entertains for the unparalleled grandeur and beauty of Cashmere, there is no escaping the fact that for rain few countries surpass it. About the beginning of May the monsoon clouds collect on the tops of the Pinjal, and continue depositing their contents for the three succeeding months. I could not ascertain an approximation to the annual amount, which, however, must be great. It often rains for weeks continuously; the valley becoming overwhelmed in cloudy vapour, and producing a moist and relaxing climate which is anything but comfortable. At that season agues and bowel-complaints are common; and yet a few days' march northwards, and you enter on the rainless country of Ladakh. So abrupt is the division between the two regions, that while the southern slopes of a mountain may be covered with luxuriant vegetation and clouds, the northern portion is bare, barren, and sunburnt. The S.W. monsoon becomes expended by the time it has emptied its contents on the northern Pinjal,* which

* "There they drop more of their moisture in the shape of snow and rain, and then pass over into the thirsty lands beyond, with scarcely enough

also accounts for the verdure of these ranges compared with the more northern chains of Ladakh and Tibet.

Although it was the 21st of May, and summer may be said to have set in, we had felt few winds more cold and cutting than that which blew on us from the Bimber Pass as we wound our way through ploughed fields, and waded over roads almost knee-deep from the incessant rains. We spent the night at the village of Mohunpora, and pitched the tents under its trees, among the foliage of which were myriads of chirping sparrows and mina birds, now busily intent building their nests in the clefts and holes of the fine old walnuts and chunars.

The breeding-season is much later in the valley of Cashmere than in the Punjaub. Birds begin to pair and build about the middle of March in the plains, whilst it is May before they commence at the altitudes of from 5000 to 7000 or 8000 feet. There is nowhere in the world where sparrows are more plentiful than in the valley; there they assemble in countless thousands in the chunar groves around the villages, and keep up a chorus of discordant sounds quite deafening to unaccustomed ears. The govind kite builds its nest of sticks, pieces of rags, etc., and always seems to prefer the highest tree around the village, where it soon renders itself notorious for depredations on eggs and young poultry. The carrion crow seeks the alpine localities to rear its young. There appears a great sameness in the ornithology of the valley compared with the forests and higher altitudes around; but that is compensated by their exceeding number. The house-sparrow, red-backed shrike, Sardinian starling, European jackdaw, and ring-dove (*Turtur humilis*), are the most com-

vapour in them to make even a cloud."—Maury's *Physical Geography of the Sea.*

mon species. Every grove has its song-thrush (*Turdus unicolor*). The chimney-swallow and hoopoe are seen at almost every turn. The hoopoe is more frequently seen on trees than on the ground. The swallow differs in no respect from the English bird, and it is noteable that I did not observe any with the deep rufous on the belly which characterises the Egyptian variety called *Hirundo rustica orientalis*. The gray titmouse, like the greater tit of the north, is seen climbing along the eaves of straw-roofed houses or suspended from the points of twigs. The yellow lark-toed wagtail is common on damp and marshy places; its habits are similar to the true Motacillæ, but its flight is not so powerful: it perches securely on the tufty tops of the reeds and grass by means of its long hind-claw. On our way we gathered a species of yellow rose growing by the road-sides, and observed again the two irises in abundance. Although the weather continued rainy, we determined on pushing across the northern Pinjal into the Wurdwun valley in quest of brown bears and ibex. The former were said to be so numerous that one European killed no less than thirty in the course of a few weeks. Accordingly we repaired with all possible speed to Islamabad, and set to work to reduce our camp to the smallest possible dimensions, as from reports it seemed that a fresh fall of snow on the pass would render it necessary to march as light as possible.

The fine grassy plain around the city has a peculiar English appearance, especially when its lawns are covered with herds of cattle. On the Veshau river, creels are placed in the rapids for the purpose of catching carp. I killed a specimen of the brown water-dipper; its European congener, however, does not seem to love the little mountain streams of the surrounding ranges. The red poppy was blooming in great abundance in fields. The poor and rich as usual crowded round my tent, many of the latter suffering from diseases quite remediable, but time would not allow, and my stock of medicine was already reduced to a few simples. It is sad to see so much misery and wretchedness in a land second to none in its natural capabilities; but it is of no use that the husbandman toils to make provision for the future; as scon as fortune is seen to smile on him, the hand of the extortioner seizes his little gains, and thus he is driven to rear only sufficient for his immediate wants. We soon learned when the tax-gatherer was going his rounds by the heaps of grain in the villages, and the groans of discontent to be heard issuing from the houses.

The strange-looking goat-antelope (*Capricornis bubalina*), known by the name "ramoo" in Cashmere, and "serou" in other districts of the western Himalaya, is perhaps the rarest of the wild ruminants. Occasionally the sportsman comes across an individual in the depths of the alpine forests, but the animal is very solitary in its habits, and seldom more than a couple are seen together. Both in figure and movements the serou is perhaps one of the most ungainly of its tribe, and so stupid is it that when come on unawares it will stand and gaze at the intruder: even the report of a rifle seldom scares it. It is fond of rocky ledges covered with pine and forest trees in secluded mountain valleys; here one may reside for years, going or returning to its feeding-grounds by the same path, which is marked like that of the musk-deer by heaps of dung. The serou has the legs of a goat, the horns of an "antelope:" its general appearance is bovine; whilst the long stiff bristles on its back, and general shape of the head, are decidedly porcine;—a sort of nondescript beast, which European sportsmen often call a "very extraordinary-looking animal," and so it is. The horns, which are present in both sexes, vary from 10 to 15 inches, and from 3 to 4 inches in their greatest circumference; they are annulated at the base, and taper backwards to sharp points. The hide is very thick, and almost ball-proof, especially at long ranges. The hair on the neck and back is long, stiff, and straight, and the general colour black, with bright rufous splashes on the sides of the body, inclining to white below. The serou is said to fight desperately; it has been known, when wounded or brought to bay, to have kept off a pack of wild dogs, and killed several by its sharp-pointed horns. A few are met with on the Cashmere ranges, and in favourable situations eastward to Nepal. On the abrupt sides of the kirawas, or ancient lacustrine deposits in the valley, the beautiful wall-creeper may be frequently seen. Its gray plumage and the bright crimson patches on the wing serve to recognise it at once; it is more plentiful, however, by the sides of streams, and in the more rocky and precipitous places towards the mountains. The gray-capped bunting is common in bushy places. Beside the roller, the gray-headed Indian jackdaw is occasionally seen about the larger towns, but it is nowhere common. A snake is often observed hunting after frogs in damp situations; the largest I have seen measured 5½ feet in length. This species is evidently the same as Mr. Vigne mentions in his Travels; it is known to the natives by the name of ajda, and it is a true python, and not the boa constrictor, as some travellers have named it, which it is needless to remark is not a native of Asia. A small adder like the common British viper infests the mountain pastures, and was very often observed coiled on footpaths; the shickarees allege that it is very venomous. A small water-snake, about a foot in length, is common on the Wulur and other lakes.

We left Islamabad on the 22d of May by way of Martund

and Changos, firmly resolved, in spite of very discouraging reports of the state of the pass, to push our way across into the Wurdwun valley. We had sent a shickaree who knew the country to reconnoitre; but he always returned with most dismal accounts of continued falls of snow on the ranges northward. After leaving Changos the road winds up a densely-wooded valley, running eastward to the village of Nabug-ney, which is situated about five miles up the valley, and composed of a few log-houses. Again we found ourselves retrograding into spring; the foliage was just out on the walnut-trees, and the cuckoo's chant was heard all over the strath. I amused myself in the afternoon watching the golden-crested wren (*Regulus cristatus*) and crested black tit, hunting among the pine-branches, whilst numbers of flammeous flycatchers were seen sporting overhead; but only for a few minutes, for they are restless little creatures, and never remain long in any situation. On the following day the journey was continued during a constant downpour of rain and sleet. The route lay up a densely-wooded valley. It was no use attempting to weather the storm, so after several hours' exposure we sought shelter in a log-house, and waited until afternoon, and then pushed on through the forest, up a gradual ascent, to a log-hut near the foot of the pass, generally used as a halting-place for travellers on their way to and from Wurdwun. A white-cheeked marten and silver fox were seen that day, and the deathlike stillness of the forest was now and then broken by the loud plaintive call of the black and yellow grosbeak (*Coccothraustes icterioides*). At dusk several woodcocks were seen crossing the clearing in the forest. We lighted a fire, and sat for hours anxiously looking for the baggage, which, however, did not arrive until near midnight. Dismal and cheerless was our condition; wet through, without food all day, and fagged by a long and fatiguing march, the alpine solitude only broken by the loud howling of the wind overhead, and the creaking of branches ; nor were our prospects promising, for after vain attempts to render the little shed waterproof, another downpour at 10 P.M. left us no alternative but to place our beds under the dripping roof, and resign ourselves to a hydropathic course of treatment for the remainder of the night.

The morning of the 27th of May was ushered in with drizzling showers and a cold and cutting wind, which blew with great force down the clearing in the forest. The thermometer was 36°. We, however, continued ascending, and soon found the pine gradually diminishing in size, and being replaced by stunted birch-trees and juniper. Great beds of snow were seen stretching across the summit of the pass, which was covered with a fresh coating. As we toiled up the steep ascent, wading to the knees, at times sinking to the arm-pits in old beds, snow began to fall; first in occasional showers, and by the time we gained the top of the pass a regular storm set in, so as to obscure objects within a few yards. The worst, however, had to come. Our way led through a large valley surrounded with steep ridges, and across mountain-sides, where the guide had to trust entirely to chance, the footpaths being all obliterated. Accordingly we formed in line, treading in each other's steps, Halkett, Young, and myself leading, with the coolies and servants in the rear. It was an anxious march, for as we advanced the snowstorm increased, until our bewildered guide reported that he had lost all landmarks, and that we must trust to Providence. On we scrambled through the snow, until suddenly the storm ceased, and we looked around on a boundless waste of white, dotted here and there in the long distance by our servants toiling through the wreaths and drifts. The old shickaree Abel Khan, who had often crossed the pass, assured us he had never before attempted the passage under such desperate circumstances. Hill-tops and undulating ridges stretched far and wide, running either in continuous slopes, into yawning gulfs, or spreading out into long valleys. As he stood on the declivity of a spur, which ended abruptly at the brink of a precipice, the guide drew our attention to the marks of a recent struggle among the snow on its brink, as if some large object had slipped over into the abyss. His accustomed eye knew the signs too well, and, shaking his head, he informed us that one of the party that preceded us a few days before must have fallen over the precipice; and his words proved true, for on our arrival at Unshun we found that a coolie had missed his footing and slipped over the precipice. In vain did the boldest and most expert of his party attempt to reach the unfortunate man. The most vigorous efforts failed from the steepness of the mountains and the great quantities of snow. At length, from a neighbouring cliff, the unfortunate man could be seen on the pinnacle of rock writhing in agony, and vultures hovering around him; but no mortal efforts were of any avail, and he was left to his fate. When the weather moderated, and the snow had partially melted, another party attempted the ascent some weeks afterwards, but were equally unsuccessful; neither from the cliff could they discern any traces of the poor man, not even a vulture hovered near. None of our party forgot the halt on that ridge, by the side of the gnarled old birch-tree. Here we held a council whether to push on or return; the guide seemed indifferent; so we decided to proceed, and once more pushed forward; now creeping cautiously along a rocky ridge, then running as fast as the deepness of the snow would allow, until we arrived at the confines of the forest after seven hours' constant toil. And glad we were to ease our aching eyes and limbs under the large boulder which had evidently served as a temporary rest for many a weary traveller. The rest of the descent was tolerably easy, until, debouching from the forest, we arrived at the banks of the Scinde river, and, looking up, saw the log huts of Unshun, a few hundred feet above us. There we found Bray and Captain Macandrew. The former had just returned from a search after bears, and was driven back by an attack of ague, from which he had been suffering in the plains, and which, strange to say, continued to molest him among the snow and cold of these arctic regions. We had scarcely finished the grateful repast prepared for us by our friends, when a sudden burst of wailing outside drew us away to witness a poor family plunged into grief on account of one of their number having been killed by a fall whilst felling trees in the mountains. We now saw our mistake in having crossed the pass at such a time of the year, and in face of the remonstrances of the natives; nor were our troubles over; for we now felt uneasy about our servants, the half of whom were still among the snow. At length the lost coolie made his appearance, bringing the intelligence that our tent had been abandoned in the middle of the pass. The night was bitterly cold, and Young and myself slept in a thin canvas tent belonging to our friends, on which the frost in the following morning lay thick and crisp, when we were aroused by the groans and sobs of the poor labourer's family next door. We started early in quest of bears, of which my companions killed two. Captain Macandrew brought me a specimen of the water-pheasant (*Parra sinensis*), which he shot on the river near the head of the valley. Wurdwun is divided into the upper and lower valley. The former is about eight miles long and scarcely a mile in breadth. The mountains on either side are of great height, and very steep in certain places. The flanking ridges run south-east, and narrow the valley a little way below Unshun, where the sides become more wooded, and the Scinde river, from its various tributaries, swells into a magnificent mountain torrent, which empties itself finally into the Chenaub a little north of the Kishtewar. I do not think I have seen the deodar cedar attain a greater size than in Lower Wurdwun, where numbers are felled and floated down the Chenaub to India. I visited this district in 1854, two years after the events I am now recording, and spent several weeks among its wild alpine valleys, where I killed two ibexes and upwards of twenty brown bears. The Wurdwun river (called also Scinde) rises in a magnificent glacier at the top of the Suru valley. There are, besides, several smaller glaciers in various parts of the Wurdwun at Sochness. Between Unshun and Pambur there are snow-beds that may be said to be persistent, with moraines of various dimensions. I was led to suppose that the boulders and collections of rock in the valley around Pambur were the remnants of ancient glacial accumulations, as there is now no appearance of anything of the kind in these situations. The result of two measurements made the village of Unshun about 9000 feet above the level of the sea, or nearly 4000 above Serinuggur : this is perhaps nearly correct.

The poor villagers expressed great fears that, between our requirements and those of our other friends and their followers, we would eat them out of house and hold, their supplies being never more than sufficient for their own wants ; besides, from the lateness of the season, their cattle and sheep were now starving, and numerous carcases lay about in the villages to be devoured by bears, dogs, and carrion-crows. The farmers assured us that the grass was above ground usually on the 20th of May. Poor wretched creatures, every one looked the very image of misery; and whenever we entered into conversation with them, it was to hear the same old tale of woe and a dread of the future. Such apathy and cold mistrust of everything connected with their government and ruler were surely never seen in any race. It was painful to look on all the wretchedness around us, which, of course, the unseasonable weather aggravated. Most assuredly here was the saying true, that "winter lingering chills the lap of May."

The season was indeed late, for few bears had yet left their caves among the ice and snow. A few herds of ibexes, driven by the severity of the late storm, had been seen lower down, and several bara-singa frequented the pine-forests about. At last a thaw for three days melted nearly all the snow of the late storm, so that we were enabled to ascend some distance, and the bears were every day becoming more numerous. On the 1st of June, while searching along the side of a steep spur, I came unexpectedly on two of the largest he-bears I had ever seen; they were within a few yards of me, feeding on the tender shoots of wild rhubarb. I fired at both, but they escaped. Another was seen feeding undisturbed about 700 yards to leeward, when suddenly the animal appeared to become restless, snuffing the air in various directions, until turning towards us, he continued moving his head from side to side, then suddenly scampered off to his cave among the inaccessible rocks. I have over and over again proved the want of acuteness of the sense of sight in these animals by following up the wind until within a few yards of a bear. Their sight is not strong, and they cannot observe objects very clearly at a hundred feet.

Young informed me that a bear killed by him on the top of a ridge rolled down some hundred feet, and was immediately surrounded by lammergeyers, vultures, and carrion-crows, all of which settled on the carcase, and commenced devouring it before his party could descend. At the beginning of the season the skins are covered with long thick hair and much woolly pileage, so that a rapacious bird can scarcely injure it except on the belly and head. Subsequently we seldom left our quarry many minutes before crows or vultures were seen circling aloft. The gyratory movement of flight, restricted to one spot, is always a signal to the others that something is near at hand. In the woods and among the decayed ferns we were constantly annoyed by a small tick, which almost buries itself in the skin and occasions great irritation.

Enormous avalanches were often seen dashing down the mountains, and carrying with them large masses of rock, uprooting trees, and pushing their way more than half-across the valley, causing thundering noises in the valleys and offshoots around. My shickaree took me to a shelf of rock to view the scene where Dr. Wray, of the 87th Regiment, was killed during the previous year. It was a narrow glen, running northwards, and surrounded by steep rugged precipices: a large bed of fallen snow covered the sides, and rose up gradually at the upper end to the peaks of the highest mountains. It had evidently slipped a few weeks before our arrival, and occupied the same position as that which entombed Dr. Wray. The officer and party above mentioned crossed into Wurdwun in April, when avalanches are most frequent. It seems they were watching the movements of a herd of ibexes from the stony bed of the stream in the bottom of the valley, when the constant rumbling noise of falling masses of snow continued to increase, and on looking up the gorge a vast avalanche was seen bounding down towards them. Bewildered by the rapidity with which the huge mountain of snow seemed advancing, they ran from one side to another; but long before they could gain a place of safety, six of the party were buried in the avalanche. The remainder, stationed a little higher on the ridge, pushed upwards, and just escaped. The bodies were found six weeks afterwards, and close to that of one of the shickarees was a large ibex, which had been overwhelmed at the same time. When I revisited this glen in 1854, upon the same wild rocky precipices I observed a herd of from forty to fifty ibexes, the greater part feeding on a grassy slope low down, but on such an exposed position that I could not obtain a nearer approach than 200 yards. Although I missed a fine old male, the loss was compensated by the scene which followed, for scarcely had the echo of my rifle died away before every pinnacle and jutting prominence among the beetling cliffs overhead was alive with ibexes gazing down in wonder. One noble old patriarch, with great curving horns, stood on the uppermost and most projecting point. He was evidently the leader of the herd, for on satisfying himself of the danger, his loud whistle resounded through the glen, and as if by magic the multitude disappeared among the shattered rocks.

On the same occasion I proceeded to Assun, a wild secluded forest-glen northwards of Pambur. As there were no hamlets within many miles, it became necessary to reduce our establishment to the shickaree, two coolies, and a small tent, which we pitched in the depth of a pine-wood at the upper end of the valley, and close to a grass-clad slope running towards some very rugged and precipitous cliffs, where herds of ibexes had been reputed to be residing. During the first night I was awoke by loud wailing cries in our immediate vicinity, and securing the rifle rushed out, when by the moonlight there appeared a large animal fluttering among the pine-tops above the tent. On discharging a barrel, a large flying squirrel dropped dead at my feet. It turned out to be the chestnut species (*Pteromys magnificus*), which the shickaree said was common in the district. Its fur was very soft, and of a deep chestnut colour above, with lower parts of a lighter hue, and the tail tipped with black. The specimen, a female, measured 16½ inches from head to tail; the latter was 20 inches in length. This flying squirrel is nocturnal in habits, secreting itself in hollows of decayed trees, and feeds on the tender shoots of the pine. Two were said to be the number of young born at one litter. In order to gain time, we took up a position on the following night on a cliff under beetling crags, to await the ibexes at daybreak, when they descended to feed on the grassy slope. As we lay rolled up in our rugs, about midnight a rush of earth and gravel awoke us, and we could hear the pattering of feet immediately above. This continued throughout the remainder of the night, and when the first dawn of day appeared, we silently reconnoitred and found an ibex and her kid lying in a hollow immediately above our resting-place. As we expected a herd, it was decided that the disturbers of our night's repose should be allowed to decamp; but our sudden appearance so electrified the old goat, that she gazed at us for a few seconds, and even permitted the shickaree to advance within a few yards before she sprang across a fissure and clambered with her kid up the face of an almost perpendicular scarp. We were cautiously picking our footsteps with alpenstock across the dangerous rents and slippery pinnacles, peering down into yawning gulfs and projecting shelves below us, when suddenly Elli Shah's eagle eye caught sight of a herd of ibexes emerging in single file from a narrow chasm underneath, led on by two fine males, one of which was standing on a spiral-topped rock, with his four feet close together in an attitude of observation. Then the shickaree, seizing a handful of dried mat-grass, tossed it up in the air to ascertain how the wind blew, and removing his turban, replaced it by a skull-cap with the gravity of a judge about to deliver sentence, and gathering up his loins and taking the spare rifle, led the way down a hollow, until, peeping cautiously over the edge of the cliff, he suddenly turned towards me crouching behind him, and with a nod and grin of satisfaction, and beaming countenance, as much as to say "We have them now," retired that I might take his place. Resting the heavy Westley Richards on the ledge, and raising the 200-yard sight, I covered the fore shoulder of a fine male. Thud went the bullet on his side and up sprang the herd ; one female strode out on a projecting rock, and whilst gazing downwards, the contents of the second barrel pierced her heart, and she sprang into mid-air and fell bumping from rock to rock down into the yawning abyss below. The male, desperately wounded, was seen following the herd, which in a few minutes disappeared among the peaks above, whilst we in wild excitement set off in hot pursuit of the former, which was discovered in a dying state, and despatched immediately. The disagreeable odour is common to the wild and tame goats, and is invariably strongest in the males. The flesh is dry and tough, without any remarkable savoury taste, unless that of young individuals. On our way down the mountain, I observed a flock of rose finches of a larger, different, and more brilliantly-coloured species than any I had before noted. Like the mountain-finches, they were feeding round the margin of the melting snow, which appears to be a favourite resort. possibly for the purpose of obtaining the tender shoots and opening buds of plants. The forest around resounded the crowing of plach pheasants, and as we neared the tent I came suddenly on a huge brown bear intently feeding on a clearing. Although his head was directed towards me, he did not seem to notice us until we were within a few yards, and it was too late to make his escape. This individual, although not equal in dimensions to the largest killed by Halkett during my previous excursion, was seemingly one of the oldest isabella bears I had seen. The canine teeth had either been broken off or ground down with the molars to the level of the gums, and one or two of the latter were wanting in the upper jaw. The fur was a dark-brown with isabella-coloured tips, showing that the white varieties are not the result of age. The claws were unusually long, possibly from want of use, and perhaps the eyesight was also impaired from age. I noticed that in one reared by Young the eyes became affected with an ophthalmia which occasioned dimness of vision; and as the disease is known to attack tamed individuals, it may also be the case that the wild animal is occasionally similarly affected. The above evidently had taken up his abode in the glen for some time, for on the following day we traced his foot-marks like steps of stairs up the face of the sward to the cliffs where his den was situated. No doubt he had continued for years pursuing the even tenor of his way to the little stream below and grassy slopes, seldom roaming beyond a short distance from cover, where in all probability these patriarchs end their days, and, like the *Ursus spelœus* of old, enveloped in earthy and calcareous deposits, and thus preserve their remains for unreckoned ages. I well remember, when on our way from Wurdwun to Pambur, halting one day on the banks of the

Scinde in the middle of a vast forest-tract, and when my servants and shickaree were employed in stretching bear-skins, I took a rifle and entered the forest in quest of musk-deer. After penetrating the wilderness for some distance, it suddenly occurred to me that I had forgot the pocket-compass, and must now trust to chance in finding my way out. After hours spent in vain attempts to discover the river, night came on, and there seemed nothing for it but to wait patiently until morning. The eternal stillness, not even the murmur of the pine-tops broke the solitude; in vain I listened for the noise of the river and longed for morning; when by the first dawn of day I was off on my anxious journey—now rushing down slopes and making my way down hollows, expecting to strike the river at every turn; but all was in vain. Horrible feelings of going directly away from the river haunted me, and the cravings of hunger began to be urgent. At length, descending a densely-wooded slope of deodar, and gaining a valley and stream, which after following for upwards of an hour, I came suddenly on the Scinde, and discovered that I had struck the river five miles below my tent. When I reached my companions I was perfectly worn out from the exertion, fatigue, and anxiety; for, except a crust of bread and a few pieces of the flesh of a musk-deer I killed in the early morn, no food had passed my lips for upwards of thirty-two hours.

The ibex (*Capra himalayana*) frequents many of the lofty ranges of the western chains, and is known to the natives by the names "skeen" and "kail," which they apply indiscriminately in the districts of Aserung, Spiti, Kenowaur, the Northern Cashmere mountains, Ladakh, Chinese Tartary, and the Altai. It is not clear that the European ibex is a distinct species. There appears to be a variety in Ladakh (and specimens of the Siberian ibex I have examined possess the same peculiarity) with shorter horns than the Himalayan. I am unable, however, to make out any further distinction. The average length of a full-grown Cashmere ibex's horns varies from 28 to 40 inches round the curve; they sometimes, however, attain a much larger size. A pair found in an avalanche measured 48½ inches round the curve of each horn. Those of the female seldom exceed a foot and a half. Like the markhore, the horns of the ibex vary much both in curvature and dimensions. They generally taper to a point, and proceed upwards and backwards, with sometimes the tips directed downwards, almost touching the animal's back; others diverge a good deal, and end abruptly, as in many European specimens. The age of the male may be generally ascertained by counting the fissures on the flat sides of the horns, and not the knobs in front, as some have supposed. The female gestates nine months, and has sometimes two kids, although one is the usual number. It is seldom that the rigors of even the severest winter drive the ibex into the lowland valleys. When forced from their accustomed haunts they seek the stunted pines at the limits of forests, and roam about in sheltered rocky situations, picking up moss, lichens, or nibbling the bark of trees. The shickarees say they are partial to clayey soils, which they lick, perhaps on account of the salts of soda, sodium, borax, etc., to which I have observed the bara-singa seem very partial. Their favourite food is a nardus, which grows in tufts at high elevations, and affords one of the means by which the adventurous hunter is enabled to preserve his footing on the dangerous and difficult situations frequented by these animals. During winter the ibex is thickly clad with hair and woolly pileage. The latter is finer than that of even the Ladakh goats, which afford the material for the shawls of Cashmere.

At the above season the ibex has a piebald appearance, from the light colour of the under-wool and hair of the outer coat, which, however, soon disappears as summer advances, and they begin to shed the woolly pile, when the colour changes to a uniform brown, with a dark line down the middle of the back. At that season they are rarely seen, and only met with on the summits of the craggy mountains. My own experience, and that of native sportsmen, show that the ibex has little sense of smell, and depends most on its sight and hearing. The iris is hazel, eye moderate and prominent, and so keen-sighted that I believe there is no quadruped excels it in that respect. The hunter soon becomes fully aware of this, and has to reconnoitre with the greatest tact before he manages to get within rifle-shot, but unless he is enabled to approach the herd from above, it is next to impossible to succeed by stalking from below upwards, as they always anticipate danger in that direction, and never expect any intruders from the region above them.

The leopards, panthers, wild-dog, and bearded vulture, are the common enemies of the ibex ; the latter preys on the kids only.

On the 1st of June I ascended a gorge running through the southern chain—one of the wildest-looking glens to be seen anywhere : its sides were formed by steep mountains, the tops covered with snow, and enormous drifts stretched down the hollows to the bottom, where they lay from 50 to 100 feet thick in many places. The northern exposure was dotted here and there with belts of pine-forest, where the snow still lay thick and hard, whilst on the opposite side the bare patches were beginning to look green, and the wild rhubarb was springing up. I had not proceeded far before two bears were seen nibbling a scanty fare on a hillside clearing. I killed one outright, but the other, although desperately wounded, was on the point of making his escape, when by good fortune I managed to hit him again on a more fatal spot, when he rolled down the mountain-side, bounding from bank to bank with great violence, now rebounding into the air a huge revolving brown mass of hair, then tumbling and tossing over rocks, and down the evener parts, until brought to a stand-still on the firm bed of snow at the bottom, some 700 feet below me. The steepness of the mountains of that glen surpassed any I had ever mounted. Our grass-shoes even were useless, and we were often obliged to make our way by digging steps across the declivities. The shickaree declared that he had seldom ventured on such dangerous places as were passed on that occasion, and I must say, although gifted with what is called "a good head," I often felt I could not afford to look below me when crossing the fearful chasms. The wild cry of the chough was often heard, and flocks were seen feeding by the sides of the melting snow; there were also numbers of the brown snow-finch flitting from one clearing to another, emitting their linnet-like chirp as the flock turned and twisted like snow-flakes in a stubble field. On the following day I revisited the glen, and after several fruitless attempts to circumvent a herd of ibexes among the inaccessible cliffs high up, we descended to the bare slopes, and killed three bears, one of which rolled down many hundred feet, but, strange to say, not a bone was broken in any of them, not even the skin injured. The shickaree killed a fine male ibex. Young had also been fortunate, for on my arrival at the tent I found him stretching the skins of four fine bears. In stalking these animals, especially in narrow gorges, the sportsman must be constantly on the out-look for sudden changes in currents of air; every gully may vary the direction, and often whilst the wind is blowing up the main opening, other currents are pursuing an opposite course down the fissures from the snow above. We found only the backbones of the bears I had killed on the previous day, and at dusk as I turned the last winding of the glen, I could see the vultures and crows intently tearing the carcases of those I killed in the forenoon. Seldom a day passed we did not observe flocks of the snow or imperial rock-pigeon (*Columba leuconota*) either feeding in the fields with the common rock-pigeon (*Columba livia*), or among the rocky parts, where it roosts and breeds. The resemblance of this species to varieties of the domestic race is striking, but I have not seen any decided variety of the snow-pigeon, which is about the size of the other, perhaps a little larger: the iris is yellow, forehead and part of neck soot-black, back of the neck, shoulders, and lesser wing coverts brownish-ash; back and part of rump soot-black; the tail moderate, and barred with white; lower parts white; legs red, and claws black.

At the village of Hafit we boiled the thermometer, and found after two trials, according to our rough mode of calculating, that the height might be about 9600. At the hamlet of Sochness, still higher up, it boiled at 194° Fahr., which made a difference of about 40° feet between the two; and as the altitude of the two places appeared so to the eye. the error may not have been very great. During the previous week the greater part of the snow on the sides of the valley had melted, the grass was springing up everywhere, and bears were plentiful, but circumstances compelled me to return to India, so I had no other alternative than to make the best of my way back. Halkett, tired of the wretchedness and discomfort of Wurdwun, made up his mind to accompany me as far as Serinuggur and wait our other friend, when they intended to proceed to Ladakh and Tibet. Young was enthusiastic enough to remain another fortnight in hopes of procuring a good ibex head, and I must say, had not necessity compelled me to beat a retreat, in spite of the dismal prospect and want of proper food (the latter a serious matter to the hard-working hunter), I would have willingly braved all the difficulties and dangers with my friend. Our bag for the previous excursion, and to the breaking-up of our party, amounted to twenty-five bears, eight deer, and three musk-deer, each contributing about an equal share

The brown or isabella bear of the Himalayas, if not a variety of, is certainly very closely allied to that of Europe, northern Asia, and arctic America. The geographical distribution of these animals has not been fixed with any certainty. In Asia we find the bear of Siberia and the Altai called the brown bear (*U. arctos*), whilst our species is said to frequent the Himalayas only. There are evidently no very clear ideas on these points, and considering the facilities for observing their habits and haunts, it is to be greatly wondered at, more especially as we find Dr. Horsfield named the Himalayan bear *Ursus isabellinus*, from a single skin brought from Nepal; but I shall presently show that the colour varies so much in specimens that seldom two are exactly alike. The distribution of this brown bear on the Himalayas is not so general as that of the black species (*Helarctos tibetanus*), which is spread over the whole extent of the lesser ranges of the Indian Himalaya, whereas the brown bear is confined to districts, and prefers high and rugged mountains near the confines of perpetual snow, and nowhere is its fancy better gratified than among the noble chains which surround Cashmere, especially the secluded glens, such as the Wurdwun valley and its offshoots: there bears were at one time very abundant, but every year shows a marked diminution in their numbers, so that, before long, we may expect to hear of the almost complete extermination of the species in the Cashmere ranges. The brown bear repairs during winter to caves in inaccessible rocks, where, forming a bed of decayed plants (usually ferns), it lies coiled up until spring; when, as soon as the snow melts and vegetation appears, it stalks forth, lean, and frequently so hungry and voracious, that it has been seen to attack tame sheep, goats, and even to attempt to kill ponies; but in point of choice it prefers vegetable to animal food. Young killed one feeding on the carcase of a Cashmere deer, which it had evidently surprised and killed when bringing forth young, as a new-dropped calf lay close by. During spring, and for some time after their first appearance, they seldom roam far from their winter abodes, and continue nibbling the tender shoots of rhubarb and such like. At that season they are fond of basking in the sun on beds of snow. The roots of the wild strawberry and a small white carrot, common in shady places, are much sought after by them. The soil in many places is ploughed up by their paws, and, like the wild boar, they dig also with their snouts. As summer advances they become very fat, and by the end of October, after feeding on wild apples, walnuts, and other fruits, greatly increase in size. It is of course then that their fat is of most value; but although we preserved a great deal, I never could remove the rancid smell which sticks to the melted fat, even after otto of roses had been added. The fat on the back and on outer parts is preferred to that of the interior of the body, having less of the offensive train-oil-like smell. This bear is seldom seen on trees, and only frequents the woods and jungles during the fruit season. The fur in winter and spring is long, thick, and shaggy, but becomes scantier and darker in colour as the season advances, so that towards autumn the under-fur disappears, and the white collar,* scarcely perceptible before, becomes now very distinct, whilst the general colour of the whole coat is much darker. These changes have evidently been the causes of many of the so-called varieties of Himalayan bears mentioned by travellers, such as the white bear, the brown bear, and the white and brown; this latter appearance is mostly observed during midsummer, when the animal is shedding its winter fur, which hangs then in matted masses on its sides. I observed, as a general rule, that the bears, on their first appearance in spring, were much lighter in colour than in autumn, and occasionally an almost white variety was not uncommon. Many old males were very dark brown, but the colour is no certain sexual distinction, as Mr. Vigne imagined, neither does it determine age. Seldom more than one or two cubs are born at one litter. The she-bear generally appears with her young in spring, and from the size of the cubs, possibly their birth takes place either during hibernation or immediately afterwards. When caught young they are easily domesticated, and become harmless and playful, but always rough and overbearing; indeed the old bears are far from ferocious, and will seldom attack their pursuers unless severely wounded and brought to bay. The eyesight is by no means good, and were it not for the extraordinary acuteness of smell, there are few animals more stupid and less alert than the brown bear of the Himalayas.

The black bear (*Helarctos tibetanus*) is not found in the Wurdwun, or at such high elevations as the last. Its favourite haunts are in the woods and jungles of the lesser ranges, where

* This gave rise to Cuvier's *Ursus collaris*, from a specimen of the brown bear of Europe procured in autumn.

it lies all day, to issue forth at nightfall and feed in fields and gardens. The black bear is not uncommon along the foot of the barrier-chains of Cashmere, and during the fruit season may be found in the valley, where its depredations among the apple, walnut, and mulberry trees are well known, and whole crops of Indian corn are sometimes completely destroyed by these unwelcome intruders. Although said to attack sheep at times, this species is eminently a vegetable feeder, and so expert in climbing trees that it may frequently be seen on the topmost branches, standing erect, and seizing the branches with its fore-paws. The shickarees have often told me that as the brown bear does not climb, he waits until the other has mounted, and then feeds on the fruit driven down by the black bear. The Tibet bear does not hibernate, and usually spends the winter in forests and dense jungles, feeding on acorns and roots. It is not partial to localities, and is constantly changing its beat. Individuals of both species, when old, often select a cave in some rocky ridge near a good feeding-ground, and continue for years to make it their head-quarters, and from constantly treading in the same footprints form a regular flight of steps towards the retreat. The black bear is much bolder than the brown species, and has been known to attack man. I need not mention that the sloth bear (*Ursus labiatus*) of the plains of India is not found on the mountains.

On the 5th of June, accompanied by Halkett, I retraced my steps towards Serinuggur. Starting at an early hour, we arrived at the "great boulder" by 9 P.M., and after breakfasting, pushed upwards. The snow had disappeared, except on the summit of the pass, where it still lay hard and crisp. A few monal pheasants, scared at our approach, swept down the ravines in all their beauty, and roused the echoes around by their wild cries. A few flocks of snow-pheasants were feeding on the bare parts. A colony of red marmots frequented the hollow between the mountains, and from the numbers of their burrows, seemed to have occupied the locality for many years. The day was very hot, and had we not worn goggles, our eyes must have suffered. Several of the followers were attacked with severe inflammation of the eyelids, which became greatly swollen; but as soon as they had cleared the pass, and entered on the green valley of Nobug-Ney, the symptoms rapidly disappeared, and the following morning nearly all were fit to proceed with the party. The natives usually fix the leaves of the plane and other trees over their eyes in the form of a shade, which seems to answer very well, but they do not suffer to the extent of fresh arrivals. Our Indian servants were always the first to become affected and the last to get well. We cleared the pass by 5 P.M. and entered the forest, debouching into the fine open valley of Nobug-Ney. The advanced state of the vegetation during the interval struck us forcibly; scarcely a fortnight had elapsed since the trees around the village of Nobug were just budding, and now all were dressed in their summer attire, offering a cheering contrast to the bare boughs we had left that day on the hill-sides of Wurdwun. On the following morning we marched through a low range of hills; the day was warm, and the surrounding scenery of the most enchanting description. I filled my vasculum with many well-known plants; amongst others we gathered *Plantago major*, *Tussilago farfara* (?) (I only found the leaf), common nettle, lady's mantle, common brake, and Dutch clover; whilst scarlet and white dog-roses bloomed in all their beauty around us. The country was for the most part thickly clad with bush, alternating with more open tracts, being the usual description of scenery in the eastern portion of the valley of Cashmere. The mountain pipit (*Heterura sylvana*), so plentiful on the Dugshai hills, was common among the grassy slopes below Nobug. The more I observed the habits of this little bird the more I was persuaded of its affinities to the titlarks. The wire-tailed swallow, Indian roller, and paradise flycatcher were all common. We turned out of our way to visit the celebrated sacred spring of Sondi Breri, which at that season, and for some weeks later, is said to ebb and flow three times a-day, but after waiting for some time, and not witnessing the phenomenon, we started off in quest of birds. Bernier and Vigne are undoubtedly correct in attributing the above to the melting of snow on the heights, and to some peculiarity in the construction of the channel of communication between the well and the melting-points, as the appearance ceases towards the end of July, when the snow on the neighbouring ranges has entirely disappeared. The well is situated in the limestone, and is fully 7 or 8 feet in depth by about double that in breadth. No doubt the noble springs of Ver Nag, Koker Nag, Atsibul, in the neighbourhood, are owing in part to the melting snow passing down fissures. Whilst waiting for the waters of Sondi Breri to flow, I shot a pretty blue warbler in the thicket of bush which covers the country around. The species I subsequently discovered to be the blue larvivora (*Larvivora cyanea*); it is by no means uncommon in Cashmere, although I never before or subsequently met with it on the lesser ranges. A restless little creature, incessantly hunting after larvæ and insects, it is about the size of the chiff-chaff: the upper parts are blue; a white streak passes over the eye; the cheeks are blue-black; lower parts are bright rufous; vent white; legs pale-brown and slender.

From Islamabad we proceeded to Kannibal, on the right

bank of the Jhelum, where we embarked in boats and dropt slowly down the river. The day was fine, and the scenery of the loveliest description: the old rustic bridges at Kannibal and Pantur; the banks fringed with mulberry-trees, now loaded with their delicious fruit; the calm, still afternoon; the varying scene at every turn of the river, were all beautiful. We had a view of the old city on the way, but enjoyed a more favourable opportunity of examining its ruins during my subsequent visit to the valley. Although what remains is almost buried under a great mass of alluvium, portions of a temple and entrance-gate were traceable, besides fragments of walls laid bare by excavators. The great thickness of soil on the top of the city is scarcely to be accounted for by supposing it to be the accumulations of roof-tops. No doubt the severe earthquakes to which the valley has been subjected, even in historical times, have produced changes of level in many parts, as is attested by these monuments.

By 9 A.M. on the 8th of June our little craft glided quietly by the shady bank of the city gardens. From the various wooden houses peeped English faces, and when we jumped out opposite the Hurri-Sing-Ka-Bagh we could not help observing the great change which two months had produced. The Maharajah's agent informed us that forty Englishmen had arrived in Serinuggur, the greater number for sporting purposes.

Every day Goulab Singh had his troops drilled on a flat near the palace. The band was composed of divers uncouth-sounding horns and trumpets, and he would attempt on each occasion "God save the Queen," and what afterwards I found out was intended for "Bonaparte's March." The scene was simply ludicrous, but the wily prince fancied he was performing a great political duty before the English officers. I asked in vain

this book has been published by asian educational services, new delhi, 2012 for a specimen of the "Cashmere Madeira wine" mentioned by Foster, but only obtained a most execrable compound which even the natives themselves agreed was by no means well-flavoured. My companion, doubting likewise the opinion of that very intelligent traveller regarding the fecundity of the women, made repeated inquiries, and, I believe, even visited the fish-market to ascertain if the latter article entered so extensively into the dietry of the female sex in Cashmere as to give cause for Foster attributing their prolificness to eating fish in great quantities. The facts, however, were all in favour of a decided decrease in the productiveness of the fair sex, and that both the men and women of Cashmere had fallen off since 1783, when Foster wandered over the Happy Valley.

I started early with my friend, Captain Rattray, 2d Regiment Native Infantry, to visit the far-famed temple of Solomon,* which stands on the summit of a little hill to the east of the city. The chief object of Captain R.'s visit was to settle some points connected with a panoramic sketch of the valley at which he was then employed, for to a name already established as a landscape-painter, from his beautiful portfolio of Afghan scenery executed during the disastrous campaign in that country in 1841, he was at the time designing another series of sketches, chiefly of Cashmere scenery.

It appears strange, from the length of time Cashmere has been accessible to Europeans, especially by its proximity to India, that no painter of eminence has immortalised its magnificent grandeur and beauty; but it is the same everywhere on the Himalaya, as Humboldt truly remarks—"He who with a keen appreciation of the beauties

* Height 6263 feet above the level of the sea.

of nature, manifested in the mountains, rivers, and forest-glades, has himself travelled over the torrid zone, and seen the luxuriance and diversity of vegetation, not only on the cultivated sea-coasts, but on the declivities of the snow-covered Andes, the Himalaya or the Nilgherry mountains of Mysore, or in the primitive forests and the network of rivers lying between the Orinoco and the Amazon, can alone feel what an inexhaustible treasure remains still unopened by the landscape-painter between the tropics in both continents" (*Cosmos*).

We could scarcely have chosen a better morning for our excursion. The sun was gilding the snow-covered peaks of the northern Pinjal as we commenced the ascent, and by the time we had gained the temple, his rays, in one flood of golden light, had illuminated half the valley, leaving the southern portion and the slopes of the Peer Pinjal yet intact. Seldom does he shine on more varied and beautiful scenery, for in all my wanderings before and since I have never witnessed its equal. There lay the capital at our feet, half-hidden among clusters of poplars, chunars, and forest trees—the Dul lake, washing the western base of the Tukt-i-Salaman, stretched westward with all its ever-changing forms. On the placid waters of the lake numerous skiffs shot either rapidly along, or threaded their way through a labyrinth of weeds, diversified by the countless floating gardens, and the Isle of Chunars, with its noble plane-trees. The shalimar and pleasure-grounds of the Delhi emperors, now faded, and fast passing into the wild jungle around them, covered portions of the northern bank of the lake. Huri Purbet, like a fortress which had undergone a siege, its walls crumbling into decay, stood on the side of a spur overlooking a scene which for loveliness and grandeur has scarcely an equal. So perfect seemed both the natural and artificial portions of the panorama, so faintly blending with each other, and yet so grand, that the eye in one sweep passed over most perfect pictures of lake and mountain scenery. Towards the city stretched a noble avenue of poplars, upwards of a mile in length, and straight as arrows; whilst away towards the east rich pastures and fields teemed with grain; villages nestled in clusters of trees, which in rows were seen fringing the banks of the classical Hydaspes, that like a huge snake twisted through the plain. Then, last of the many beauties, rose those grand and noble mountains, encircling the whole panorama, and shielding the paradise from the northern blasts, whilst from their rugged sides dashed a thousand rills to fertilise and beautify its soil. On the palace parade-ground Goulab Singh's soldiers were at drill—a curious-looking, ill-dressed, and badly-accoutred mob. The loud discordant bray of their instruments grated harshly on our ears as they marched past in review order, before the chief. We thought, would the British soldier ever march past on that same plain? and what a happy day for Cashmere it would be when the old flag of England waved on the ramparts of Serinuggur! We paid a visit to the Isle of Chunars, and sat in Nourmahal's bower, now only traceable by a few hewn stones. In the fragment of a wall was the tablet erected by the travellers Vigne, Henderson, and Baron Hugel to commemorate their meeting in the valley some fifteen years previously. The inscription was much defaced; and when I revisited the island two years afterwards the entire slab had been removed, possibly thrown into the lake.

CHAPTER XII.

Return to Punjaub—River Scenery, and its Ornithology—Day Haze or Mist—Lakes of Cashmere—Visit to the Heir-Apparent—A Frightful Accident—Maury's Theory of Monsoons—Return to the Valley—Start for Ladakh—Scenery—Bultul Pass—Marmots—Tartars—Birds—Plants—Scenery—Buddhist Temples—Birds—Tibetan Magpie, its Allies—Redstarts—Familiar Birds—Discovery of a New Species of Mountain Finch—Lameru—Jolly Lama Priests—Wild Sheep—Natives—Leh—Birds—Yak, and Wild Quadrupeds of the Region—Tame Animals—Tang-Lang Pass—Plains of Rupshoo—Nomadic Life—Oppressive Sensations at High Elevations—The Dog of Tibet—Salt Lakes and Wild Fowl—Wild Ass—Burrel, or Wild Sheep—The *Ovis ammon*—Chaits—Tibetan Antelope—Sudden Variations of Temperature—Tibetan Sand Grouse—Tailless Rat or Lagomys—Alpine Hare—Tibet Ravine Deer—Hotch-Potch—Sulphur Mines—Chumouraree Lake—Wilderness—Birds—Tibet Partridge—Ibex.

On the 11th of June, with many regrets, I turned my steps towards Rawul Pindee, Halkett accompanying me as far as Baramula. The day was hot, but our boats were well thatched, and we sat under the chopper all day, admiring the scenery as we dropped down the river. The skeletons in their cages at the entrance to the city looked if anything more grim than before. The mid-day haze, so often observed on the plains of India, was very apparent on the surrounding mountains. In the Punjaub it makes its appearance about nine A.M. like a slight mist. I have seen the clearest of mornings become in an hour so hazy that objects then distinctly visible were shrouded in gloom by mid-day. By some authorities emanations from the soil are said to be the cause, whilst certain electrical changes are put down by others; but I am not aware that either afford a correct explanation of this somewhat singular phenomenon. From the lowness of the river's banks we were enabled to view the surrounding scenery to advantage. I strolled along the sides of the marshes, and killed a few castaneous ducks. This species and the mallard remain in the valley during the summer months, and breed, when geese and other water-fowl are rearing their young on the Tartarian lakes, from whence they return in November. We passed the pretty little village of Shadepoor on the left bank, and anchored close to Simbul, which is a little farther down; from thence paid a flying visit to the lake of Manasa Bul, one of the most beautiful tarns in Cashmere. On its banks were the remains of the once noble palace and gardens of the famous Nur Jehan. The clearness of the water, and the grandeur of the mountain scenery northwards, render this a most perfect little picture of Cashmere beauty. We pushed on the following morning towards Sopur, through the Wulur Lake, halting to take luncheon on its little island, where the remains of one of the ancient temples of the Martund description were observed. There was a monotonous stillness on the placid waters more calculated to weary than entertain; the immense sheet, not even ruffled by a breath of wind, and without one living object on its surface save the little water-snakes, about a foot in length. This active creature, with head a little elevated, propelled itself by twisting, and dived immediately we came near. The contrast is great between the unruffled smoothness and absence of birds during the summer months and the busy scene in November, when wild fowl crowd the lake. Then gusts, sudden gales, and hurricanes make the navigation much dreaded by the boatmen, who will seldom venture to cross unless the weather is fine, preferring to proceed by the Shadepoor Canal, which opens into the Jhelum near Sopur. The lotus and singara-nut grow in abundance around the shallow parts on its southern side, where rushes and reeds offer excellent retreats for rails and water-hens. On our arrival at Sopur, we paid a visit to the heir-apparent, Prince Rhunbeer, who was living in the dirty old fort on the river. He received us with all the *suaviter in modo* of an Oriental, and with apparent gravity talked of his being our humble, obedient servant, and that his father's country was ours, and we might just do what we chose with anything or any one in his dominions. He wanted the cunning, restless eye of his father, and for a youth of twenty-four he looked ten years older; he had a sallow, dissipated, but handsome countenance, which appeared to advantage in a helmet sort of head-dress, surrounded by a turban with a plume of heron's feathers. The nobles of the court all wore shields and swords, and the guard a nondescript uniform, with flint muskets. Our interview was of short duration, for the Prince tired us out with his fulsome compliments, which came forth with a drawling voice as if talking was a very trying effort to his Royal Highness. We were amused at his stating that he had often hunted ibex and bears, and could scarcely retain a courtly gravity when we conceived the Prince in the tights generally worn by the Sikh's nobles clambering up the bare rocks of Wurdwun. I subsequently discovered he did once "go a-shooting," and after an attempt to mount a hill, was finally borne up on the backs of his followers, and that he actually fired at a bear and missed it. This was the first and last of Rhunbeer Singh's hunting expeditions. After several extra compliments on both sides we withdrew, the guard at the door nearly knocking us down by their violent attempts to "turn out" and "present arms" to the "Sab-Logues." We entered our boat at the Sopur log-bridge at 2 P.M., and continued moving slowly down the stream, arriving at Baramula at dusk. The palms* mentioned by Bernier seem to have disappeared: not one was observed. Several dwarf species are common on the ranges near the plains of the Punjaub, but never to my particular inquiries was a palm-tree seen in the valley.

The want of loyalty on the part of the inhabitants of Baramula towards the young heir to the throne was very striking. With the exception of the soldiery, a great majority of the poorer classes fled into the mountains on the arrival of his Royal Highness. The reason, we were informed, was partly owing to the imperial decree of the previous year, by which several hundred coolies were pressed for the purpose of carrying the baggage of the ill-fated army that left more than half its numbers before Chulas, in the unsuccessful raid against the rajah of that country. This state visit was evidently made with the view of restoring public confidence, but the wretched inhabitants had been so often called on to give their services to the state on short notice and no pay, that they had little trust in any demonstrations of royal affection. I have seen Goulab Singh's palkee (litter) surrounded by numbers of petitioners, all eager to gain an audience, and begging most earnestly to be allowed to tell their grievances; indeed it was seldom he went abroad or made a tour through the provinces that he was not followed by a motley crowd of sufferers pressing forward to solicit a hearing for some alleged injustice on the part of himself or his dependants. I recollect a scene of this description immediately on the Maharajah landing at

* "When day had hid his sultry flame
Behind the palms of Baramoule."
Lalla Rookh.

Islamabad, when several respectable well-dressed zemindars were most unmercifully beaten by the sepoys of his guard for attempting to follow the royal palkee. The Prince's arrival at Baramula was celebrated by the usual marks of regal munificence. A feast was given to all the dirty fakirs within miles, when half-naked wretches, like as many carrion crows, usually at hand on such occasions, now flocked in from all quarters, and were seen seated around fires, gorging on rice and curry, whilst hundreds of the labouring classes were skulking dinnerless among the rocks in the vicinity. It was state policy, however, to propitiate the fakirs.

I now, to use a South African expression, began "to make tracks homewards." Accordingly after once more enjoying the magnificent scenery of the Baramula Pass, I was descending the pathway which debouches on the Uri plateau, when I came on a handsome native woman lying by the wayside, insensible, and bleeding from several wounds on the head and other parts of her body. Beside her was a small bundle of clothing, and her slippers, which were placed on the edge of a precipice some 200 feet above the Jhelum, whose waters were dashing furiously below us. I had scarcely time to look around before her husband, with an infant in his arms, came out of the bush, and informed us in the most indifferent manner that she had attempted suicide by leaping from the cliff, and that he had just carried her up from below, where he found her lying with her head half-immersed in water by the rocky side of the river. How she had not been dashed to pieces I could not understand. The bleeding vessels were stanched as well as the circumstances would allow, and we had her conveyed to the nearest hut, where I dressed her wounds and put up two fractures of the bones of the left arm. I was strongly apprehensive of some foul play, and after the poor woman had been placed on straw and made as comfortable as the hut would allow, I took her husband aside, and by the aid of a Sikh sepoy of my guard, interrogated him respecting the circumstances. The husband's story was that she had been in love with a soldier at Noushera, and in consequence he had reproved her, and was on the way to take up his residence at another village, when she preceded him and his child for the alleged purpose of preparing their dinner before their arrival at Uri, and that his attention was directed to the occurrence by the appearance of her bundle and slippers on the edge of the precipice. He told the story with such *sang froid*, and looked altogether so much the villain, that I had great misgivings as to his telling me the truth. My servants, after making further inquiries, were of the same opinion, and that he had pushed her over the cliff and placed the shoes and bundle in the above situation in order to make it appear that the act was her own doing. The poor woman recovered so far by the following morning as to be able to recognise her infant, but I had no time to wait, and when I passed Uri a week afterwards I heard that she died on the day after my departure. When the circumstances of the case were mentioned to the chief official at Uri Fort he shrugged his shoulders, and in true Indian pathos exclaimed, "What can I do, she was his wife?"—as much as to say that matrimonial differences of whatever description were beyond his jurisdiction. Pilgrims on their way to the caves of Umernath passed us in parties constantly, and a number of these nomads encamped under a mulberry-tree close to our bivouac at Uri. They informed us that they had been wandering all over India for the last four years, visiting sacred shrines, and had come direct from Ajmeer, in the centre of Hindostan, to pay their respects to their gods in the gypsum cave of Umernath. A few of their women were exceedingly beautiful; the slender forms, dark-brown faces, black eyes, and long flowing hair of the girls were very characteristic of Zingari descent. They spoke Hindostanee, but the conversation between themselves was carried on in a dialect said to be peculiar to the gipsies of India. At night they lay in a circle under a tree, where they spread mats, and placed their goats, goods, and chattels in the centre. When I awoke at 5 A.M. the following morning they had gone on their pilgrimage. At Chacar I was met by a courier with a letter informing me that I had been granted three months' additional leave of absence. Accordingly, with a light heart, we turned our faces once more towards Cashmere, and by forced marches were enabled to rejoin Young and Halkett at Serinuggur on the 25th of June, in time to make preparations for the expedition to Ladakh. The monsoon had fairly set in, and the clouds we observed before banking up in large dark masses on the tops of the mountains were now showering down their contents on the valley. Scarcely a day passed without rain, which more or less confined us to our log abodes. I found a rest requisite on my own part after the heat and fatigue of the previous fortnight, and was only too glad to avail myself of a week's rest among the society of many excellent friends; amongst others, that of Major M'Gregor, government political agent, and his kind lady. Young joined from Wurdwun with a bag of twenty-seven bear-skins, and by dint of his indefatigable industry and perseverance had managed to outnumber every one in hunting trophies.

The theory of monsoons has been so ably discussed by Dr. Maury that one need have no hesitation in quoting his authority on this subject. He says—"The south-east winds from the Indian ocean and the Arabian sea, on the other side of Hindostan (which would be, of course, the south-west wind and south-west monsoon), after deluging the Ghauts, proceed as dry winds to the Himalaya, in crossing which they are subjected to a lower temperature than that to which they were exposed in crossing the Ghauts. Here they drop some of their moisture in the shape of, snow and rain, and then pass over into the thirsty lands beyond with scarcely enough rain in them to even make a cloud. Thence they descend into the upper air, there to become counter-currents in the general system of atmospheric circulation." As before noticed, in this way the differences can be accounted for in the climate and appearance of the Cashmere mountains and those of the rainless and cloudless regions of Ladakh and Chinese Tartary. On the 1st of July 1852 we witnessed a total eclipse of the moon, which the Cashmerees attributed to a huge animal, somewhat in the shape of a bird, interposing its body between the luminary and the earth. On the occasion in question they were too glad to indulge their superstitious ideas with a sort of hope that, as more Europeans were in the valley then than had visited it before, it was an omen of the long-cherished wish, that before another year the English would be masters of their country. On the following day we commenced our march towards Ladakh by the Shalimar gardens and up the valley of the Scinde river. The scenery was enchanting, and so home-like, that I do not wonder Mr. Vigne and every English traveller should rave about the resemblance. He says—"As we advanced, the scenery increased in beauty ; the river becomes larger ; the verdant and forest-clad mountains are indented by straths and defiles ; smaller valleys send down their tributary streamlets to the waters of the Scinde; here and there were seen the cottages and walnut-trees of a retired village, or the thatched roofs of an English-looking farm-house would peep out where the forest was the least dense. We travelled forward, threading our way through a natural plantation of walnut, peach, apricot, mulberry, plum, apple, pear, and other trees, that rose upon the mountain-side with surpassing beauty and extent." Our third day's march was to the village of Khund, situated at the entrance of one of the great gorges, and near the Scinde, the waters of which are white from the light-coloured clay forming its bed and banks. Patches of snow still covered the tops of the highest mountains in the neighbourhood, and seldom a day passed without a shower. I employed a few leisure hours at Khund in exploring the fine wooded valley, having been detained there a day from want of coolies. I was struck with the absence of birds in this dense mountain solitude; indeed the district seemed almost deserted by living beings of any sort. I wandered over miles of forest and jungle without seeing anything beyond the orange-coloured bullfinch already noticed and the trail of a few bears. A small black scorpion was very common under stones, and upwards of twenty were killed by our servants in clearing a little spot sufficient for the accommodation of our tents. As we journeyed on, the valley of the Scinde became narrower, and the wooded scenery gave place to grassy hill-sides or rocky and precipitous gorges, now and then presenting a patch of forest or jungle. At the little guard-room in the defile of Guggen Ghere we rested at mid-day before ascending the rocky bed of the river, which was half-choked by huge masses of rock and beds of snow; the latter sloping down from the surrounding mountains at a low angle. Many in the higher regions would have become glaciers but for that reason; consequently they totally disappear before the end of

August. We encamped at dusk on a grassy glade surrounded by vast towering and perpendicular mountains, several of which were covered with snow. The scenery was magnificent, especially towards sunset, when their snowy tops looked one mass of red and golden yellow. We had now reached the Sonamurg, or Valley of Golden Flowers, one of the chief pasture-lands, and capable of affording every advantage in the way of rearing cattle or horses. Herds of both were seen roaming over the vast savannahs, which teemed with a countless variety of plants—

"Billowy bays of grass ever rolling in shadow and sunshine."

Among the gorgeous flora of Sonamurg I recognised the gigantic umbelliferous *Ferula asafœtida*, which furnishes the well-known medicine of that name. Whether this species is identical with the celebrated Cyrenic plant, the σιλφιων of the Greeks, I cannot say, nor am I certain that it is the same as the *Prangos pabularia* mentioned in Moorcroft's *Travels*. The wild onion and garlic were abundant, and the handsome shining-leaved thistle-like *Mima persica* was common. The *Rheum emodi* and two other species of rhubarb (*webbianum et speciforme?*) were often observed. We were constantly meeting with gangs of good-natured Ladakees on their way to Cashmere with loads of merchandise, carried by their half-bred yaks. As we proceeded up the valley the vegetation began to decrease, and by the afternoon of the 6th of July, when we arrived at the foot of the Bultul pass, the fair scenery of the previous days was entirely changed. We were now about to cross the great watershed, and a few hours would bring us into the rainless desert regions of Ladakh. The sun was declining as we commenced the ascent, and by the time we arrived at the summit of the pass had dipped behind the lofty peaks of Haramuk. We had gained an elevation of 10,500 feet above the level of the sea, and were now in the region of snow. All was desolation, and a cold cutting wind blew in gusts down the narrow mountain-gorges, which were filled with ice. In vain we attempted to peer through the gloom of the rapidly-advancing night for our baggage and servants; but darkness came on, and found us still expectant on the mountain-top. We had descended the northern face of the ridge to a clump of stunted birch in search of a level spot on which to pitch the tents, when all at once, in the dismal solitude around, screams burst out of the ground; louder and louder became the cries; the rocks sent back the sounds; we stood in astonishment, wondering what animal could be producing such unearthly noises, and various were our surmises, until one of our servants arrived and informed us we were in the centre of a colony of red marmots (*Arctomys tibetanus*). The "drun," as the red marmot is named by the natives of these regions, is confined to certain situations at high altitudes, and prefers fertile and secluded valleys, where vegetation returns rapidly and is luxuriant. There this active creature spends the summer months, surrounded by a plentiful supply of food, until again forced to its burrow by the cold and snow of winter. Their excavations are formed on gentle slopes or under stones and rocks, where they delight to sit erect and scream. Often the burrows are scattered over the valley, where loud wailing cries may be heard for miles along the mountain-sides. It is seldom they wander for any distance from their habitations, and usually take up a position close to the entrances, darting thereinto on the approach of danger. They frequently leap during progression, at times using their tails to assist them. Wild garlic, onions. and particularly a species of the former with yellow flowers, constitute their favourite food, which they store up in autumn. The hibernation lasts from four to five months, or even longer when the snow lies for any lengthened period. The bearded vulture and larger eagles are among their chief enemies. I have seen the former bear off a marmot with great ease. The total length of an adult drun is from 2¾ to 3 feet; the colour, chestnut, with black splashes on the back and hips. It is seldom met with under 8000 above the level of the sea.

After a dismal night's bivouac on the Bultul Pass, we rose at 6 A.M. on the following morning, July 7th, when the thermometer stood at 36° Fahr., and after breakfast continued our journey over a large glacier, at the further end of which a stream of some magnitude gushed forth, and in conjunction with other tributaries formed the Dras, a fine river flowing northwards. The scenery was desolate and dreary beyond belief; the mountains rugged and steep, with little verdure on their sides, and that confined to the lowest levels—to wit, narrow valleys and banks of streams. All actual vegetation had disappeared except a few clumps of birches, from which the well-known chaunt of the cuckoo resounded. Several flocks of goldfinches, the black redstart and white-fronted species, sand-martin, and the roseate finch, were seen. Marmots in numbers continued their wailing calls all day at broken intervals, and, like as many jacks in boxes, popped into their holes as we approached. The plain of Minimurg, at the foot of the pass, was covered with wild onions; besides which the Salep orchis, with its large yellow flowers, was not uncommon. The Dras river, now a goodly stream, flowed down the valley, the sides of which were marked by descending glaciers and beds of snow fast melting round their dank margins. As usual in these situations, the pretty purple and rose-coloured primroses were peeping up, and a third species, perhaps *Primula elliptica.* The short-stemmed rhubarb, with rough leaves (*Rheum moorcroftii*) was common; also the *R. emodi* and another species. The mountains were mostly composed of schistose rocks and a gray limestone. The boulders of the latter, which had fallen down on the banks of the Dras, had a polished or glazed appearance like trap, but doubtless this was owing to the action of the weather. It was evident we had now fairly passed the limits of the monsoon, for not a cloud was visible, and the sky was of that deep impenetrable blue characteristic of this region and high elevations. The village of Pandras is situate on a rocky eminence near the river, and is composed of small flat-roofed hovels scarcely distinguishable from the heaps of stones on the mountain-sides. The Caucasian type of countenance had now disappeared, and given place to a coarse Tartar visage. The women were in general very ugly, their dress consisting of a round pork-pie cap of black material, fitting close to the head, a thick woollen gown reaching midway beyond their knees, with their legs wrapped in bandages of cloth, and boots, reaching above the ankles, of the same material, with under-surfaces covered with leather. The females muffle up in piles of clothing, and both sexes frequently clad themselves in sheep and goat skins with the woolly side inwards. The little fort of Dras is situate on the river, and is the only respectable-looking building in the valley; the native dwellings being, as already stated, small square-roofed hovels, with only a door, and not above 8 feet in height. They are built of stone, and crowded together on ridges and wherever there is security from avalanches, which occasionally overwhelm the valleys during winter and at the melting of the snow in spring. The raven of Ladakh is a larger bird than that of the Northern Punjaub, owing most likely to the climate being better adapted to its habits and constitution. I scarcely think there are sufficient grounds to consider this species distinct from *C. corax*, the differences in what Mr. Hodgson calls this variety (*C. tibetanus*) being only in a somewhat larger size, the wing measuring 18½ inches, tail 11½, and the bill to gape 3 inches. The common sparrow of Ladakh differs in no respect from *P. domestica*. The pied and gray wagtails, hoopoe, brown mountain finch (*M. nemoricola*) —perhaps the gelinok of Moorcroft—and blue rock-pigeon, were observed in the valley of the Dras associated with a flock of the latter. I observed what I took to be a pied variety, but Mr. F. Moore, of the Indian Museum, London, has since proved it to be the *Columba rupestris* of Pallas.* It is easily recognised from the other, and its congener, the *C. leuconota*, by the white band across the middle of the tail and the bluish-white of the belly and lower parts.

The long-billed variety of the blue thrush is common among the rocks ; it would seem this is a permanent race of *Petrocincla cyanea*, and peculiar to the more northern regions, inasmuch as all I procured in Ladakh and Cashmere belonged to the above variety. The song-lark (*A. arvensis*) follows up the valleys to the limits of verdure. I saw one at Dras, but not subsequently. I do not think it visits Ladakh.

Our next day's march was to the village of Kirboo, about eighteen English miles. On the roadside, near Dras river, were two erect stone pillars, with figures and characters, apparently Chinese ; but we afterwards discovered that both were Buddhist. The scenery, as usual, was exceedingly wild, the mountains being perfectly bare, and with steep sides. The Dras river, a powerful stream, was seen dashing furiously through a narrow channel, more or less choked up

* See *Proc. Zool. Soc. of London*, and Pallas' *Zoogr. Russo-Asiat.* p. 560, plate 35.

with fallen masses of rock, which (as before observed) were covered with glazed incrustation, owing to the action of the weather, which had formed a stalagmitic deposit on their surface. Boulders of granite, with hornblende predominating, were also often observed. It was during this day's march that I met with the magpie for the first time in Asia, and quite unexpectedly, for, judging from former experience, the locality seemed unsuited to its habits; but nevertheless, here it is found, and the Tibetan magpie prefers the bleak and sterile regions of Ladakh and Tibet to the wooded and cultivated tract of Cashmere and the Lower Himalayas. Mr. Hodgson has separated this species from the British bird, as he has done ravens of India and the Himalayas, and, to my mind, on very doubtful grounds, inasmuch as he makes no allowance whatever for climate and locality; and because the Tibetan magpie is only a little larger, and has not so much white on the quills, he has given it another name; consequently, reviewing the magpies of Europe and Asia, we find a host of different species, all so closely similar, both in the regions they frequent and in their plumage, that unless we draw very fine distinctions, I see no possibility of separating one from the other.

I conceive the term *race* or *variety* as applicable to the following, but that they are what naturalists usually consider distinct species, I cannot allow. The *Pica bactriana* is acknowledged by Mr. Blyth to be a variety or race of the European magpie; also the Chinese variety he considers almost identical. The Bootan bird is at present shown to be the same as the *P. megaloptera*, and that we are now considering. It is a great pity, where a species is found somewhat different from a given type, that we should not allow it a place among the *varieties* of that type and species, until such time as proper comparison has been instituted between them. This rage for "species-making" is not confined solely to cabinet naturalists, but I regret to think, for the sake of science, that rather than be behind-hand, or that another should make the discovery, it is the custom with even many of our best-known field ornithologists to give a separate specific name to every individual that differs in the slightest degree from another.

The common and allied swifts (*C. apus et affinis*), and a little white-rumped martin with a forked tail, and apparently like *C. urbica*, were often seen among the rocky cliffs on the banks of the Dras. I did not procure specimens of the latter, and cannot therefore vouch for any differences between it and the *C. cashmeriensis*, noticed elsewhere. The white-capped redstart, common on the more southern rivers and streams, although occasionally observed, was becoming every day more rare. I mention this as being the last occasion on which I observed it during my journey to the lakes of Ladakh. The chestnut-bellied redstart evidently takes its place on the rivers and streams of Central Asia.

The little fort of Kargil is situate near the junction of the Zakut and Kartse, which flow into the Dras a short way to the north of Kargil. The scenery of this day's march was very wild. Several peaks of great height were observed; that of Karstee, 14,000 feet, was seen rising in majestic grandeur to the south of our route. Opposite Kargil is the village of Sileste, with its pretty little terraced fields, irrigated by a canal which runs along the side of the hill. A few willows and poplars, and a species of tamarisk, with abundance of red roses, were observed; also wild currants, the fruit of which was unripe, and, I believe, is never fit for use, being dry and very acid. The Kartse is crossed by a bridge near the above village, and passing over a broad valley, you come to the banks of the Zakut, which has to be crossed and recrossed several times. This latter stream is also called the Buchee by the natives, who do not appear to know it by the name given in maps. A small stream called Tafee joins the Buchee near the picturesque-looking village of Shergol, situated on an eminence overlooking a somewhat broad valley. The chief lion of Shergol is its strange Lama temple, formed in the face of a rock above the village. The mountains appeared to consist chiefly of granite, and a conglomerate of a porphyritic structure. I shot a kestrel, and Young saw several chuckore. The black-throated wheatear was common in stony places. The carrion-crow was frequently observed, and the lark-toed wagtail (*Budytes citreola*) in the irrigated fields. The pretty little red-fronted finch (*Metoponia pusilla*, Pall.) is a tenant of waste places, and usually seen singly or in small flocks feeding on the seeds of a species of wormwood, on which goldfinches, house-sparrows, and one or other of the roseate grosbeaks also feed. This finch is easily recognised by its small size, a red spot on the forehead, and yellowish-brown of the upper parts; the females and young are darker in plumage. Its song is sweet and melodious, and, in consequence, it is in great request as a cage-bird in the Punjaub, to which it is brought from Afghanistan. On the Buchee I killed a European dipper (*Cinclus aquaticus*). The houses in the villages are built as close together as possible, even one on the top of the other, in consequence of occasional avalanches, and very rigorous winters, that shut out all communication with their neighbours. These arrangements as to crowding, in a sanitary point of view, bid defiance to all ideas of ventilation and cubic space; and we found, on inquiry, that as in more civilised life, death often stalks silently through these villages, and numbers of their inhabitants pine away and die, no one knows how. Severe epidemics have also visited these people, and great mortality took place some years before our visit from smallpox, which has raged more than once in Ladakh, and committed terrible havoc. Avalanches destroy whole colonies, so that ruined and deserted villages are often observed, although not all resulting from this cause alone; hence, for safety, commanding situations are chosen along ridges or projecting cliffs. The pagoda-shaped buildings were common, and we passed a colossal figure, 15 feet in height, cut out of the solid rock. In the desolate-looking country around I discovered a new species of mountain-finch, which we subsequently found to be pretty common around the salt and fresh water lakes. It resembles the *M. gebleri*, but it is larger; head and back are grayish-ash, upper tail-covers white, primaries black, tips and inner webs of the secondaries white (the two last having both webs white), chin and throat pale gray (below white), auxilliary feathers pure white. In habits this finch resembles the true larks; it is generally seen in flocks, and builds in the long dykes (*mani*), where I have found its nest of dried grass.

The alpine chough (*Pyrrhocorax alpinus*) was seen here, and subsequently a flock was observed feeding on mulberries near the village of Khaletse. This species is easily distinguished from the Cornish chough (also a native of Ladakh) by the bill being shorter, and yellow instead of red. The young of the former have the bill and legs not so yellow and red as the adult specimens; my specimen measured 16 inches in the flesh. The scenery after leaving Kirboo was exceedingly dreary, and the heat in the narrow gorges and valleys very oppressive. Not a tree was visible for a long march of upwards of twelve miles, and until we arrived at the

Lamastry of Lameru, which is situated on the top of a ridge: the houses are built close together on points of the rocks. The immediate scenery around was really picturesque and fine, chiefly from the cultivated valley and rows of willows by the banks of its stream. The long dykes (*mani*), so plentiful in this country, were as usual covered with slate slabs, bearing the eternal words "Om mani Padmi om,"* cut out upon each. One of the priests or gelums came out to meet us, bringing dried apricots, walnuts, and a mug of chung; his jolly red nose, short-cut hair, and general *en bon point*, might have fitted well for "a friar of orders gray." He wore the usual red loose robe, adorned with amulets and strings of beads; cloth boots of divers colours, and a praying-box in his hand, which he kept revolving like a child's rattle, now stopping to listen to our interpreter's request regarding provisions, then (as if to make up for lost time), setting to work to grind his prayers with redoubled energy. The head-dress of the natives consists of a long cap of black cloth, which falls negligently and not ungracefully on one side. Pig-tails are worn by both sexes; that of the women consists of divers plaits, ornamented with blue and green pebbles, resembling turquoise—none, however, appeared of any value. The chung, or ale, is evidently much used, and the only intoxicating liquor known to the Ladakhees. The bloated looks, watery eyes, and red noses of many of the better classes sufficiently testify to their partiality for this "good cheer," which at best is not equal to sour cider. The mode of making it is by boiling barley, adding dough, and then allowing the whole to stand until fermentation has taken place. As usual with passers-by, we paid a visit to the lamastry during the after-

* "Hail to him of the lotus and jewel."—See Hooker's *Himalayan Journal.*

noon, escorted by our jolly-nosed friend. After passing through several dark galleries and apartments, containing divers deities, figures on the walls, inscriptions, and so forth, we were ushered into a long low-roofed room, surrounded by piles of records, and many most uncouth images. On each side of a long table were seated eight old men, who, immediately on our appearance, commenced a most diabolical uproar—shouting and beating drums, and blowing blasts on huge brass trumpets. More and more uproarious they became ; in fact—

> "They screwed their pipes, and gar'd them skirl,
> Till roof and rafters a' did dirl."

The first notice of the shapoo, or wild sheep of Ladakh I can discover is in Moorcroft's *Travels*, where he mentions seeing one killed near Lameru. We had not time to procure specimens, but on a subsequent occasion I was enabled to examine several entire skins and heads which had been procured in the surrounding mountains. These I compared with the houriar (*Ovis vignei*) in my own collection, from the salt range of the Punjaub, the details of which will be found elsewhere,* and also in my paper in the *Proceedings of the Zoological Society of London* for 1858. The shapoo is said to be common on the Ladakh mountains, and extends northwards to Dardu on the Indus, and the countries to the west and south.

The road, after leaving Lameru, passes through a wild-looking gorge by the side of a mountain-torrent called Winlin, which, after a short course through the range, empties itself into the western branch of the Indus, or Sinh-kha-bab, at which point the road turns up the left bank to a log-bridge and custom-house, where, crossing to the opposite side, we

* See pages 138, 143, 144.

were soon at the little village of Kelatse, with its fields of barley, apricot and mulberry trees forming a little oasis in the otherwise barren waste. The Indus here is a powerful river, full eighty yards in breadth. The surrounding mountains are mostly composed of granite, slate-rock, and a coarse conglomerate. A few miles farther on is the village of Nemla, composed of a few stone huts; here we had to wait several hours before the arrival of our baggage, in consequence of having made a forced march of fifteen miles. On the following morning, July 16th, the remainder appeared on the shoulders of women, who, on account of the absence of their lords and masters in the sulphur-mines, had joyfully undertaken to carry the *kiltas*, and for the next three days all our baggage (amounting to twenty-four coolie loads) was carried entirely by these hardy, good-natured dames, whose contented (I wish I could say prepossessing) faces bore always a good-natured grin, no matter how heavy the load, or steep the hill up which they had to toil with it. Some of the women wore skull-caps and pigtails like the men; among these latter we saw a few approaching to good-looking, but, like angels' visits, they were few and far between.

The road from Himis continues along the bank of the river, over low hills and across ravines, until, debouching into a rather broad valley covered with round pebbles and flints, you enter a plain of alluvium, which, after passing the picturesque village of Likur, suddenly terminates in another some hundred feet below its level. Fields of peas and beans surround the villages. The raven and hoopoe were the only tenants of the arid waste. After leaving the pretty little village of Bazgo, the usual mani and graves were observed for miles along our route; also a noble range of snow-capped mountains running parallel with the river. In August the gardens at Nimo are stocked with apples and apricots. After leaving Nimo the footpath winds through a sandy ravine near the Indus, now much reduced in size and velocity as compared with its course below Kalatse. In the shallow parts natives were catching Himalayan trout, some of which were above half-a-pound in weight. The common tern (*S. hirundo*) was seen hovering over the river. On emerging from the valley of the Indus an extensive plain is seen stretching north and south, surrounded by great snowy mountains. At the northern extremity stands Leh, the capital. It is situated upon a rising ground, at an elevation of 11,000 feet above the level of the sea. Like the generality of the fortress-looking towns and villages in Ladakh, it has an imposing appearance from a distance. The old palace, fort, and ruined wall on the face of a ridge are striking enough, but, in common with every one of Goulab Singh's conquests, tyranny and neglect have sadly changed Ladakh since the time of its legitimate rulers. A broad street, with a few wretched shops and wares, are all worth noticing. One is struck with the vast numbers of women hanging about the streets, some carrying heavy loads, others apparently waiting for employment. The men, it is said, are chiefly employed in the sulphur and borax mines, so that the greater part of the cultivation and manual labour in and about Leh is performed entirely by women. At stated times caravans from Yarkund arrive with brick-tea, shawl-wool, China silks, ponies, etc., which are exchanged for grain, English calicoes, and the like ; so that Leh is but a market-place for Cashmere and Yarkund merchants. The Yarkund pony is a hardy little animal, and fetches a high price, being in request for the hill-stations in the north-western provinces of India. The variety called the Tangun piebald is common. They are shy and timid at first, and evince a strange dislike to

Europeans, but soon get accustomed to their new masters; and for their strength, endurance, and sure-footedness are well adapted for alpine travelling. While crossing the Kara Korum mountains, whole caravans are sometimes overwhelmed by snow-storms; and I was told by Billah Shah, the chief merchant of Leh, that in many places the route to Yarkund is only traceable by the bones of horses. Billah Shah was exceedingly civil to us, and was much more popular than the commandant of Goulab Singh's fort in this neighbourhood, a certain Bustee Kam, who had the repute of being very cruel and tyrannical. We paid at the rate of three shillings per pound for a cake of black or green brick-tea, which, although mostly composed of leaf-stalks, was rich-flavoured. The tent was pitched in a grove of poplars and willows called the "town garden," where we were soon surrounded by all the idlers of Leh, including a Yarkund fakir, dressed in a quilted blanket and sugar-loaf hat of the same material. This strange-looking individual amused us during dinner by dancing a sort of jig, to which he kept time with a not unmusical song and two rods covered with loose iron rings; the latter he beat constantly against his padded shoulders, whilst the intervals between each performance were occupied in earnest devotions, the length of which depended on the alms he received.

The sameness of the scenery began to get tiresome, for the eye found no relief from one eternal repetition. This continued day by day, soon produces depression rather than exhilaration, more especially when there is no time to examine objects which, on closer acquaintance, would doubtless prove both interesting and instructive.

On the 20th of July we continued our journey in a southerly direction, across the great valley and to the left banks of the Indus, on which we kept for several miles, passing through a rich and cultivated district, studded here and there with well-built villages—a few of these, as usual, occupied projecting cliffs on the ridges and off-shoots. In the far distance the lofty peaks of the Kara Korum mountains rose against the northern horizon. We noticed porphyritic rocks near the village of Opshee, at which point the footpath leaves the Indus and turns to the right up a narrow gorge and by the side of a mountain stream, on which the common sandpiper, Asiatic and common water ousels, were observed. The chestnut-bellied redstart was noticed for the first time near Ghia; it is easily distinguished from the white-capped species by the broad white band across the centre of the wing. The female and young have no white on the forehead, and are less brilliant in colouring. The tame yak now takes the place of its half-bred, called "zho." The cold and climate of these upland regions do not seem to agree with the latter. The yak is therefore the chief beast of burden in Rupshoo, and furnishes the Tartars with nearly all their wants. The wild animal does not come so far south, but a few are met with during winter and early spring on the Nobra ranges; they migrate, however, to the loftier slopes of the Kara Korum before the end of April. The yak wanders about singly or in small herds, preferring secluded valleys to open hillsides, passing the day among the snow, where, like deer and bears, it may often be seen at mid-day stretched out at full length asleep. Captain Peyton's collection contained an entire skeleton and a few magnificent heads, procured by himself. The horn of the largest measured 2 feet 4½ inches round the curve, 1 foot in its greatest circumference, and between the tips 1 foot 8 inches. I learn, however, that much larger measurements are recorded. The prevailing colour of the wild yak is black, with a grayish tinge on the head. In its native state it is shy and timid, and the same to some degree when domesticated. It would appear, however, that the wounded animal is ferocious, as Peyton informed me that one wounded by him charged impetuously with its head down, and that he saved himself only by jumping aside, when the infuriated animal, pursuing its headlong course, fell down a precipice and was killed. The zho, pronounced " zo" by the natives, is the hybrid between the female of the common shorthorn of Ladakh and the male yak, and is the chief beast of burden in the southern districts. We were informed by the Ladakhees that the cross is fertile, but Moorcroft, who devoted much attention to these subjects, says the progeny soon degenerates.

The shawl-goat, and a dwarf variety (black, with short horns), also a race of black-faced sheep, and the dumba, or broad-tail, are reared in great numbers. Four horned varieties of this sheep are not uncommon. The "black-face," or hunniah, stands much higher than any I have seen elsewhere, and is a handsome animal. We brought a herd of shawl-goats and two of these sheep to the Punjaub. Although the former throve very well, all the sheep rapidly lost flesh and pined away within a month after their arrival on the plains. Moreover, the yak seldom survives beyond a few months, and even rapidly degenerates in the valley of Cashmere. The heat and insects are evidently its greatest enemies in the tame as well as wild state; and we observed that none of these animals, not even the goats, seemed to care for the luxuriant vegetation of the lowlands, preferring whatever resembles their Tartaric furze and bent to the rich clover and grasses of Cashmere.

After leaving Ghia the pathway leads up a wild-looking valley to the Tang Lang Pass, at the foot of which we encamped for the night, surrounded by beds of snow. At sunrise the thermometer stood at 31° Fahr ; and a little stream close by was frozen over. The pass is crossed by a narrow gorge between two mountains, and the ascent is by no means difficult. Several blocks of a pure white marble strewed the bottom, and the hillside was covered with a rather deep bed of glacial clay. The summit of the pass is said to be 15,500 feet above the level of the sea. From the little flat on which our tent was pitched we looked down on the plains of Rupshoo stretching through the mountains; in fact nothing else than flat-bottomed valley, with the mountains rising abruptly on either side. These dreary-looking plains are for the most part covered with scanty herbage and patches of furze. Here and there we could discern the black tents and the herds of the nomadic Tartars, and for the first time we began to experience the effects of the high altitude, and soon found that slight exertion caused an oppressive feeling in the chest, fatigue, and weariness. At night I was frequently awoke by a sudden sensation which passed off on taking a deep inspiration. By some these sensations have been attributed to the necessary exertion consequent on attaining such elevations, but in our instance this could not have been the case, as the ascent had been gradual, and exertion far less in the Rupshoo plains than we had undergone in gaining that altitude. Moreover, the fact that the feeling continued as long as we remained in these elevated regions, and disappeared on the very day we recrossed the Tang Lang and got to Ghia, which is upwards of fifteen hundred feet below the level of the pass, is a proof that the feelings were associated altogether with the rarefied atmosphere of high altitudes. I am far more inclined to believe with Humboldt that the weariness and sense of fatigue in the limbs, especially in the joints, is the result of the low atmospheric pressure. I allow that the above condition is influenced in a very great measure by the state of health, and that a disordered stomach or such like will cause the sensations to become more intense.* Indeed I feel persuaded that no one subject to organic or functional disorder of the heart ought to attempt to travel in elevated regions, in as much as violent action of that organ is of frequent occurrence in healthy persons, and in the stout and robust bleeding from the nose is by no means rare. The year after our visit an officer affected with a diseased condition of the heart crossed the Nagpogonding Pass, when he became suddenly ill, and died on the banks of the Chumouraree Lake, where his solitary grave remains as a guide to the traveller along the shores of that wild and desolate region. It is somewhat strange, however, that the natives do not complain of this feeling, and seem to go up these steep mountains without any unusual sensations of fatigue; also that those who ascend to great heights in balloons do not appear to suffer. That, however, may arise from there being no demand for exertion, for, except sense of oppression in the chest during sleep, we did not experience any uneasy feelings when at rest.

The bearded vulture was seen hovering over the Tartar tents. At their entrances were stationed several Tibetan mastiffs (*Molossus tibetanus*). These fierce-looking animals commenced barking on our approach, and had several times to be driven back by their owners. One old dame succeeded in silencing a savage-looking monster by putting his huge uncouth-looking head under her petticoats. The natives are a good-natured and jovial race, but very filthy. In the tents there seemed

* This I have repeatedly observed with reference to the sirocco wind in the Mediterranean: to the healthy it has little effect, but the weak and diseased are materially injured by its depressing influence.

no attempt at privacy, and, judging from the number of sleeping-mats observed in those we inspected, crowding appeared to be excessive, yet they seemed a hardy-looking people. As usual, however, the blear eyes of the old, and inflamed condition of others, showed that ophthalmia prevailed. I saw no goitre anywhere in Ladakh, although it is prevalent among the natives of the ranges which border the Indian plains. The women were exceedingly ugly, and among all the squalid-looking children about their various encampments I could not discover one with even the slightest approach to good looks. The raven was stalking unconcernedly about the tents, and so tame as to approach and feed on the refuse of our dinners. I found the pied wagtail, and once saw an individual of the gray sort (*Motacilla boarula*). The red-fronted finch, also the mountain-finch (*Montifringilla adamsi*), kestrel, black-throated wheatear, alpine chough, and chuckore, were met with in about the same numbers on the plains of Rupshoo as on the less-elevated districts we had left. Several fresh and salt water lakes were passed, around the borders of which were quantities of borax, crystallised and in powder ; the latter is often borne aloft for several hundred feet by whirlwinds, which are very common around the lakes and sides of the plains. One lake, called Tooskee, was covered with Brahminy ducks (*Anas rutila*) and their broods, the latter being almost fully fledged.

July 24.—On the plain near the lake a herd of kiangs or wild asses (*A. hemionus*) were feeding. On our approach they scampered off to a safe distance, and, turning, gazed at us intently until we again advanced, when, wheeling off at a trot, they kept halting occasionally, and, turning towards us, advanced a few steps on each occasion as if for the purpose of reconnoitring. We attempted to get within range, but the want of cover intense heat, and reflection from the plain, together with the oppression and sense of weariness consequent on the elevation, soon obliged us to give up the chase. Young fired at a herd of kiangs, which he calculated was about 200 yards off, but found afterwards that they had been nearly double that distance. There is unquestionably an ocular deception on these plains, for I have been told by hunters that at such high altitudes objects look much nearer than they are in reality. Possibly the clear and cloudless atmosphere may be the cause; however, it is a fact that sportsmen in these regions, at first, very seldom calculate distances correctly. One of our servants, a native of Koloo, who had visited Chinese Tartary, assured us that he saw there a kiang used as a beast of burden; however, all the natives we interrogated in Ladakh denied the possibility of any approach at domestication, and that the young always died in confinement. The chief food of this species appears to consist of the stunted fescue grasses common on the plains and mountains, together with a red-flowered vetch, possibly *Oxytropis chiliophylla* of Hooker.* The speed of the kiang is great. I did not see it gallop: its action seems to consist of a long step or trot, which is never varied. I was surprised to see the agility with which a herd bounded down a steep hillside.

The Tooskee Lake is about two miles long and half-a-mile in breadth; its waters are highly impregnated with soda. No fish were obtained in the lake nor in the fresh-water streams which run into it. I procured specimens of Temminck's sand-piper and the little sand-lark, both of which were common along the shore. Halkett's mountain-barometer made the lake 15,000 feet above the sea-level. This is probably a little under the mark. The hills around are said to abound with large game; but although I tried to ascend one

* *Himalayan Journals*, vol. ii. 164.

of the highest peaks, I saw none, and became dead beat long before we got half-way up. My companions also experienced the same unconquerable oppression. Young saw a herd of nahoor or wild sheep, and several herds of kiang. The nahoor, if not identical, is very closely allied to the burrel of the Borendo Pass.* It is called the naboo in Ladakh, and is the sna of Tibet; and, judging from the quantities of its horns on the chaits and cairns of both countries, it would appear to be their most common wild ruminant. Mr. Blyth's distinctions between the two sorts of burrel have reference chiefly to the form of the horn. He says the burrel's is more rounded, the annual dents are better marked, with larger bulgings between them. The outline of the horn is more graceful, and the whole configuration of the animal more imposing. I must confess I have not observed these distinctions, although I have compared horns of the nahoor with its more eastern congener; and I question the propriety of taking such equivocal points as a means of separation. My own experience has taught me to place little reliance on the shape of the horn, for both in this and the other wild sheep and goats of the Himalayas the horn, as I have had occasion to remark, is subject to considerable variation in each species, both as to shape and appearance.

The argali, or *Ovis ammon*, is not uncommon in this district, but is more plentiful on the northern ranges. A few remain about the Tooskee Lake and neighbouring hills during summer; the majority, however, migrate to Nobra as the snow melts. I had an opportunity of examining a magnificent collection of skins and heads made in Nobra by

* *Proc. Zool. Soc.* 1840, p. 68. *Ann. and Mag. Nat. Hist.* 1841, vol. vii. 249.

my friend Captain Peyton during the spring of 1854. He informed me that he found them in herds, chiefly on low hills, and almost invariably in the open places, where an old ram was always on the alert when the remainder were lying down. Its alarm consists of a loud whistle, which, as in the case of the other wild species, is the signal for instant departure. They run at great speed. Lieutenant Smith, 75th regiment, informed me that he attempted to run down a wounded *Ovis ammon* with Persian hounds, but with no success, as the dogs became breathless in a short time, he supposed from want of water, but in all probability from the high altitude, as the locality was at least 14,000 feet above the level of the sea. Besides, from the stony nature of the mountains, they soon become footsore. I have seen enormous horns of the *Ovis ammon* on the chaits, where, I believe, the finest are to be procured. These cairns are mostly made up of horns, of tame yak, wild sheep, and goats, which are piled up in the shape of a cone, with stones, pieces of quartz, pebbles, and sticks, to which rags are attached. They are considered to be the abodes of spirits, and when a Tartar arrives at one, he walks round it several times, repeating a prayer, of which the everlasting "Om mani Padmi om" forms the chief part. An adult male argali stands about 12½ hands high at the shoulders. The horns of the female seldom exceed 20 inches in length, and are flat, narrow, and curve backwards. The horns of a ram's skull, taken off a chait near Tooskee, measured 39½ inches around the curve; but specimens much larger have been procured.

The sous or Tibetan antelope* (*Pantholops hodgsonii*) rarely comes so far south as Tooskee Lake; its favourite haunts are among the lofty ranges northwards, where, according to my in-

* For a full description of this animal, see *Jour. As. Soc.* 1846.

formants, Peyton and Smith, it is met with in herds. In the former gentleman's collection from the northern part of Nobra, I observed one with a horn much distorted and stunted in growth, which would show that these slender members are apt to get damaged, and possibly one might drop off occasionally, which would give the animal the appearance of being one-horned, and account for the Messrs. Huc and Gabet's* assertion with reference to a unicorn, even as Dr. Hooker justly remarks a profile view of the animal might to careless observers carry a like impression. The Tibetan antelope is swift-footed and graceful in its movements, and by no means shy in situations where it has not been often hunted. The height of an adult male is 3 feet 3 inches, and the average length of horn about 24 inches. One of Peyton's trophies measured 27 inches. It was remarked that in nearly all his skins, amounting to upwards of twenty, there was found clusters of the larva of an insect, each of the size of a sparrow's egg, deeply embedded under the skin of the back and hips. Like the other wild ruminants of these regions the sous repairs to the snow during mid-day to escape the flies and insects, which seem to annoy it in a great degree. The two slit-like openings in the groin, which Peyton informed me formed pouches capable of containing the clenched fist, are certainly strange appendages, and like the infra-orbital openings their uses seem by no means apparent We had scarcely pitched our tents near a spring in the immediate vicinity of the lake, when the excessive heat and oppressive state of the atmosphere suddenly changed, and a cold breeze came down the mountains, where a thunder-storm was seen raging with great violence. Gradually it moved along the northern shore of the lake towards us. In half-an-hour the thermometer came down from 82° to 34°, and snow

* *Travels in Tartary.*

fell in quantity sufficient to cover the surrounding mountains several inches in thickness. These sudden changes of temperature are of frequent occurrence during the sultry heat of midsummer, and are doubtless owing to the different states of the atmosphere of the plains and valleys, compared with the mountain-tops, both as to temperature and electrical condition.

The Tibetan sand-grouse (*Syrrhaptes tibetanus*) repairs in large flocks to drink at the fresh-water springs; two were killed by a party of Englishmen at our encamping-ground on the day previous to our arrival. The plumage of both sexes is much alike, but the long tail of the male is distinctive. A fine eagle, with white head and neck, black body, and long wedge-shaped tail, was seen on a cliff near our tents. The tailless rat* (*Lagomys hodgsonii*) is plentiful, but I did not see the other species (*Lagomys roylii*) so common on the Cashmere ranges. One or both may be the Pharaoh's mouse mentioned by Marco Polo. The lagomys is said to be eaten by certain tribes in Tartary. Some persons have supposed the marmot to be the animal referred to by the above traveller, but I have not been able to discover that it is ever used as food by the natives.

The alpine hare (*Lepus oiostolus*) was common among the fallen boulders, and along the stony bottoms and sides of the valleys leading towards Poogah Lake. This species very much resembles the alpine hare of Europe. It makes forms under rocks, and is said to burrow in banks, where we saw several holes partially filled up with soil, after the manner of rabbit-burrows. Like its congener just mentioned, this species changes colour with the seasons. It is said to be almost white in winter. In midsummer it is a light-brown, ex-

* Waterhouse's *Rodents*, vol. ii. p. 20.

cepting on the hips, which are bluish, and the lower parts white.

The Tibet ravine-deer of Europeans (*Procapra picticauda*) is met with on craggy mountain-sides, and, like the goral and chamois, delights to sport among cliffs and precipices. The ruddy or Brahminy goose, and its broods, are plentiful on this lake and around its stony sides. The flesh of this bird, although generally considered unpalatable in India, is by no means so when stewed with mountain mutton and alpine hare in the regular "hotch-potch" style. I recommend every Himalayan traveller to adopt this plan with game in general, and provide himself with a good-sized stew-pot; for it is wonderful how few incompatibles enter into the hunter's fare when seasoned with a good appetite. You may mix fish, partridges, hares, ducks, and venison, and, if well served up, nothing can be more savoury. Near the little green plot at Poogah on which travellers generally encamp is one of the sulphur and borax mines. Here we found several men and boys employed melting the minerals, the former in shallow basins. The hollow in the rock was only a few feet from the surface, and lined with beautiful octohedral crystals of sulphur, more or less mixed with white powder or crystallised borax.

After a tedious march of upwards of twelve miles over a low range of hills, and across a dreary stony plain, we passed a small lake, and soon afterwards a large sheet of water was seen extending southwards for upwards of ten miles—its greatest breadth might be about two. Gerard, the first English traveller who visited the lake, calls it Chuinoninil, and makes its elevation 15,000 feet above the level of the sea. My own impressions are that this is under the mark, although Halkett's mountain barometer gave nearly the same altitude.

It is called Tsümureri by Moorcroft, which the Tartars at the Poogah mines pronounce Tsomoreree. Of late years English travellers have been accustomed to name it Chimouraree, which is likely to supersede the others. There is much difficulty in being able to find out the names of places in these uninhabited districts, for one may journey for days and not meet a single native; and when any are encountered they are generally non-residents, or travellers on their way to or from distant countries.

A noble amphitheatre of mountains surrounds the lake on one side, whilst at its northern extremity is the Nagpogoding Pass, which, according to the above authority, is 17,000 feet above the level of the sea. Halkett made it 800 feet higher, but his calculations were not studiously exact. The shores of the lake are stony, and the high-water marks seem to indicate considerable elevations at certain seasons—perhaps during the spring and winter months, when evaporation is least. Several good-sized streams run into it, but there is no outlet. No doubt the waste and supply are balanced by evaporation. The idea of a subterranean communication, as surmised by some authorities, has no support from any appearances observable on the lake or neighbouring country.

Excepting one rude stone building, occasionally occupied by the gopa of the district, and that scarcely worthy of the name of a human habitation, we had not seen a house of any sort since leaving Ghia. The solitary grandeur of the scene was at first impressive, but soon became wearisome in the extreme, for the eye got tired of the unbroken sheet of water, then scarcely ruffled by a breath of wind, and of the vast barrier-chains which, like those we had been accustomed to see for weeks, presented the same monotonous similarity; whilst the stony desert plain around the lake showed not one.

object more than another to attract the eye, and no sound to break the stillness around.

The highest peak (Prang-la) is said to rise 4000 feet above the level of the lake. No fish were seen in its clear waters, although a small species, perhaps the fry of the Himalayan trout, were common in the little mountain-streams where they empty themselves into the lake. The water of the lake had a soft brackish taste. As usual, the alpine pigeon (*C. rupestris*), black-throated wheatear, raven, Ladakh mountain-finch, were common on the hills and plains around. The lesser tern was seen occasionally, and I shot, for the first time, a brown-headed gull (*Larus brunnicephalus*), which was now and then seen hunting along the margin of the lake. This handsome bird is not unlike the black-headed gull, from which, however, it is distinguished by the colour of the iris, which is white. The head and neck are grayish-brown, turning to black on the lower part. The first six primaries have the proximal half white and the distal half black, with white spots on the tips of the two first quills. We observed the rufous-breasted dotterel (*C. leschenaultii*) and young, a brood of which were seen running along the pebbly side of the lake. An adult male measured in the flesh 7 inches. Forehead is black, with a white spot in front of the eye. A black band passes from the bill through the eye; throat and neck are white; breast and sides of the neck light rufous. The black-headed mountain-finch (*Montifringilla hæmatopygia*) is often seen around the lake, usually feeding with the short-billed variety of the mountain-linnet, which is common in Ladakh. The young of the latter have the edges of the quills more marked with white, and the pink on the rump is paler than in the bird of Northern Europe; otherwise there is no apparent difference. The smaller bill, which has given the Asiatic bird a character is called *L. brevirostris* by Gould, somewhat different from the other, was by no means very apparent in my Ladakh specimens. As far as I can make out from comparison of skins, there does not seem sufficient grounds for separating the above and *L. montana*. Sir William Jardine, who has likewise carefully compared Ladakh specimens with the above, is of the same opinion.

The black-headed mountain-finch is usually seen singly; its flight is powerful; the seeds of an artemisia constitute its favourite food. The male in the flesh measures 7 inches. The eye is small; back and wing-covers grayish-black; rump thick and tinged with pink; tail black, margined with white; lower parts are dirty-white. The plumage of the back and belly is soft and downy, which is the case with many of the indigenous birds of these high altitudes, evidently to serve as a protection against the cold of winter. In fact, the extra down takes the place of the woolly pileage of the mammals of these regions. The rufous-breasted accentor (*Accentor strophiatus*) frequents the furze bushes, where I found its nest, with four eggs of a white colour, beautifully speckled with light-brown like those of the yellow bunting (*E. citrinella*). Its call somewhat resembles the siskin's. The upper parts are brown, with longitudinal striæ of a darker colour; throat and neck mouse-brown; breast rufous; belly and lower parts dirty-white. The brown and common water-ousels were again observed; also a solitary Philippine dotterel. We saw a flock of geese settle on the lake, but could not discern the exact species. However, by the aid of our telescopes, we could recognise mallard and teal, but they were likewise a great distance from the shore. I shot a small sand-martin, which at first sight appeared to be identical with the common bank-swallow (*H. riparia*), but turned out, on closer inspection, to be an allied species (*Cotyle subsoccata*) also met with in winter in the Punjaub.

The Tibet partridge (*P. hodgsonii*) was first discovered by Mr. Wilson of Mussouree* in 1841, and subsequently described by Mr. Hodgson.† It was still later (1854) met with by Lieutenant Smith, 75th regiment, near the Pangong Lake in Little Tibet.‡ Since the above date I observe several more specimens have reached Europe. It seems this partridge is common along the western slopes of the Tibetan Himalaya, and affects barren mountain-sides. When the Rupshoo mountains are properly explored, it may be found there likewise. The skin of Mr. Smith's specimen, from which Mr. Gould's delineation was taken, measured 10½ inches in length. A white band crosses the forehead, and, passing over the eyebrows, meets the opposite at the occiput. Throat white; black patch at the corners of the lower mandible; breast and belly barred irregularly with black and rufous, the former in greatest abundance on the breast, the latter on the neck and sides of the belly and breast; vent and lower party of the belly dirty-white; the feathers as usual are soft and downy; crown rufous; occiput mottled with black and rufous, which is continued over the back and wing-covers, resembling closely the same parts in the Indian gray francolin, whilst the quills of the birds assimilate in appearance with the same parts in the black partridge. Many sportsmen who saw Mr. Smith's specimen pronounced it a hybrid between the two last-named species, and certainly at first sight the similarity is striking.

The ibex is found on certain ranges in Ladakh, especially

* *Calcutta Sporting Review* for December 1848, p. 163.

† *J. A. S. Bengal*, vol. xxv. p. 165.

‡ Gould's *Birds of Asia*.

on the chains northward of Leh. I have examined various specimens from the district lying between the latter and Iscardoh, on the Indus, none of the horns of which equalled in size those of the same animal from the Cashmere ranges. A like remark having been frequently made to me by both European and native sportsmen, I made a note of this difference at the time, and when subsequently inspecting the collection in the British Museum, and a fine specimen of the *Capra siberica* from the Altai mountains in the Derby Museum, Liverpool, was struck with the similarity of the latter animal and the Ladakh variety. At the same time, as they differed in no other particular, I cannot see any just cause to consider the latter otherwise than a race of *Capra himalayana*, which comes very close to the European ibex (*C. ibex*). Indeed, specimens of the two are often exactly similar in every respect.

CHAPTER XIII.

Foxes of the Tibetan Plateau—Leopards—Discomforts of the Region—Return—White Marmot—Old Acquaintances—Degradation going on in the Ladakh Gorges—Scenery and Change in Fauna and Flora—Suru Valley and its enormous Glacier—Glacier action—Scenery in the Northern Ranges of Cashmere—Wurdwun Valley again—Snow-storm—Snow-partridge—Varied and beautiful Scenery—Start from Pilgam after Deer—Unsuccessful Expedition—Birds—Flora—Rain—Bears, and their Habits—Wretchedness of the Natives—The Sporting-bag—Return to Serinuggur—Departure for Rawul Pindee.

THE mountain-fox (*V. montanus*) was not seen beyond the wooded regions of Cashmere, and is evidently replaced by the silver fox (*V. flavescens*), which is not, however, partial to the barren regions of Ladakh, but, as has been noticed elsewhere, is also to be met with on the tops of the southern Pinjal. The ounce (*L. uncia*) is perhaps the most common of the large Felidæ. I have seen the skin of a black variety, said to have been procured in Ladakh; and the natives of Tibet and Chinese Tartary mention a leopard without spots. The tiger does not apparently frequent these regions, and is said to be very seldom seen farther northward than the first ranges of mountains which border the plains of India. I believe, however, that individuals wander into the valley of Cashmere. I recollect at Changos, near Islamabad, one evening during my second visit to the valley, we were startled by the barkings of the mountain-foxes, which, my shickaree said, were tormenting a leopard in a bare scrubby jungle near our tent. I had not time to mark the characters sufficiently, but on going to the spot, I observed a very large animal skulking through the cover. It had no spots on its sides, and from its great size I felt certain it was a tiger. The natives, however, positively deny that the tiger is ever seen in the valley; but, judging from their accustomed timidity, I can fancy it is seldom they wait to note the appearance of such visitors.

Our little party broke up on the 29th of July, Halkett proceeding to Simla, by Piti and Konawar, whilst Young and myself made up our minds to hurry back to Cashmere and employ the few remaining weeks of our leave of absence in hunting the Cashmere stag. It is painful at all times to part with a good companion, especially one who has shared your discomforts as well as pleasures, and deeply so when you feel that there is no hope of that good fellowship being renewed under the same pleasant circumstances.

On the 30th of July we bade farewell to our kind friend. Shortly afterwards it commenced to rain, accompanied by a cold biting north wind, which at last ended in a heavy snow-storm, and we were driven to seek the shelter of the rocks, until approaching night compelled us to encamp on the cheerless hill-top without the means of preparing our dinners. On the following morning we were off again by another and nearer route across the mountains to the Tooskee Lake, where we just arrived to encounter another heavy snow-storm, as sudden in its onset as on the previous occasion. The thermometer sank 30 degrees in half-an-hour, and hail and snow lay thick around us. All rushed towards the little stone hovel near the spring, to find it occupied by a party of Tartars and their asses and sheep, which were laden with bags of salt and flour. It is a serious matter in these regions to get caught in a storm, as dried yak's dung and furze are the only fuel procurable. On the above occasion it came hard on us to be obliged to dine on milk and cakes, especially as several ruddy geese and hares were in our larder. Shortly after leaving Tooskee we overtook the party of officers we had met on our way to the Chimouraree Lake. They seemed to be taking it easy, and enjoying their English luxuries in the shape of pig's faces, port, and beer—delicacies to which we had long been strangers. It was, however, somewhat mortifying to us, who had purposely come in the lightest marching order, to find, in spite of all our plans to secure easy access to the game, that one of these gentlemen on the previous day had scarcely walked off the beaten path when he killed two fine specimens of *Ovis ammon*, whilst with all our trouble and preparation it had not been our fortune to see even one; but "the race is not always to the swift, nor the battle to the strong;" at the same time there can be no doubt that to cultivate an intimate acquaintance with the denizens of these rugged mountains, one must be content with a small commissariat. I have done many a hard day's work on porridge and milk, but it is not wholesome to use every sort of hill-flour for that purpose, especially the coarse grain of the Wurdwun and other valleys northward of Cashmere. When crossing the Tang-Lang Pass we came on a colony of white marmots (*Arctomys tibetanus*). This sort is distinguished at once from the red species by its lighter colour, being a yellowish white, and also its call, which more resembles a whistle than a scream. One side of a spur was riddled by their burrows. The white seems to take the place of the red marmot on the more barren and high ranges above 10,000 and 12,000 feet.

We arrived again at Ghia on the 1st of August during a heavy snow-storm, which delayed the baggage for several hours, and obliged us to beg for shelter from the natives, who kindly put us into one of their temples, where we spent that and the following day surrounded by images and idols. It was a frequent subject of remark, how much our friends at home would wonder to see us all seated on the floor surrounded by these grim-looking figures, and not much less grotesque-looking Tartars crowding around the door to watch us at dinner. I have a vivid and pleasant recollection of that day, and of the wild and unbounded delight of two Irishmen and two Scotchmen meeting by chance in such an out-of-the-way place, all brimful of news and adventures.

The feeling of oppression and lassitude, which had affected all of us during our travels in Rupshoo, left us as soon as we recrossed the pass and got to Ghia. It seemed as if a heavy load had been removed from off our bodies. To me the sensation had been unusually troublesome for the last few days, in consequence of suffering from over-fatigue in attempting to ascend the mountains in quest of birds.

It is dangerous to penetrate the defiles of Ladakh immediately before or during a fall of rain, as masses of rock get loosened, and roll down the mountain-sides into the valleys. During our march to Opshee we were kept in constant dread of falling rocks, the noises of which sounded like thunder through the narrow gorges. It was, therefore, a great relief to get clear of the pass and once more debouch on the open. Being desirous of witnessing one of the fairs which annually take place at Leh, we delayed a day or two, waiting for the caravan expected from Yarkund, but to no purpose, and as the fair could not commence until the Tartar merchants arrived, we took our departure for Cashmere. Continuing by the former route as far as Kargil, we then changed the direction and proceeded by another road which leads across the Suru glacier into the valley of Wurdwun. Accordingly, on the

13th of August, having started from Kargil, we passed up the banks of the Kartse, through a fine broad valley, which lies to the south of the village. The country was somewhat densely populated, and well watered by means of canals, the banks of which were covered with rows of fine spreading willows. The surrounding mountains are very steep, and for the most part scarped, especially towards their summits, whilst their hollows and fissures lower down were green with grass or filled with snow. Large detached masses of rock, with the same vitreous exterior as observed near Dras, strewed the bottom of the valley and bed of the river, and reflected the heat strongly in our faces. We passed the noble peak of Kartse, rising from the bed of the river to an altitude of 14,000 feet above the level of the sea in one shattered and scarped spire, both its summit and hollows covered with perpetual snow. At the base of the mountain is the pretty village of Lang Kartse, and a mile or so further on the fort and little hamlets of Sanko. Several torrents had to be crossed, one of which delayed us some hours in consequence of its bridge having been carried away by the melting of the snow on the high mountains. The more we advanced southward, it became apparent that we were fast leaving the barren region of Ladakh, and were entering again on the rich and fertile valleys of the south. Both flora and fauna proved this. Yesterday, at Shergol, we had seen the magpie, chestnut-bellied redstart, alpine chough, and Tartar rock-pigeon ; to-day their places were taken by the roller, white-capped redstart, Cornish chough, and blue rock-pigeon ; moreover, the Tartar visage had now give place to the Caucasian.

It was sunset before we arrived at the fort of Sanko, where its fat little commandant was ready to receive us, and had spread a mat on the green, on which we all sat down and chatted together until after dusk. Whilst our host was intently narrating to us a story eulogistic of his lord and master Goulab Singh, some one by mistake let off the water in a garden close by, so that before we knew what had taken place the whole green was inundated. My companion and myself were soon on our feet, but the commandant, being very portly, required assistance, which, however, arrived too late to save his nether garments from a thorough soaking. To us the scene was ludicrous in the extreme, especially on seeing the fat little man waddling like a duck through the wet in his dripping tights, with his heavy sword dangling by his side, and the large shield (part of his state costume) slung on his shoulders like a tortoise-shell. The dignity of our friend had evidently received a serious blow, for he fumed and swore most vehemently at some imaginary enemy, for none could persuade him but that the whole affair had not been done on purpose.

The Suru valley narrows in some parts; at others spreads out into prairies clad with dense and luxuriant vegetation, like that of the Sonamurg. It was delightful to wander through the long grass and pluck wild flowers, after the dismal sterility of the country we had just left. Several mountain-torrents had to be crossed on the way, and a few by means of rope-bridges made from the twisted branches of willows. A few miserable-looking stone hovels were seen in clusters on the ridges, and in situations where they were not likely to receive injury from snow-drifts and avalanches.

The green sandpiper, roseate finch, hoopoe, and chough were observed, also a whinchat of a species I had seen on one occasion near the Poogah Lake. Several colonies of red marmots occupied the hill-sides and valleys, whilst on the Kartse

I observed the red-billed curlew (*Ibidorhynchus struthersii*). A few bearded vultures were hunting along the slopes in quest of small animals, whilst the Indian vulture was soaring overhead, and numbers of the common swift wheeled around the precipices. It was late in the day when our baggage arrived at the foot of the glacier, and fearing we might not be able to cross before night, encamped close by on a green sward, down which ran a rapid torrent from the glacier, forming one of the chief tributaries of the Kartse. Like many other streams of glacier origin, we noticed a great difference in its size in the morning compared with mid-day and afternoon, which was doubtless owing to thaws and heat; consequently, several streamlets which had flowed in the afternoon were frozen at night and up to mid-day.

The view from the tent was unquestionably very grand. Above us rose a towering peak, with its summit hidden in clouds; whilst half-way down a tremendous icebed filled the valley, and stretched in one huge tortuous mass between two perpendicular ridges. The surrounding mountains presented a succession of rocky and scarped sides, whilst a series of noble-looking ranges filled up the background, and stretched away as far as the eye could penetrate. It had snowed off and on during the day, and now cold drizzling showers were continually recurring, so that the servants and coolies, for want of better shelter, were driven to seek the cover of any projecting rock. Their little fires sent clouds of smoke upwards in dense masses, whilst our Rupshoo goats and sheep, and my jaded pony, grazed silently around our little canvas home, all of which consorted well with the grandeur and wildness of the surrounding scenery. On the following morning the party started in mist and rain, and after an hour's scramble gained the summit of the pass, which is said to be 13,000 feet above the level of the sea. The descent was very difficult, in consequence of great transverse fissures, over which the coolies and animals had to leap. These great gaping ice-rents continually obstructed our journey, and frightened my pony by the hollow noises occasioned by the torrents of melted ice which flowed into them from the surface of the glacier. Our course was therefore tortuous, and had to be directed as it best could by seeking the narrowest portions of the rents. In this way four hours were spent toiling over the broken and irregular surface, for the most part covered with masses of rock, gravel, and debris from the surrounding slopes. At times we had to slip down abrupt declivities, at others to scramble through great hollows. The grandeur of the scene, in spite of the hazy state of the atmosphere, was most impressive, and I more than once turned and gazed upwards at the vast contorted mass of ice and rock, wondering how long the huge boulders lying on the top of the glacier would take to move to the bottom; and wondrous as glacier motion seems, there is certainly something in its general appearance which suggests the idea of a frozen river. The sweeping slope, dirt bands, and lateral moraines, have, even to the unscientific observer, some significance of motion. I believe we would have appreciated the grandeur of the scene a great deal more had we then been intimately acquainted with the discoveries of Agassiz, Forbes, Tyndall, and others, or what is so truthfully and so sweetly portrayed in the following lines :—

"A sunny glacier on the creviced slope
Its icy talons fixed, and down the hill,
With annual progress, like a tortoise crawled;
Doubtless is crawling now, while summer noon
And its relaxing ether smooth the path—
A path more slowly travelled in the frosts
Of winter, yet incessantly pursued

By night and day the varying seasons round.
The feet of destiny are not more slow
Than that mute creature, haply not so sure."*

The Suru glacier terminates abruptly in a vaulted cavern, from which the Scinde or Wurdwun river takes its rise. As we descended, the surrounding mountains began little by little to show approaches to verdure commencing with birch, which was succeeded by grassy slopes covered with pasturage, dense and luxuriant as any we had yet seen. Abundance of wild onions and rhubarb covered these slopes, and although it was the 16th of August, the cuckoo's chaunt sounded sweet from the birken woods around, and the wild scream of the red marmot was heard shrill and loud above the roaring of the cataract. Continuing our course down the mountains gradually sloping towards the valley of Wurdwun, either by rugged pathways or wading knee-deep through long grass, we at length gained the banks of the Scinde river, and after toiling over its rugged bottom, and picking our way through the forest we found ourselves once more at Sochness. The snow had long since disappeared, and the valley of Wurdwun was now clad in verdure, presenting a strange contrast to what we had witnessed in May; however, the misery and wretchedness of the inhabitants continued as before, such utter apathy and grovelling indigence as the most degraded of Oriental races present. The men, dressed in their long loose gowns, presented a most effeminate appearance. One cannot help feeling that, even making every allowance for the tyranny and oppression of their rulers, the Cashmerians are naturally a phlegmatic and spiritless people. Everywhere in Cashmere you see the inhabitants indolent to a degree, filthy in their

* *Sir Lanceolot: a Legend of the Middle Ages*, by F. W. Faber, D.D., Priest of the Oratory of St. Philip-Neri.

habits, mean, cowardly, shabby, irresolute, and indifferent to all ideas of reform or progress; so much so, that I verily believe it would now take a century of the most liberal government to bring them on a par with their neighbours, for among all the advantages possessed by a land overflowing with milk and honey, the Cashmerians are about the least enterprising of Oriental races. With the Sikhs they have nothing in common, and as to personal bravery and warlike character they never had any pretensions, but, on the contrary, their deficiencies in these respects have long since passed into a proverb. It is vain, however, to hope that there can be any progress under the present ruler, who, like his father, is bent on self-aggrandisement, and that of the worst description; so much so, that were it not for the natural beauties of Cashmere the land would have long since been turned into a wilderness. Whether to ascribe the above defects in the Cashmerian character to long and continued oppression, to themselves, or, as some have supposed, to their moist, enervating climate, one thing is certain, that as long as the present system of government continues, so long will this unfortunate people retrograde, for advance they cannot. The grain in Wurdwun valley was still green, although we had seen the barley reaped and thrashed at Kargil only four days before. The rigor of the seasons is always most severely felt in secluded valleys, as the snow lies long, and, coupled with the constant clouds and rain of the monsoon months, makes the climate, especially that of Wurdwun, most disagreeeable, at least until August.

After several tedious delays, we left Sochness in a pelting rain, but only too glad to get away from the filthy log-house, where we had spent two days among the poultry and such a collection of vermin as we had never before witnessed. Being anxious to reach the Duchinpara by the nearest route.

we struck up a steep hill in a northerly direction, behind Sochness, and passed over several beds of snow. When near the top of the ridge rain fell in such torrents, and the clouds became so dense, that we were obliged to encamp on the nearest bare spot, where, with our servants and eight coolies, all huddled together on the floor of the little tent, we braved the pitiless storm for the remainder of that and the whole of the succeeding day. The coolies were most averse to proceed any farther; indeed it was with great difficulty they had been procured, and had not a sharp look-out been kept by our servants we would have been left on the hill-top without the means of transport; as it was, two or three deserted, and had to be replaced by sending all the way to Sochness for others. They feared the weather, and dreaded being storm-bound on the summit of the pass; so that, on the following day, when the last portion of the ascent was being made, several flung down their loads and would not proceed. Moreover, it was only with the greatest persuasion we could get the remainder to continue the journey. Matters looked desperate, but we had no alternative but to push on to the nearest village, and despatch a servant to Sochness once more. The summit of the ridge is 13,000 feet above the level of the sea, and forms one of the highest practicable passes of the Northern Pinjal. From the top we looked down the opposite side on a field of snow, ending in verdant mountain-sides, which in their turn gave place to the woods and forests of the Duchinpara and its offshoots. In a gorge near the top is seen the pretty little lake Sonsernag, from whence gushes a small stream which falls into the Lidur a short way farther down. In bare stony places in and around the snow I saw several wrens (*Troglodytes himalayanus*), a species closely allied to the familiar European bird, from which it differs in scarcely any appreciable degree. It is common at high altitudes all over the Cashmere ranges. A flock of snow-pheasants were seen, together with the quoir monal or snow-partridge (*Lerva nivicola*), which at a distance resembles the other, but it is very much smaller. This handsome bird is not uncommon in certain localities and at high altitudes on Cashmere, Ladakh, and northwards. Mr. Wilson of Mussouree, whose long and intimate acquaintance with the habits and haunts of the larger animals and game birds of the Western Himalayas, entitle him to be considered a good authority, says: "The snow-partridge breeds near the limits of vegetation, and lays from six to seven eggs."* Its wild plaintive whistle very much resembles that of the snow-pheasant, to which bird it assimilates likewise in habits. Both it and the other Tetraogalli of these regions are hardy, and I imagine would stand the climate of Northern Europe. We saw flocks of a starling-like bird flitting from one bare patch to another on the confines of the snow; they ran with much celerity, but no specimen could be procured. What appeared to be the male had long pointed wings, was a fine glossy black above, less so on the lower parts; the others, possibly females or young of the year, were less brilliant, and of a sombre blackish-brown, like that of the Asiatic water-ousel. There are light and dark coloured varieties of the latter to be seen both in Ladakh and on the lesser ranges near the plains of India. As usual at such elevations, flocks of the brown mountain-finch (*M. nemoricola*) were plentiful.

The scenery of this day's march, taking it all in all, from the snow-clad mountain-top to the grassy hill-sides and

* *Calcutta Sporting Review* for December 1848 contains an excellent description of the habits of many Himalayan game-birds by Mr. Wilson ("Mountaineer").

magnificent forests of the Duchinpara, was among the most beautiful and varied we had hitherto trodden. The wild-looking grassy glades and groves of pine and birch, undulating for miles, and sloping downwards into densely-wooded valleys, are among the most delightful and captivating of Cashmerian mountain scenery. We passed near the caves of Umernath, and along the pathway by which many a footsore pilgrim was hastening towards the sacred shrine in the gypsum rock. At Pilgam we found our old shickarees, Barshah and Ellishah, who by previous arrangements had come to accompany us to the deer-forests. In the meantime, while our commissariat was being replenished, we employed a few days in hunting the neighbouring forests and hill-sides, and Young killed a black bear near the village One day, when crossing a mountain-top, I came on an isabella bear and cub feeding intently on wild carrots and roots of strawberries, which both were tearing up with their fore-paws. Desirous of trying how near I could approach unobserved, as the wind was very favourable and the animals busily engaged searching for food, I crept on hands and knees within 10 feet before either took any notice of me, when the old dame gave a grunt, and scampered off as fast as her legs would carry her, followed by the bewildered cub, which, astonished at its mother's timidity, turned round several times and gazed at us in astonishment. I have observed that this bear's powers of vision are by no means good, and of little use to the animal beyond 12 or 15 yards. I believe they depend almost entirely on smell and hearing for their safety. I discharged the contents of my double-barrelled rifle into the old dame as she rushed down the steep, but neither bullet brought her down. Ellishah would, however, persist in asserting that we would find her, and led me a wild-goose chase through the forest and long ferns, with no better result than the satisfaction of finding out by the bloody trail that I had not missed my mark. Both species of bears commence to shed their winter coats in June, which are not again attained until the middle of October.

Although the weather was very unsettled and rainy, we determined to push up the valley; so, on the 26th of August, having left Pilgam, we proceeded northwards, over hills and down grassy slopes, through belts of forest or clumps of birch, where I saw several flocks of my orange-coloured bullfinch and many fresh trails of deer. The ground was likewise ploughed up in many places by bears, one of which was killed by Young, who procured a considerable quantity of grease. The external fat is always preferred to that of the internal parts. I noticed the fat from the region of the kidneys had a strong smell of urine, which our shickarees said no refining will remove.

Being desirous of securing good deer-shooting at any price, we left the direction of our movements entirely to the shickarees, who shifted our encamping-ground as they thought fit. But all was in vain; although up before daylight, and hunting late at night, not a single head of deer was visible. Thinking they might be found at the little ponds or springs at dusk or early morn, we repaired to the situations, and lay in wait, in anxious expectation of meeting with a herd when they came to drink. Even on moonlight nights we would wander through the copses and by the sides of the forest, but to no purpose. Every morning disclosed fresh footprints, and even sometimes close to our encampment. Nor were we more successful in the forest; for although we waded up to the middle in tall bracken, and sought the deepest solitudes, not a sound was heard or a stag visible. It is notable that, like the profoundest regions of the sea, the interior of these great pine-forests contains little or no animal life. There is apparently a similar gradation in the distribution of the fauna of forest tracts as there is between the littoral and abyssal regions of the deep. An occasional nutcracker was seen, but birds were remarkably scarce in all the forest parts. We plucked abundance of raspberries in the clearings, and a stone-bramble, possibly identical with, if not very closely allied to, the *Rubus saxatilis* of northern Europe. Wild currants were also plentiful, but sour and unpalatable. One day we encountered a string of natives carrying loads of asafœtida to the markets of Serinuggur. This plant, as before stated, grows in abundance in certain defiles and valleys running southwards, and is most plentiful on the more sheltered ridges. It is a large umbelliferous plant, seldom under 6 feet in height, with yellow flowers and thick stem, apparently the same as that we had met with in the Sonamurg.

The Lidur river, a moderate-sized mountain torrent of a few yards in breadth, had to be crossed, and to our disappointment we were forced to retrace our steps some distance to enable us to get across, in consequence of the log bridge having been destroyed on the previous day by a party of natives who had fled from the tyranny and oppression of the ruler of Cashmere, and, with their cattle and household gods, had pushed on by this route with the intention of becoming subjects of Sher Ahamid Khan, a neighbouring rajah. On the opposite bank we were shown a heap of stones, from which the fugitives pelted the Maharajah's sepoys who had been sent to bring them back. It was told us, moreover, that with a few old muskets they managed to keep the military at bay whilst their main body was retreating across the Kullohoy glacier at the top of the valley. In 1849 this Sher

Ahamid Khan attempted to dispute the sovereignty of the valley with Goulab Singh, but gave up the project from a fear that the Cashmerians in his army would show the white feather when it came to blows. I was assured of the truth of the above statement by a native merchant. It is likely, however, that the rajah was afraid of British interference. Be that as it may, there can be no question that the making away of the Cashmere valley was one of the grandest political blunders of its day, and one which will be constantly felt as long as we hold the Punjaub. Independent of the vast addition to our Eastern revenues by opening out a magnificent field for English enterprise, Cashmere would have secured advantages in a military point of view of the greatest importance, by affording splendid and healthy sites for a reserve army, which, on the shortest notice, might have been made available for any emergency in the North-western Provinces; but instead, its noble prairies, plains, and forests, scarcely surpassed by those of any other country, have been sold to rulers whose whole end and object have been to reap and never sow.

The continual wet state of the weather was apparently the chief obstacle to our success, and the higher up the mountains the more unpleasant it became; but, determined to give every region a trial, we made for the top of the ravine to a wild sequestered spot at the foot of the glacier. Several brown bears were seen, and I killed a male, from which a large quantity of grease was obtained. There was an old bullet wound in his hip, and another through his flank. We had now reached the *Ultima Thule* of our wanderings in quest of deer. Never did hunters work harder, for we toiled across the steep mountain-sides, over melting snow-beds and slippery slopes, but with no good results; for no sooner did one mass of cloud clear off the hillside than another took its place. One morning I espied a fine stag on a cliff above us, and just as I was getting within range, a cloud came rolling down the mountain and enveloped us. It was useless advancing in hopes of the dense mass clearing away, for there was no discerning objects within a few yards. I crawled, however, up the steep ascent to within a short distance of the deer, whose feet I could hear clattering on the stony ridge close by. Thus ended our futile attempts at deer-hunting; and as the weather had every appearance of continuing in the same state for a week longer, we struck camp on the 2d of September, and, leaving the inhospitable region, retraced our steps to Pilgam, where a very different state of matters existed. From thence we could discern the clouds still hovering over the tops of the Kullohoy mountains, while all around the village was in bright sunshine. By our former route we continued our journey down the Duchinpara to the village of Gannisbul, situate among orchards of fruit-trees, under one of which our shickarees had spread bears' skins, and prepared for us a feast of apples and pears in celebration of our visit to their native village. In the evening we repaired to a neighbouring jungle to wait for black bears, which at that season descend from the mountains in numbers to feed on wild apples, grapes, and walnuts. Although we saw several, none were killed.

This species has been known under cover of night to enter the orchards in the very centre of the villages, and we were surprised one morning at Kullohoy to find that on the previous night one had been digging up the turf within a few yards of our tent. Their aptitude for climbing enables them to mount to the tops of the tallest trees, where they may be often found at night standing on their hind-legs on a branch, and seizing the boughs laden with walnuts, which they crunch, rejecting the shells. They descend tail foremost, and if suddenly startled, will drop to the ground from a considerable height, or, as sailors say, "let go by the run."

Never did the splendid valley of the Duchinpara look to greater advantage. The rainy months had now passed, and everywhere nature seemed to wear its choicest garb. Every animal looked happy except man. It was painful to observe the misery and wretchedness of the poorer classes, with teeming plenty around. Painful scenes were constantly intruding themselves on us, either in the shape of a revenue officer beating a farmer for being short of the rent, or numbers of poor, miserable, half-starved men and women searching for mushrooms and wild plants by the road-sides. Even the fruit of the walnut and other trees in the jungles was not exempt from the avaricious grasp of the ruler. In vain we turned away from these scenes, but to no purpose; if we managed to evade one, something more startling took its place. Here, as elsewhere noticed, ophthalmia was rife, and particularly among the women and children, whose wan and pale faces but ill assorted with the profusion and healthy aspect of nature's productions around them. Now that the sporting portion of our excursion was at an end, my companion, who had noted carefully every item of our six month's work, produced the following game-list, which, considering that we were more intent on sight-seeing than the chase, is perhaps by no means contemptible:—To Young's rifle fell 29 bears, 2 deer, 2 ibex; to mine, 7 bears, 5 deer, and 1 musk-deer; Halkett bagged 8 bears, 1 deer, 2 musk-deer;—grand total, 57 head. During my subsequent excursion to Cashmere in 1854 I was more successful, having killed 17 bears, 2 ibex, 2 markhore, 1 tare, and 6 musk-deer. These were great days for the hunter. I fear, however, that from the annual migration of English sportsmen to the valley, it is seldom now that even the most expert and persevering are so successful. We reached Serinuggur on the 6th of September to find the quarters in City Gardens filled with European visitors, chiefly officers returned from shooting excursions, none of whom had been more successful than ourselves; and among the various competitors for the honour of having made the best bag of the season, Young stood pre-eminent.

The grapes of Cashmere are not equal to those of Cabool, possibly from the little trouble taken in rearing them. Unless in the gardens about Serinuggur, it is no uncommon sight to see them growing in great profusion in the jungles. The peaches are excellent; so are the mulberries and walnuts; but the apples are spongy, and the pears have not the flavour of the European fruit, doubtless from want of due attention.

The prince, in the absence of his father, who was reported to be seriously ill at Jamoo, gave a state dinner, to which all the English residents were asked. The festivities, as usual, were preceded by a natch, after which we retired to the banqueting-room, where upwards of thirty English officers sat down to dinner. The prince, of course, was debarred on religious grounds from eating with us, but he stood by and saw the lions feed. After dinner a comedy verging on the improper was performed by a very dirty-looking company on a temporary stage in the reception-hall. The prince wore a finely-worked turban-like head-dress with heron's plumes, after the Sikh fashion, with a jacket of blue and white velvet, magnificently ornamented with precious stones. I never before saw him appear to such advantage, and could not help admiring his becoming costume until he rose from his state chair, when the close-fitting tights (rather baggy posteriorly) and the meagre proportions of his lower extremities appeared so perfectly out of keeping with the assortment of the upper part of his person that I could scarcely contain my gravity.

One of our shickarees, who received the name of Jungulee from our servants on account of his wild and savage aspect, announced his arrival, accompanied by a young brown bear which Young had caught in Wurdwun, and entrusted to the care and tuition of Mr. Jungulee during our excursion to Ladakh. Accordingly Bruin was added to our herd of Rupshoo goats and sheep; and on the 11th of September we bade farewell to the land of Nourmahal, and proceeded by the former route to Murree, from thence to Rawul Pindee, where we arrived on the 22d of September 1852.

CHAPTER XIV.

Scavenger Animals—Their Utility—Hyena and Jackal Grave-Diggers—Swine—Dogs—Sheep—Their disgusting Mode of Feeding—Measled Pork—Tape-Worm—Antiquity of the Dog—Climate of Rawul Pindee—Degradation of Alluvium—Storms—Heats of Midsummer—Effects on Europeans—Agency of Storms and Removal of Organic Remains—Their Relation to Fossil Remains—Moon-rise on the Himalayas—Death of Captain Colby by Tiger—Departure for Peshawur—Elephant—Traits of Character—Peshawur—Lawless Natives—Murders—Khyber-Pass—Scenery—Dangers of Travelling—Mammals and Birds—British Birds—Migrations—Conclusion.

THE part played by certain mammals and birds in the removal of refuse, more especially in hot climates, is far more important than generally supposed. As regards India and the East, the chief actors in this great sanitary movement, or what might justly be designated Nature's first-class scavengers, embrace, among beasts, the jackal, hyena, domestic swine, dog; and among birds, vultures, kites, crows, minas, and the well-known adjutant (*Leptoptilos argala*, Gmel.) I have noted many facts in connection with the habits of these useful animals in South-eastern Europe, North Africa, as well as Asia, and been strongly impressed with the belief that, if the time should come when the most prominent actors in the scene become extinct, or greatly reduced in numbers, there will needs be some means of making good the loss; for most assuredly, if Eastern cities were at present denuded of their carrion quadrupeds and birds, there is no system of conservancy on the part of the human occupants at all equal to take their place. The nocturnal, bold and sneaking habits of the jackal and hyena are well known. The last is decidedly far less numerous, and hunts generally singly, whilst the jackal does so in packs. The one appears, however, frequently to accompany the other, for at night, among the discordant yelps of the jackal, may be heard the hoarser bark of the striped hyena. Over South-eastern Europe, Central and Southern Asia, both are more or less plentiful, affecting also the mountainous regions to pretty high altitudes. Whether it be the climate or not, I have observed both species attain a larger size on the Himalayas, and are invariably in better bodily condition than on the plains of India. The exceedingly lean and half-starved aspects of both these animals, as met with in many districts, would seem to indicate that they have often a hard struggle for existence. It is said that the pariah dog assists them to rifle graveyards; at all events, it is no uncommon circumstance to see the results of their depredations. One frightful example came under my notice at Rawul Pindee, where a grave in the cemetery was opened and a body torn to pieces by a troop of jackals. On the occasion in question they had removed several heavy stones placed above the body in order to prevent their attacks, and I noticed that, besides using their fore-paws in removing the soil, they had evidently lifted many of the stones with their mouths. Withal, however, these sacrilegious deeds are more than compensated for by the vast amount of scavenger-work they accomplish. Although anything in the way of flesh, putrid or otherwise, is acceptable, I am not aware that the jackal betakes to the dung-eating habits of the dog, swine, and even sheep, of India. The two first play an important part in the removal of the excreta in and around many Oriental cities, where no such institution as either a public or private latrine is known. Indeed the swine of many parts of India are maintained entirely in this way, and driven daily to the purlieus of the towns. The domestic animal strongly resembles the wild species in its outward form, but its lean appearance and excessively loathsome habits present an equally opposite contrast. Its flesh is very often "measled"—that is, contains the germs of the tape-worm, which are supposed to be the result of its foul feeding. This circumstance came forcibly before my notice at Rawul Pindee, where the diseased flesh of the animal was sold in quantities to the soldiers. The result was a marked prevalence among them of the parasite, which, on microscopic examination proved to be the species known as the hookless tape-worm (*Tænia mediocanellata*). No doubt mutton is frequently contaminated in this manner, as, strange to say, the sheep, and even goats, of many parts of the East, take to the same abominable mode of feeding. It is strange to observe how the poor rejected pariah becomes sensible of kindness or any attention from man. Once persuaded that no harsh measures are intended, his erect ears droop, and he crouches at your feet. This predilection for man seems almost inherent in the dog, and when we trace back its history as far as the refuse-heaps of Denmark and the pile-folks of the Swiss lakes, or what is still more suggestive, the representations on the Egyptian temples and tombs, the great fact is irresistible, that man and the dog have shared each other's company for possibly a longer period than any other; and whether the love at first was gradual or not, it has now at least, as far as the brute is concerned, become instinctive. Moreover, when we think of the vast periods embraced by the Egyptian monuments of antiquity, and the time it must have taken to develope even one variety from the feral stock, and note the fox-hound or turnspit of 4000 to 5000 years ago, it may well be conceded that the dog, of all four-footed beasts, has a claim to our kindness and protection. The Himalayan wild dog, when taken young, is easily tamed, and this rule would seem to hold good with the wild races of other countries; indeed, although not generally acknowledged, the wolf, jackal, and hyena, get much attached to man, if carefully reared and treated with kindness. The semi-domesticated dogs, in common with the wild species, have erect ears; and this would seem to become more 'pronounced' the nearer they assimilate to the latter. This circumstance I have noted in respect to domesticated sheep, goats, etc., when left more or less to shift for themselves, as is apparent on the Himalayas and Alps.

The proximity of the snow-clad ranges creates frequent and sudden alterations in temperature along the sub-Himalayan valleys and adjacent plains. The cool weather suddenly sets in at Rawul Pindee about the end of September, and continues up to the beginning of May, when the strong heats commence. The harvest is now over, and the quails that had congregated during the ripening of the grain disperse among the scrub and wastes. Now the soil gets baked and cracked, so that when rain falls the thick mass of surface alluvium becomes thoroughly saturated, and at length disintegrates and is carried to lower levels or into watercourses, to be swept by the sudden freshets to the main-drainage channels that empty themselves into the Indus. This accounts for the very uneven and broken-up aspect of the country around Rawul Pindee, more especially in the direction of the Himalayas. Although the heat of midsummer is often intense, and as high as 100° Fahr. in well-built houses, and 140° in the sun, it is not of long duration, being frequently broken by thunder-storms, which are connected with the atmospheric conditions taking place at the same time on the high ranges.

There is no regular rainy weather at Rawul Pindee, but only the south-west monsoon clouds, as they drop their moisture on the Pinjal, affect the heated atmosphere of the torrid plains below. Then furious storms, accompanied or not by electric discharges, sweep along the north-western frontier of the Punjaub. Sometimes these phenomena assume imposing aspects. The storms are usually preceded by prolonged droughts and successions of intensely hot weather, when an unusually close and oppressive day is characterised by a peculiar stillness of the atmosphere, during which the leaves are seen to droop, and all animated nature becomes exhausted, and the soil is parched ; when, about sunset, a huge dense gray cloud of dust, several miles in breadth, is seen advancing from the north and hugging the mountains on the one side and the plains below, creeping stealthily but steadily onwards, preceded by hot scorching blasts, which raise the thermometer several degrees. The sensations are stifling for a short time, then suddenly the blast feels cool, and at length, as the mass approaches, and the thunder and lightning draw nearer, the dust envelopes you, and for a few minutes all is darkness, when down comes the rain, which the thirsty soil drinks up almost instantaneously, and the glass falls some 25° to 30° in the course of a few minutes.

The cold of the winter months does not begin to affect the leaf until the end of November, when frosty nights, succeeded by delightfully cool days, invite exercise, and strive to recompense the European for the long summer spent in darkened rooms and under punkas, where he had dragged out a monotonous existence, panting from heat and pallid from want of exposure to the air outside. The generally bleached aspects of Europeans in India, and women in particular, are doubtless attributable in part or wholly to this cause; and although the habit of closing doors and windows by day—bottling up the cool air of night—does certainly reduce the heat considerably, and prevents the entrance of dust and hot winds, it may be questioned if the constitution would, in the long run, suffer more if subjected to a few degrees of higher temperature, with that indispensable requisite, light, which of all necessaries of animal life is one of the most important.

In countries subject to sudden and violent storms, it is suggestive to note how easily organic remains can be transported in situations where no regular river or stream exists. I have often picked up bones of sheep and cattle among the debris in the bottoms of dried-up watercourses, many miles distant from Rawul Pindee, and under conditions that clearly showed they had been conveyed by floods and freshets. Such occurrences are common in Central Africa, as shown by Sir Samuel Baker in connection with the Blue Nile and rivers of Abyssinia, where entire carcases of the elephant, hippopotamus, tortoise, etc., are borne along the watercourses for long distances, and deposited pell-mell where sufficient resistance is presented. The arrangement of fossil remains of like quadrupeds, in the rock-fissures of Malta, seem to indicate a similar origin, as likewise the wonderful assemblages of living and extinct animals in the caverns and rock-fissures of Gibraltar. Thus the presence of organic remains, under conditions such as have just been stated, do not necessitate the supposition that a perennial stream or river once flowed on or near the deposit.

There could be no finer picture for the landscape-painter than the view from Rawul Pindee of a full moon crowning the top of the Peer Pinjal. That enormous barrier-chain, illuminated by the glorious orb, whilst the intervening space is hidden in gloom, presents a scene of almost unparalleled grandeur and majesty.

A fine specimen of the panther (*F. pardus*) was shot on the low hills, near Rawul Pindee, which I afterwards identified. It was during our residence at this station that a frightful accident occurred to Captain Colby (98th Regiment), when out tiger-shooting in a jungle, about twenty miles distant from Rawul Pindee. He mortally wounded a large tiger which had infested the district for some time, carrying off cattle and whatever came in its way. The brute, however, escaped into a thicket, and both elephant and beaters refused to enter; when, dismounting, Captain Colby proceeded in quest of the tiger, which he came on suddenly, and before he could bring his rifle to his shoulder, the infuriated animal sprang upon him and felled him to the ground. Several hours afterwards the unfortunate gentleman was found with his right arm torn to pieces, and several severe wounds elsewhere from the paws and teeth, whilst within a few yards lay the tiger, dead. The injuries sustained necessitated amputation of the arm, but other internal wounds proved of such a serious nature that he died a few days after the accident.

Our regiment left Rawul Pindee towards the end of 1853 for Peshawur, crossing the Indus at Attock by means of boats. Here the river is rapid, and its channel considerably narrowed by rocks. The transport of the baggage and camels occupied two days, whilst the commissariat elephants were made to swim across—all of which took to the water without much persuasion excepting one. No force or coaxing would induce him to enter, and so he was left behind. It was a strange sight to observe the huge brutes steering their way across the river with the whole body perfectly immersed excepting the trunk. Sometimes the current during the inundation proves too strong, and thus more than one fine elephant has been carried away. One old male, employed in carrying the officers' mess-tent, had been rather unruly ever since leaving Rawul Pindee, and now broke away from his picket, and made off to a neighbouring jungle, when it became necessary to bring him back by two others, in the mode usually adopted in capturing the wild ones. These furious fits of ill-temper and insubordination, called "must," resulting from excited passion (ἀφροδισιακός), are sometimes developed to a dangerous extent, and apparently very sudden in their onset. I knew a gentleman who nearly lost his life by a "must" elephant—one of six that were engaged in beating a tiger-jungle. He had dismounted, and was standing in front of the line of elephants, when one of them, with enormous tusks, rushed at him and made a vigorous attempt to impale him. Being of a spare habit of body, the elephant missed his mark, and the gentleman escaped by retreating to the rear of the others, whilst the infuriated animal made off with his driver and two persons for some distance, before he could be persuaded to rejoin his companions, which, however, he did that afternoon, and remained perfectly quiet and docile for the remainder of the excursion. There was one of the largest Indian elephants I have ever seen, chained for many months in the open air at Rawul Pindee, in consequence of his excessive ill-temper. He used to fall into periodic attacks of rage, when he continued trumpeting often all night. I have seen this animal amuse himself for hours by tossing a large heavy log of wood, some 20 feet in length and upwards of 10 inches in diameter, into the air as if it were a crowquill, and seize his "dhurra" (*Sorghum vulgare*), straw, and fodder, which he flung about, and sometimes amused himself by digging up the ground with his tusks. During an expedition into the Hazara country, among the lower Himalayan ranges, N.W. of Rawul Pindee, several of the baggage elephants died very suddenly, but whether owing to climate or change of food could not be ascertained. The drivers told me that the climate of the hills does not agree with the animal.

A residence at Peshawur, after a sojourn in other parts of the Punjaub, is not by any means pleasant; and perhaps, of all other stations, this is the least inviting to the naturalist, but not in any way from the absence of objects of interest as the unfortunate circumstances that prevent Europeans from travelling in the valley or surrounding mountain-ranges. My excursions were therefore confined to a few miles around the station, and even on these occasions it was always doubtful whether or not an Afredee or one or other of the bloodthirsty hill-men, might not be lying in wait with matchlock or tulwar, ready to despatch you. This year matters assumed a more than usually serious aspect from the assassination of the chief commissioner, Colonel Mackeson, by one of the lawless and fanatical natives of the surrounding mountains, who stabbed him in the verandah of his house. Unintimidated by frequent and severe chastisements, these tribes continued their depredations among the peaceful inhabitants of the valley, and sneaked at night into the British lines, where they coolly murdered sentries on their posts. One morning, whilst searching for birds within a stone's throw of the military cordon that constantly surrounded the camp, my attention was directed to a group of natives assembled about a small mud-hut in a hollow, where a person had earned a livelihood by grinding corn with a hand-mill. It was a wretched little hovel; nevertheless, for the sake of the few handfuls of flour, one of these ruffians had murdered the poor old man, whose body, despoiled of clothing, lay half out at the doorway, presenting frightful gashes in various parts, and, excepting his little mill, not a particle of grain or any of his goods and chattels remained. It was only a short time previously, whilst a lady and gentleman were taking a ride in the vicinity of the station, an Afredee fired on them; the lady escaped, but her unfortunate companion was cut down and killed. The entrance of the Khyber Pass, of unpleasant memory, is distinctly visible, more especially in clear winter days; and also from the lines may be observed the fortress-like village of Jamrood, on an elevated ground, and covering the mouth of the pass; westward, rising one above another, are the magnificent Afghan and Kaffir mountains, including the Hindoo and Sufeid Koh; whilst northwards and east, in long ridges, with dark intervening valleys, and running into the Peshawur plain, are the abodes of the rebellious hill-tribes, who, were it not that they quarrel a good deal among themselves, would in combination make a formidable enemy. All these vast mountain-ranges have been unexplored by the naturalist; indeed, few Europeans have ever managed to penetrate the great valleys northward of Peshawur. Frequent inquiries made of natives who had visited some of the higher and more secluded mountain-valleys elicited scant information, and that altogether with reference to the most common large quadrupeds. The markhore was stated to be abundant in certain localities near the western bank of the Indus, above Attock, and around the Khyber Pass. Many of its horns, some almost exactly like corkscrews in form, and upwards of 2½ feet in length, were sent me; others, not nearly so much twisted, presented also a more flattened appearance. A wild sheep, seemingly identical with that met with on the Salt Mountains and around Attock, is also common in these situations; but, as far as I could learn, not on the same ranges with the former. The tiger and panther are found along the skirts of the Himalayan chain, the former increasing in numbers to the south-east and banks of the Indus, especially near Kala Bagh. I have noted a fox distinctly different from the *Vulpes bengalensis* in the ravines around Peshawur, but never obtained a specimen, so as to ascertain if it is the same as the one observed on the Salt Mountains.

Both the gray and red ichneumons (*H. griseus et ruber*) are plentiful. Skins of the pine-marten (*M. abietum*) are imported from Afghanistan and sold in the bazaars of the city, where also those of the ermine are occasionally observed. Pigs abound along the sub-Himalayan valleys and in the Eusofraye country. Ravine or Bennet's deer is said to be plentiful. Hares (but the exact species was not determined), and a very large bustard (*O. nigriceps ?*) the *O. macqueenii*, is a regular winter visitor, and the little chukore (*A. bonhami*), is met with in suitable places.

It was interesting to note the cold-weather arrivals. The *lapwing, teal, gray lag-goose, cranes, rooks, European jackdaws,* the *bittern, chimney swallow, gray wagtail,* either taking up their residence, resting for a short time, or pushing southwards—some in long trains, as is the case with the large water-birds. The rough gabbling of the geese and cranes lasted often throughout the night, whilst the guttural sounds of the sand-grouse were frequent; both the common and large species (*P. exustus et arenarius*) were often seen in flocks by day, and seemed to be regular migrants. There was a small thrush that evidently arrived in the gardens and orchards in the cold months, and is very common. It is 9 inches in length, with the upper parts olive-brown; throat and front of the neck dirty-white; the sides of the neck and breast are thickly spotted with olive-brown; belly and lower parts dirty-white; legs light-brown. I marked again during winter, in the Valley of Peshawur, the white-rumped martin, so closely allied, if not identical with, the bird of Europe, but did not obtain a specimen. Snipes are common in March, and quails in October.

Here the narrative of my travels must cease. The loss of the greater part of the notes referring to the subsequent portion of my sojourn in Peshawur, and second expedition to Cashmere, and my return to England in 1854, has brought about this abrupt termination. I fain hope, however, that what have been here recorded may be the means of arousing some youthful minds to an appreciation for the works of Nature, or mayhap create an ardour in the pursuit of such knowledge. If these ends are attained, I shall feel so far rewarded for all the difficulties I have had to combat with in the compiling of the notes and determination of many of the natural objects; and this, in conclusion, leads me to expect from my readers some consideration for any defects in diction or scientific accuracy, considering that the delay in publishing the contents of this volume has been altogether brought about by the constant change of place, that left me few opportunities of consulting libraries or museums, and made me more than ever grateful to many distinguished masters of science for substantial aid, and to none more than to my friend Sir William Jardine, Bart., who has revised the proof-sheets and corrected the nomenclature; also to Adam White, Esq., who in my absence has given material assistance towards the completion of the work.

NEW BRUNSWICK, NORTH AMERICA,
April 1867.

INDEX.

THE END.